W9-CDH-490

# Predict, Observe, Explain

## Activities Enhancing Scientific Understanding

John Haysom

Michael Bowen

**NSTApress**

National Science Teachers Association

Arlington, Virginia

National Science Teachers Association

Claire Reinburg, Director
Jennifer Horak, Managing Editor
Andrew Cooke, Senior Editor
Judy Cusick, Senior Editor
Wendy Rubin, Associate Editor
Amy America, Book Acquisitions Coordinator

ART AND DESIGN
Will Thomas Jr., Director
Cover illustration: Lushpix Illustration/Unlisted Images, Inc.
Interior illustrations: Tim French

PRINTING AND PRODUCTION
Catherine Lorrain, Director

NATIONAL SCIENCE TEACHERS ASSOCIATION
Francis Q. Eberle, PhD, Executive Director
David Beacom, Publisher
1840 Wilson Blvd., Arlington, VA 22201
*www.nsta.org/store*
For customer service inquiries, please call 800-277-5300.

Copyright © 2010 by the National Science Teachers Association.
All rights reserved. Printed in the United States of America.
14  13  12  11      5  4  3  2

**Library of Congress Cataloging-in-Publication Data**
Haysom, John, 1938-
Predict, observe, explain : activities enhancing scientific understanding / by John Haysom and Michael Bowen.
    p. cm.
Includes bibliographical references and index.
ISBN 978-1-935155-23-2
1.  Science--Study and teaching (Middle school)--Activity programs.  I. Bowen, Michael, 1962- II. Title.
Q181.H37555 2010
507.1'2--dc22

                       2010027459

eISBN 978-1-936137-59-6

*NSTA is committed to publishing material that promotes the best in inquiry-based science education. However, conditions of actual use may vary, and the safety procedures and practices described in this book are intended to serve only as a guide. Additional precautionary measures may be required. NSTA and the authors do not warrant or represent that the procedures and practices in this book meet any safety code or standard of federal, state, or local regulations. NSTA and the authors disclaim any liability for personal injury or damage to property arising out of or relating to the use of this book, including any of the recommendations, instructions, or materials contained therein.*

**PERMISSIONS**
Book purchasers may photocopy, print, or e-mail up to five copies of an NSTA book chapter for personal use only; this does not include display or promotional use. Elementary, middle, and high school teachers may reproduce forms, sample documents, and single NSTA book chapters needed for classroom or noncommercial, professional-development use only. E-book buyers may download files to multiple personal devices but are prohibited from posting the files to third-party servers or websites, or from passing files to non-buyers. For additional permission to photocopy or use material electronically from this NSTA Press book, please contact the Copyright Clearance Center (CCC) (*www.copyright.com*; 978-750-8400). Please access *www.nsta.org/permissions* for further information about NSTA's rights and permissions policies.

**About the Cover**—Safety Issues: The cartoon image on the cover depicts the excitement that often accompanies hands-on science investigation and the dawning of new knowledge. During actual school lab investigations, teachers and students should always maintain a safe learning environment, as described on page xiv. Most notably, teachers and students should wear personal protection equipment such as indirectly vented chemical splash goggles, aprons, and gloves if the demonstration or activity has any potential for bodily harm.

# The Story of a Curriculum Development Project

## Acknowledgments

This is a brief story of a curriculum project designed to produce learning materials that enhance students' understanding of important scientific concepts. It is not the story of a traditional curriculum project but, rather, of a project designed to involve practicing teachers in a meaningful way. Many teachers contributed in different ways, and this story is an expression of thanks for the efforts they made at different stages of the project. It also acknowledges the help received from science teacher educators in Canada, the United States, Australia, New Zealand, and the United Kingdom.

The story begins at a conference organized by Gaalen Erickson at the University of British Columbia (UBC). It was here that I learned about the power of Predict, Observe, Explain sequences (POEs) from two teacher-researchers, Jim Minstrell and Ian Mitchell. These people unknowingly planted the seed for this project.

Upon returning from my sabbatical at UBC, I made a request to Saint Mary's University for support. Over the course of the next three years, the university provided graduate assistantships to Clayton Coe, Judy Reynolds, Bob Dawson, Nevin Jackson, and Norma MacSween, all practicing teachers who were studying for their master's degrees. I also received invaluable help in the design and preparation of the trial materials from Sue Kent. On reflection, it is easy to recognize that this sort of support is crucial; without it, the project struggled to keep going.

The first task in Year 1 involved the design of sample learning sequences. This began with an extensive and comprehensive search of the research literature on children's scientific ideas. It was carried out by Clayton Coe with the assistance of librarian Doug Vaisey. In many instances, the research procedures used to elicit students' ideas stimulated the design of POE sequences. In addition, we scoured the products of other curriculum projects, especially SciencePlus by the Atlantic Science Curriculum Project, for ideas for activities that would lend themselves to being presented in the form of POEs. In subsequent years, many others contributed their ideas for learning sequences, notably Dick Gunstone and the Monash Children's Science Group.

Even though the learning sequences we had designed were far from perfect, we launched the field testing and evaluation of the materials at the end of the first year. We invited teachers to select a topic they would be teaching and return their evaluation of each sequence they used. The evaluation form was a simple one: We asked the teachers to rate the sequence on a five-point scale, provide their reasons for the rating, and note any problems they encountered

# Acknowledgments

when using the sequence, along with suggestions for making improvements. In addition, we had the hunch that the teachers themselves would benefit from using the POEs. Judy and Clayton examined their responses, and many reflected on the way in which they taught science. Here are some sample responses.

> *POEs have given me more insight into the misconceptions students bring with them into a science class.*
>
> *They have shown me that it is important for all students to reflect on their understanding of concepts and to verbalize it before and after the POE experience.*

Their findings were presented at a meeting of the Canadian Society for the Study of Education.

In the second year, Bob Dawson and Nevin Jackson focused on field testing and evaluation. Following a number of presentations at inservice meetings, which received enthusiastic responses, we invited the teachers to select a booklet of POEs on a topic they would be teaching. In return they undertook to send their evaluations of each POE they used, together with the students' scripts. However, by the end of the year, the return had been patchy, especially regarding the students' scripts. We attributed this to the demands we were making on the teachers' time, especially regarding the photocopying of the student worksheets.

As a consequence, in Year 3, we made contracts with a number of committed teachers and provided workbooks for all their students. Chuck McMillan, Bill Reid, and Frances Wallace undertook the bulk of the testing. This worked very well, even though we were unable to test all the POEs and we finished up with a pile of workbooks about two meters high. Norma MacSween began analyzing these. This project—coupled with revising the materials, checking the literature, and preparing for publication—proved to be an enormous task.

The writing of this book was brought to fruition when I renewed a long-standing professional relationship and brought my former student Michael Bowen on board to work with me in finalizing the POEs, organizing the writing, sourcing reference literature in the teaching guides, and honing the final text and images.

In addition to the people mentioned above, I would like to acknowledge the invaluable efforts of all of those who have assisted in this project. They have all helped bring together curriculum development, classroom teaching, and education research in a way that we hope will make an important contribution to science education.

*—John Haysom*

NATIONAL SCIENCE TEACHERS ASSOCIATION

# Using POE Sequences

POE sequences provide an important way to enhance your students' understanding of important scientific ideas. We believe that POE sequences are an important tool in every science teacher's repertoire. If you are teaching a traditional curriculum, one based on a textbook, the sequences can enliven the enrichment you provide. If you are teaching an activity-based curriculum, they can help provide a firm basis for understanding. POEs are based on a sound theoretical foundation that has been researched extensively.

Children live in a world of sense impressions. They see, hear, smell, touch, and taste. From infancy they spontaneously make sense of the world in which they live. They form concepts and try to link one concept with another to explain the world around them. For example, they might come to think that matter disappears when substances dissolve or burn, or that plants take in food through their roots, or that heavy objects such as stones or nails sink, or that heavy objects fall more quickly than lighter ones. They find such ideas useful in their lives. The idea that children—or all of us, for that matter—construct such understandings of the world is fundamental to the constructivist view of learning.

Scientists also try to make sense of the natural world of sense perceptions. This is their collective mission. They do this deliberately and carefully. They extend our sensory world by using instruments to measure mass, length, and time more accurately. They use instruments to measure the large and the small, the hot and the cold, the soft and the loud, and so on, to enhance our sensitivity. They expand the natural world by carrying out experiments, enabling them to observe phenomena that do not occur naturally. They formulate concepts such as density and gravitational force and arrive at powerful generalizations, such as that an object floats when its density is less than that of the liquid in which it is immersed, or the acceleration of all falling objects is the same in a vacuum.

There are thus two types of interpretations of the world in which we live: everyday, commonsense interpretations and those of the community of scientists. It is part of a science teacher's job to help each student build on everyday, commonsense interpretations so that the student can adopt and internalize scientists' interpretations. This can be a very challenging task, especially when the scientific interpretation is at odds with students' interpretations. For example, some students believe that electricity gets used up as it goes around a circuit, or that vacuums suck. These ideas have worked well for the students concerned. So why should they change their ideas now?

How can the science teacher respond to this challenge? A variety of teaching strategies have been developed to complement the constructivist view of learning. As you would expect, they have many features in common. The POE sequences we have developed embrace many of these features. They are included in the suggestions for using the POEs that follow. As you read about the steps in the sequence, you might find it useful to refer to one or two POEs to provide examples.

## Step 1: Orientation and Motivation

The POE usually begins by drawing on the students' past experiences or previous understanding and raises a challenging question that can be addressed through the experiment that follows. A few minutes of full-class discussion will provide the students with the opportunity to reflect on their past experiences and understanding.

## Step 2: Introducing the Experiment

Introduce the experiment. Linking it to the previous discussion will help make it meaningful.

## Step 3: Prediction: The Elicitation of Students' Ideas

Before doing the experiment, ask the students to write down on the worksheet what they predict will happen, along with the reasons for their predictions. This exercise is valuable for both the students and the teacher. Making their reasons explicit helps the students become more aware of their own thinking. It also provides the teacher with useful insights and an opportunity to plan ahead. Hence, while students are writing, you might stroll around so as to prepare yourself for the discussion that will follow.

## Step 4: Discussing Their Predictions

This is a two-stage process. First, ask your students to share their predictions in full-class discussion, using a chalkboard or SMART Board to highlight the range of predictions and reasons for them. This needs to be handled with sensitivity on account of some students' feeling anxious about seeming "wrong." Hence, you will need to be supportive and encourage as many students as possible to express their viewpoints. There are no poor ideas! All ideas are valued because they represent our best efforts to make sense of the world. You might explain that making our predictions explicit helps us learn.

After this has been done, you might invite the class to discuss which predictions and reasons they now think are best. When students reconsider their reasons, some may begin to change their minds and reconstruct their thinking. Immediately prior to the experiment, it's often fun and illuminating to have a straw vote about the outcome.

## Step 5: Observation

Most of the experiments in this book are designed to be done as demonstrations, although some make good student explorations. If you demonstrate the experiment, invite the students to help out whenever appropriate. Ask them to write down their observations.

## Step 6: Explanation

Students often reshape their ideas through talking and writing. We have frequently found that it's useful for students to discuss their explanations of what they observed with a neighbor or in a small group before formulating a written explanation. They seem to find this action reassuring. After they have done this, collect a sample and invite a full-class discussion of these as appropriate.

## Step 7: Providing the Scientific Explanation

Introduce the scientific explanation by saying, "This is what scientists currently think," rather than, "This is the right explanation." Many teachers choose to ask their students to write the explanation in their notebooks or on the back of their activity record sheets. The students might then be invited to compare their explanations with those of scientists, looking for similarities and differences (another opportunity for them to reconstruct their ideas).

## Step 8: Follow-Up

Researchers have found that students' ideas often are resistant to change and there is no guarantee that a POE will do the trick, even though it might provide a valuable beginning. This also was evident in the field testing, when student explanations before and after the experiment were compared. Hence, in some POEs, we have included a follow-up at the end. This often is designed to help the students reconsider or apply the scientific ideas they have just encountered and begin to appreciate how useful they are for explaining natural phenomena.

So many steps may seem to make POEs complex and unmanageable, but this isn't the case in practice. The underlying pedagogy resonates with the beliefs held by most teachers, and after a little experience you will probably find the procedure becomes routine for both you and your students. This is liberating and will enable you to focus your attention on facilitating learning by responding to your students. Incidentally, many teachers have found that they can complete Steps 1 through 7 in a 40-minute period. Sometimes they take a break after Step 5: Observation, and set the next step for homework.

A major strength of POEs is that they can continuously provide you with insights into your students' thinking: Steps 1 through 4 probe your students' initial conceptions, Steps 6 and 7 enable you to monitor your students' efforts to reconstruct their thinking, and Step 8 provides you with feedback on your students' progress. POEs thus can offer you "authentic responses" from your students, provided that judgment and assessment do not come into play. It's important, therefore, to encourage your students to share their thinking, which for the time being may or may not be scientifically acceptable, and to value their responses. In this way, it becomes possible for you to adjust the pace of your teaching and to plan for subsequent instruction, thus optimizing your effectiveness.

## The Teacher's Notes

Alongside each POE, you will find the scientific explanation; students' explanations: field experience; students' explanations: research findings; and apparatus and materials.

## Scientific Explanations

We have tried to express these in a student-friendly form, one you might choose to use in Step 7.

## Students' Explanations: Field Experience

These might well be worth reading before you use the POE because they can help you anticipate what your students might say. Even though your class of students will be unique, it could well be that they will have similar ideas to those we have found. On account of the way in which the field testing was conducted, it was not possible to provide these students' explanations for all of the POEs. In these cases, we hope you might make time to analyze some of your own students' scripts.

## Students' Explanations: Research Findings

The research findings similarly provide you with an idea about the responses that your students might give, and you might find it interesting to check these out not only before but also after using a POE. When you do this, you will be locating your personal experience alongside the body of knowledge about teaching, and this can be professionally enriching.

In most cases, we expect that you will find it sufficient to simply refer to these summaries. However, some teachers, perhaps those engaged in further study, might find it worthwhile to go into greater depth. As was mentioned before, this area has been extensively researched, and literally hundreds of papers have focused on children's ideas. *Making Sense of Secondary Science* (Driver et al. 1994) is a wonderful resource that summarizes the findings through the date of publication. These days, the research literature is much more accessible, and fortunately this has removed much of its esoteric nature. Accessibility of the literature has been made possible by the arrival of Google Scholar. If you have a reference, you may view a summary or abstract of the article simply by filling in a few key words on the Advanced Scholar Search page. Sometimes the whole article is available, but if it is not and the article looks promising, many libraries, especially university libraries, will be able to help you access it. (A comprehensive bibliography of students' and teachers' conceptions and science education up to 2009 by Reinders Duit is available online: *www.ipn.uni-kiel.de/aktuell/stcse/stcse.html*.)

During the field testing, we were intrigued to find many similarities between our experience and these research findings, and it was illuminating to compare the two. Because many of our POEs and elicitation procedures are original, we have incidentally added to these findings. Moreover, we hope that in the future some teachers will take time to analyze their students' scripts, especially where we weren't able to do so, and thus add to this body of work by becoming researchers themselves.

## Apparatus and Materials

Teachers often have difficulty acquiring and storing the necessary apparatus. With this in mind, we have tried to keep the requirements simple and have recommended the use of everyday items wherever possible. We would like to offer these two ideas, which may help teachers overcome the problem:

1. You might organize a curriculum night for parents featuring POEs. We are confident they would enjoy participating in a simulation of one or two sequences themselves. At the end, you could solicit their help in acquiring the materials you need, dividing up the apparatus and materials lists between them.

2. We have found that shoe boxes, fish trays, and other similar containers are useful for storing the items needed for most POEs. They can be labeled and kept on a shelf, ready to use at a moment's notice.

Finally, a few comments about your use of the student activity sheets. It is our intention that teachers who own this book should be free to copy the activity sheets for their own students' classroom use. To facilitate this, the publishers selected a binding that makes it possible to easily open the book and keep it flat. However, we gather that in some schools and districts there are strict policies about making limited photocopies. In such cases, many teachers have reported that they copy the student POE pages onto overhead transparencies or PowerPoint slides and have students answer the questions in their notebooks. To us, this would not be as effective for learning; we carefully considered the layout and space allotted for writing to enhance student engagement and provide students with a record of the activity. Nevertheless, it certainly helps overcome the problem.

## Reference

Driver, R., A. Squires, P. Rushworth, and V. Wood-Robinson. 1994. *Making sense of secondary science*. London and New York: Routledge.

## Safety in the Classroom Practices

Although most of the experiments are designed to be done as demonstrations, some make very good student explorations. It is important to set a good example and to remind students of the pertinent safety practices when they do perform an experiment.

1. Always review Material Safety Data Sheets (MSDS) with students relative to safety precautions in working with hazardous materials.

2. Remind students to only view or observe animals and not to touch them unless instructed to do so by the teacher.

3. Use caution when working with sharp objects such as scissors, razor blades, electrical wire ends, knives, or glass slides. These items may cut or puncture skin.

4. Wear protective gloves and aprons (vinyl) when handling animals or working with hazardous chemicals.

5. Wear indirectly vented chemical splash goggles when working with liquids such as hazardous chemicals. When working with solids such as soil, metersticks, glassware, and so on, safety glasses or goggles can be worn.

6. Always wear closed-toe shoes or sneakers in lieu of sandals or flip-flops.

7. Do not eat or drink anything when working in the classroom or laboratory.

8. Wash hands with soap and water after doing the activities dealing with hazardous chemicals, soil, biologicals (animals, plants, etc.), or other materials.

9. Use caution when working with clay. Dry or powdered clay contains a hazardous substance called silica. Only work with and clean up clay when wet.

10. When twirling objects around the body on a cord or string, make sure fragile materials and other occupants are out of the object's path.

11. Use only non-mercury-type thermometers or electronic temperature sensors.

12. When heating or burning materials or creating flammable vapors, make sure the ventilation system can accommodate the hazard. Otherwise, use a fume hood.

13. Select only pesticide-free soil—commercially available for plant labs and activities.

14. Many seeds have been exposed to pesticides and fungicides. Wear gloves and wash hands with soap and water after an activity involving seeds.

15. Never use spirit or alcohol burners or propane torches as heat sources. They are too dangerous.

16. Use caution when working with insects. Some students are allergic to certain insects. Some insects carry harmful bacteria, viruses, and so on. Use only biological supply house insects and wear personal protective equipment, including gloves.

17. Immediately wipe up any liquid spills on the floor—they are slip-and-fall hazards.

# About the Authors

After completing his doctorate in chemistry at Cambridge University, **John Haysom** taught science in various schools before becoming a member of the faculties of education at five universities: Oxford University, Reading University (United Kingdom), University of the West Indies, Saint Mary's University (Canada), and Mount Saint Vincent University (Canada).

John has gained an international reputation as a teacher educator and curriculum developer. In the United Kingdom, he was coordinator of the groundbreaking Science Teacher Education Project, funded by the Nuffield Foundation. This was probably the first teacher education curriculum project in the world and was adapted for use in Australia, Canada, Israel, and other countries. At the University of the West Indies, he was responsible for the design and implementation of an innovative, theme-based inservice B.Ed. curriculum. As a professor of education at Saint Mary's University, he initiated and helped lead the Atlantic Science Curriculum Project's SciencePlus textbook series. This curriculum was highly rated and became widely adopted in the United States. He has acted as a science curriculum consultant to the government of Trinidad and Tobago and to a number of projects in the United States.

He is the author of many books for teacher educators, teachers, and schoolchildren, as well as academic papers in curriculum design, evaluation and implementation, and teacher education.


**Michael Bowen** completed his doctorate at the University of Victoria. After studying the research practices of field biologists, he developed a curriculum for middle school students. This was tested with grade 6 and 7 students in the classroom. Following a postdoctoral fellowship in the sociology department at Trent University, he became a member of the faculties of education at three universities: Lakehead University, the University of New Brunswick, and Mount Saint Vincent University (where he is now an associate professor).

Michael's ongoing research has many facets, including studying student learning from participation in science fairs, the development of competency with science inquiry practices in student teachers, and the creation of online communities of learners where participants conduct and share research projects in a science-project-specific social networking site. His research has been presented at national and international conferences in Canada, the United States, and Europe and has been published in journals in jurisdictions throughout the world. The work he is most proud of is that which has been published in professional teachers magazines. His science teacher preparation classes are known for using innovative approaches to teacher preparation.

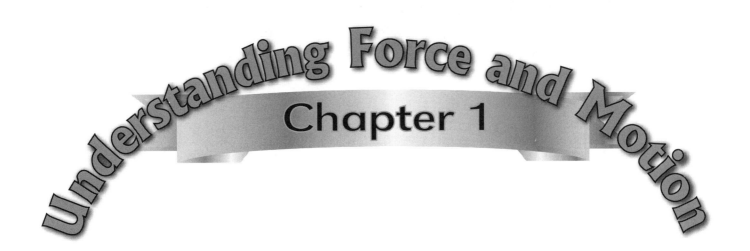

# Understanding Force and Motion
## Chapter 1

## Contents

## Scientific Explanation

The objects will not change position from their initial rest positions because the downward force on each side of the pulley (ignoring the weight of the string) is the same and the net force on each side of the pulley is zero. The gravitational attraction is the same on each object. An object remains in constant motion (or at rest) unless a net force greater than zero acts on it. This is Newton's first law of motion.

## Students' Explanations: Field Experience

This POE was used with 40 grade 7 students. Fifty-seven percent (57%) predicted correctly that the objects would not move (a), 35% predicted (b), and 8% predicted (c). Those predicting correctly, (a), often were able to articulate an explanation that was scientifically acceptable:

> *I think it is (a) because gravity is pulling down on them and since they weigh the same there will be equal force and they won't move.*

And, very perceptively,

> *There is more weight on the one that is lower because there is more string.*

A few introduced the idea of friction:

> *I think (a) is true because there is friction on the rope and this stops movement.*

The types of preconceptions underpinning incorrect predictions were as follows. Many students seemed to think of the pulley system as a pair of scales:

> *The weights are equal and they want to be at the same height.*

A few explained their observations in terms of gravity varying with height:

> *The gravity on the top will have a greater pull on it so this (c) will happen.*

## Students' Explanations: Research Findings

Seventy-eight percent (78%) of 125 14-year-olds thought that the unaided objects would move until both were at the same level. For some, this was a normal consequence of the objects being equal:

> *The objects are the same weight so they will lift each other to the same height.*

> *Both weigh the same but if one weight is pulled slightly over to one side, the other will be able to even it out.*

> *Because when the short side is pulled toward the Earth and when they are even there is no force so they don't move. (Watts and Zylbersztajn 1981)*

Similar research was carried out with 466 first-year university students (Gunstone and White 1981). Thirty-five percent (35%) predicted that the system would return to the original position, with the objects at the same level. Only a few (13%) of those predicting incorrectly were able to reconcile their observations scientifically.

## Apparatus and Materials

- Stand
- Clamp
- Pulley
- 2 equal masses
- String

Note: Gunstone and White (1981) favor using a bicycle wheel instead of a pulley and a bucket of sand and a wooden block instead of the objects. This suggestion has much to recommend it. Set up the apparatus so that the two objects are at the same height, Position B. To begin the experiment, pull one mass down to Position A.

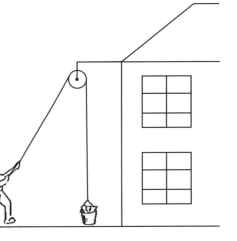

## Balanced Forces

### The Bricklayer's Problem

A bricklayer is building a chimney. He sets up a pulley at the edge of the roof. He fills the bucket with bricks. It weighs the same as he does. He wonders if he will be able to lift it. Can he haul it to the top? He tries!

### An Experiment

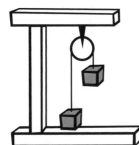

Attach two equal objects to a piece of string and loop them over a pulley as shown in the diagram. Let go of the bottom object and wait one minute to see if anything happens. What do you predict will happen?

### Predict

Which drawing below do you think will show the position of the objects one minute from now? Check one [√].

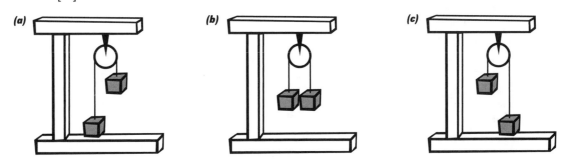

Please explain._____

_____

_____

### Observe

What happens when you do the experiment?

_____

### Explain

Try to explain what actually happened.

_____

_____

_____

## Scientific Explanation

In the "pulley problem," there is no movement. The downward (gravitational) force on each side of the pulley must therefore be the same. The mass of the bucket of sand and the mass of the wooden block are therefore the same. (Newton's first law of motion states that an object will continue to move at a constant speed [or remain at rest] unless it is acted upon by a net force greater than zero.)

If just a little sand is added to the bucket, the downward force on that side is greater; however, there will be no movement if it cannot overcome the frictional force between the pulley and its axle.

If more sand is added, the downward force increases and the bucket begins to move when the frictional force is overcome.

Because the bucket accelerates, the speed at Point B is greater than at Point A. If even more sand is added, the acceleration is even greater. (Newton's second law quantifies the relationship between force and acceleration: $F = ma$).

## Students' Explanations: Research Findings

This POE is based on research done by Gunstone and White (1981) with first-year university physics students.

1. In the "pulley problem," 27% of students thought the block would be heavier. Some attributed this to the block being closer to the floor.

2. Just more than half made correct predictions about what would happen when sand was added; however, 30% predicted a "new equilibrium" position would result, as if position and not just net force affected the system.

3. Ninety percent (90%) of students correctly predicted that the speed of the bucket would be greater at the lower mark.

A similar study by Hakkarainen and Ahtee (2005) found that the majority of students in grades 5 through 9 thought that the lower-hanging object was heavier.

## Apparatus and Materials

- Pulley (or bicycle wheel)
- Cup (or bucket) of sand
- Block of wood
- String (or cord)
- Stand and clamp

Note: Before carrying out the experiment, demonstrate that the pulley or bicycle wheel moves freely, and that the block and bucket can pass without bumping each other. Check that the apparatus is stable.

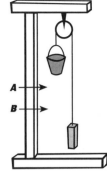

## *Balanced and Unbalanced Forces*

### Pulley Problem

A bucket of sand and a block are connected by a string. The string is then placed over a pulley so that the bucket is higher than the block. Nothing happens!

Question: Which do you think is heavier? Check one [√].

(a) Bucket **[    ]**          (b) Block **[    ]**          (c) About the same **[    ]**

Please explain. _____

_____

### Two Experiments

1. Add a small amount of sand to the bucket.

2. Add a larger amount of sand to the bucket.

### Predict

What do you think will happen in each experiment? Do you think the block will move? Please explain.

Experiment 1: _____

_____

Experiment 2: _____

_____

### Observe

What happens?

Experiment 1: _____

Experiment 2: _____

### Explain

Try to explain what happened.

Experiment 1: _____

_____

Experiment 2: _____

_____

### Hey!

Do you think the bucket will move faster as it passes Point A or Point B, or will the speed be the same? Please predict and explain. _____

_____

Let's take a closer look! _____

## Scientific Explanation

The two carts apparently experience the same gravitational force. There would be, theoretically, an extremely small but imperceptible difference: The gravitational pull between two objects decreases as the distance between them increases. Because the upper cart is slightly farther away from the center (of gravity) of the Earth, the force acting on it is slightly, albeit immeasurably, less.

## Students' Explanations: Field Experience

This POE was used with 34 grade 7 students. Their predictions were as follows: 38% believed that the upper cart would experience more force on it (a); 12% believed that the lower cart would experience more force on it (b); and 50% thought that both carts would experience the same force (c).

Many reasons were given for both carts experiencing the same force: same mass, same weight, same slope, same friction, same gravitational pull:

> *... because there is the same amount of mass.*

> *... because they are both carrying the same amount of weight and it has the same force.*

> *... because both are on the same angle, both the same car, same amount of friction.*

> *Gravity is the same wherever the car is.*

There appeared to be three major reasons underpinning incorrect predictions. Some students believed gravitational pull varied with height:

> *The higher the car, the more force of gravity will be on it.*

Other students felt differently:

> *... because the top cart is higher and gravity is far away.*

Some students perceived that the slope of the ramp was greater at the top:

> *The top one has a steeper hill to get down.*

Some students associated the force on the cart with the speed the carts would have at the bottom of the hill if released:

> *... because it is higher up and will have more force and speed. The lower won't have enough time to pick up speed.*

## Students' Explanations: Research Findings

Forty-eight percent (48%) of 125 14-year-old students chose the option suggesting that the upper car would be pulled down the hill with a greater force than the other (Watts and Zylbersztajn 1981):

> *... because the car is farther up the hill and will have more force pulling it down.*

> *... because the car is higher there is a bigger force.*

> *... if you are lower the force is weaker.*

> *The hill is very steep and gravity pulls things down to Earth ... is much higher so the force is greater.*

## Apparatus and Materials

- Meter board or plank
- Dynamics cart or toy truck
- Weight (e.g., 500 g)
- Force meter

## *Parking on a Hill*

The only place to park the car was on a very steep hill.

"It'll be OK if you put on your emergency brake and turn in your wheels," Jesse said to her mom.

There were two parking spots available: one halfway down, the other toward the top.

"Do you think it matters which one I take?" Jesse's mom asked.

### An Experiment
Set up a board on an angle (about 30 degrees). Put two carts each containing the same mass (say 500 g) on the board (as shown) and attach force meters to them. Read the force on each cart.

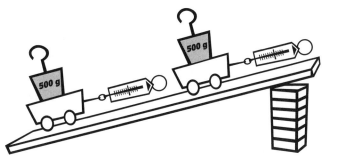

### Predict
Which of the following statements will be true? Check one [√].

(a) [   ] The upper cart experiences more force on it.

(b) [   ] The lower cart experiences more force on it.

(c) [   ] Both carts experience the same force.

Please explain your thinking. _____

_____

_____

### Observe
Attach the force meters to the carts and read the force each registers. Write down your observations.

Force on upper cart _____        Force on lower cart _____

### Explain
Try to explain the readings you observed on the force meters. _____

_____

_____

## Scientific Explanation

The washer is kept in circular motion by the force of the string pulling it toward the center. The washer, once released from the pulling force of the string will continue in a straight line (tangential to the circular path)—that is, it will follow Path B. Newton's first law states that an object will continue to move in a straight line unless acted on by a force.

## Students' Explanations: Research Findings

Fifty-one percent (51%) of college undergraduates interviewed by McCloskey (1983) predicted correctly.

A similar study was carried out with 315 grade 9 students (Berg and Brouwer 1991). The majority of the students theorized that a "circular force" would be given to the object and that it would therefore continue in a circular path.

## Apparatus and Materials

- Piece of string (15 cm long)
- Washer

# Sling Shot

Have you ever whirled something around your head on the end of a string?

What would have happened if the string broke?

## An Experiment

Tie a washer to the end of a 15 cm piece of string.

Twirl the string around and let it go.

## Predict

Which path do you think the washer will take when it is let go at point P? Check one [√].

Or if none of these fit your thinking, draw your own direction arrow on (d).

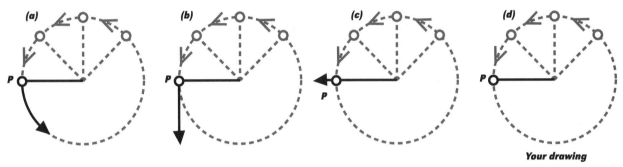

*Your drawing*

Please give your reasons. _____

_____

_____

_____

## Observe

Let's give it a go! Be careful not to hit someone with the washer, though!

What happens? _____

## Explain

Can you explain why the washer went in the direction it did?

_____

_____

_____

## Scientific Explanation

Keep it going: It usually requires very little force to keep a trailer going—just enough to overcome the friction between the wheels and the axles. (You can coast on a bicycle for a long way.) Newton's first law says that an object will continue to move in a straight line at constant speed unless it is acted on by a force.

Speeding up: If you apply a constant force to the trailer, it will speed up, provided, of course, that the force is greater than the friction. (You speed up on a bicycle when you pedal. It is only when friction and air resistance balance your push that you reach maximum speed.) When you apply a force to a moving object, it accelerates. This is a natural extension of Newton's first law.

Double the pull: If you double the pull or the force applied, the acceleration is doubled. (If you push harder on your pedals, your bicycle will accelerate faster.) Newton's second law says that the acceleration ($a$) is proportional to the force ($F$) applied. It is often expressed in the form $F = ma$, where $m$ is the mass of the object.

Double the load: Doubling the load increases the mass of the trailer. Hence, applying Newton's second law, the trailer does not accelerate as fast. (A heavy cyclist will have to push harder than a lighter one to accelerate as fast.)

Downhill disaster: The two trailers reach the bottom of the hill at more or less the same time. (Different frictional resistance accounts for any variation). The effect of doubling the pull is balanced by the effect of doubling the load. (Ignoring any difference in friction, a heavy cyclist coasting down a hill will reach the bottom at the same time as a lighter one.)

Note: The same reasoning explains why all falling objects accelerate at the same rate.

## Students' Explanations: Field Experience

We noticed that students encountered considerable difficulty when being taught this topic, so we devised this POE to help them, hoping that they would find it less counterintuitive.

## Students' Explanations: Research Findings

In their review of children's ideas about force and motion, Gunstone and Watts (1985) identify five intuitive rules that children frequently use. Two of these are pertinent here: First, many students hold the so-called Impetus Theory of Motion. This intuitive rule says that "constant motion requires a constant force." For example,

> *If he wanted to keep moving along here (the horizontal), he would have to keep pushing, otherwise he'd run out of force and just stop.*

> *To keep going steadily, you need a steady push. If you don't force something to move, its not going to go along is it? (13-year-olds)*

Second, many students also believe the following rule, which is an extension of the first idea: "[T]he amount of motion is proportional to the force" (or the harder you push something, the faster and farther it goes). Findings of this type are remarkably stable over time and across cultures and are identified with what is known as an Aristotelian framework that comes from basic intuitive models grounded in children's everyday lived experiences (Mildenhall and Williams 2001). These models are generally non-Newtonian (and, consequently, noncanonical) understandings of mechanical relationships and are remarkably resistant to change (Mildenhall and Williams 2001).

## Apparatus and Materials

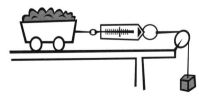

- 2 dynamics carts
- String
- 1 Newton force meter
- Set of weights
- Table pulley
- Board (about 1 m long)
- Blocks (to make an inclined plane)

## *Towing a Trailer*

### Keep It Going!

True or false?  Once the trailer is moving, it takes next to nothing to keep it going (at constant speed).

Predict _____  Observe _____

Explain _____

_____

### Speeding up?

True or false?  If you pull with a constant force, the trailer speeds up (that is, moves faster at B than A).

Predict _____  Observe _____

Explain _____

_____

### Doubling the Pull

True or false?  If you double the pull, the trailer speeds up (accelerates) twice as fast.

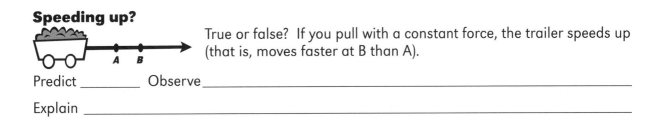

Predict _____  Observe _____

Explain _____

### Doubling the Load

True or false?   If you double the load, the trailer doesn't accelerate as fast.

Predict _____  Observe _____

Explain _____

### Downhill Disaster

True or false? If two trailers break free and roll back down a hill, the trailer with double the load reaches the bottom at more or less the same time as the trailer with a single load.

Predict _____  Observe _____

Explain _____

## Scientific Explanation

It's the blowing force that makes the seeds move. In the larger tube, the force acts for a longer time. Hence the seed continues to accelerate, builds up more speed, and goes farther.

Note: This POE can also be used when considering energy concepts. The expanding gases do more work in the longer tube (work = force × distance). Hence, more kinetic energy is produced in the longer tube.

## Students' Explanations: Research Findings

In their review of children's ideas about force and motion, Gunstone and Watts (1985) identify five intuitive rules that children frequently use. Two of these are pertinent here.

First, many students hold the so-called Impetus Theory of Motion. This intuitive rule says that "constant motion requires a constant force":

> *If he wanted to keep moving along here (the horizontal), he would have to keep pushing, otherwise he'd run out of force and just stop. (13-year-old)*

> *To keep going steadily, you need a steady push. If you don't force something to move, its not going to go along is it?*

Second, many students also believe the following rule, which is an extension of this statement: "The amount of motion is proportional to the force" (or the harder you push something, the faster and farther it goes).

Hakkarainen and Ahtee (2006) stress the importance of pupils' experiencing the same concept in different contexts for them to reach understanding.

## Apparatus and Materials

- Plastic straws
- Sunflower seeds
- Scissors

If you wish to explore the effects of force acting for a longer time, you will need the following items:

- Truck or dynamics cart
- 100 g weight
- Table pulley
- String

## Sunflower Shooters

Susan was watching a show about World War II. She was amazed at the artillery that was used at the front. The gun barrels were so long! Could it be that the long barrels are more accurate? Maybe they are more powerful. What do you think?

### An Experiment

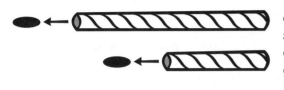

Take a plastic straw and cut a piece off the end about 5 cm long. Blow a sunflower seed out of it and see how far it goes. Try blowing a sunflower seed out of a regular straw and observe how far the seed goes.

Note: Both straws should be horizontal.

### Predict

What do you predict will happen?  Check one [√].

(a) [   ] The seed will go farther using the short straw.

(b) [   ] The seed will go farther using the long straw.

(c) [   ] They will go the same distance.

Please explain your thinking. _____

_____

_____

_____

### Observe

Let's be fair!  Color the seed in the long straw red and the seed in the short straw blue, then launch both at the same time. Which straw shoots farther?

_____

### Explain

Try to explain the results of your experiment. _____

_____

_____

_____

_____

## Scientific Explanation

When we walk, our feet push on the ground, the ground pushes back on us, and we go forward. A push in one direction is matched by a push in the opposite direction. Forces always come in pairs. When the rope was attached to the tree, the tree was pulling as hard on the rope as the students were pulling on it. Try holding one end of the rubber band: You will be acting as if you are the tree. (In passing, we have found it useful to do this with students—it seems to help them.) Newton expressed these ideas in general terms in his third law of motion: For every action there is an equal and opposite reaction. Or if Body A puts a force on Body B, then Body B puts an equal force on Body A, but acting in the opposite direction.

When both teams are pulling and the rope is stationery, Team A will be pulling as hard as Team B. In the experiment, the rubber band is the same length as when one team is practicing. It may seem strange, but the same is true when Team A is moving slowly and steadily (Newton's first law). Interestingly enough, the team that is able to push harder on the ground is the team that wins! You can check this by adding a small weight to one team. You will notice two interesting things: (1) The length of the elastic remains the same, and (2) the whole apparatus begins to accelerate (Newton's second law).

## Students' Explanations: Field Experience

In the trial, a spring scale was used instead of the elastic band and a 5 N force applied to each end. However, it was subsequently modified because we found that the way a spring scale works sometimes puzzles the students.

When this POE was used with 86 grade 7 students, their predictions were as follows:

Nineteen percent (19%) predicted that the scale reading would be 0 N. Typically these students reasoned that the forces at each end of the scale would balance out:

> *I think it will measure 0 N since there's balanced forces working on it not allowing it to be pulled either way.*

Thirty-one percent (31%) predicted that the scale reading would be 10 N, typically arguing that both the forces would act on the scale:

> *(10 N) because there is 5 N on each side pulling it.*

Forty-three percent (43%) correctly predicted that the scale reading would be 5 N. Some evidently found it difficult to articulate their reasons:

> *I think it will read 5 N. I don't know why. I just think it will.*

Others were able to express their thinking very clearly:

> *I think it will weigh 5 N because one side will hold it while the other side puts weight on it.*

## Students' Explanations: Research Findings

Watts and Zylbersztajn (1981) tested 125 students who were 14 years old. They found that 82% of the students believed that the team exerting the greater force on the rope would win. None of the students mentioned the forces between the people and the ground.

## Apparatus and Materials

- 2 pieces of string (paper clips fastened to each end enable them to be clipped on and off quickly)
- 2 identical weights
- 2 table pulleys
- Elastic band
- Ruler

## *Tug-of-War*

The A Team was practicing for the tug-of-war. They tied the rope to the large oak tree in the field behind the school. The tree held up, but the rope looked as if it would break.

"With both teams pulling, I bet the rope will break when they use it in the tournament!" Joey laughed.

What do you think?

### An Experiment

First, hang a weight from an elastic band. Measure the length of the stretched elastic. _____ cm

Then set up the apparatus below. Attach a second weight (same mass) to the other end of the elastic band.

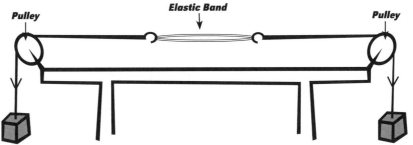

### Predict

Do you think the elastic will stretch    [  ] More    [  ] Less    [  ] The same?  Check one [√].

Don't forget to explain your thinking. _____

_____

_____

### Observe

Let's check! How long is the elastic band now? _____ cm

### Explain

Try to explain what actually happens. _____

_____

_____

### *Hey!*

So, do you think the rope will break in the tournament?

Try these brainteasers! The A Team is winning! They are slowly moving backward.

Do you think the elastic will stretch if you slowly pull one end of the string?
Prediction _____        Observation _____

Describe carefully what you think will happen if you add a small weight to one end. _____

_____

Let's try it! _____

## Scientific Explanation

The golf ball and the Ping-Pong ball appear to hit the ground at the same time. Similarly, the legend about Galileo culminates with the two balls hitting the ground at the same time. However, even though the legend often appears in science textbooks, it is almost certainly fiction. Nevertheless, it was Galileo who carried out some brilliant experiments with inclined planes. These led him to the conclusion that the acceleration of all falling objects is the same.

Because gravitational force acts continuously on an object as it falls, the object falls faster and faster. It accelerates. The two balls hit the ground at essentially the same time. This can be explained by Newton's second law: $F = mg$, where $F$ equals the force on an object, $m$ is the object's mass, and $g$ is the acceleration due to gravitational attraction. This can also be expressed as $F/m = g$; because the ratio of force to mass is constant, all objects dropped from the same height should hit the ground at the same time.

Many people find this hard to believe. They know a piece of paper falls to the ground slower than a book. Indeed, if the two balls were dropped from a higher elevation, another factor would be seen to come into play. This is air friction. The friction the falling object encounters slows the acceleration until, given some time, the force of air friction, which increases with speed, equals the force due to gravity. At that point, the object doesn't speed up because there is no net force on it (in accordance with Newton's first law). It falls at a constant speed—its terminal velocity. The Ping-Pong ball will be slowed down faster than the golf ball because it is lighter. If you dropped the two balls from a second-floor window, the golf ball would hit the ground first!

## Students' Explanations: Field Experience

This POE was used with 42 grade 7 students. Eighty percent (80%) predicted that the golf ball would hit the ground first. The majority of these attributed this to the golf ball being heavier. One articulate student put it this way,

> **The golf ball will hit the floor first because it is heavier than the Ping-Pong ball so the gravitational force is stronger on the golf ball.**

After the students had observed the balls hit the floor at the same time they evidently struggled to construct reasons, e.g.,

> **They were the same when they fall because of buoyancy.**

> **They have about the same surface and no wind effecting [sic] them.**

> **... because of the same gravitational pull. And the wind or air couldn't interfere.**

No students were able to provide a scientifically acceptable explanation.

Their teacher was clearly concerned and wondered if this POE should be used only after Newton's laws had been taught. She also was concerned about how to present the scientific explanation.

## Students' Explanations: Research Findings

In a study of 67 grade 5 students, Nachtigall reported that 91% expected a heavier ball would fall faster and that 47% described the fall as being at a constant speed on account of the force of gravity being constant (see Driver et al. 1994). Gunstone and White (1981) reported that 25% of 176 first-year university physics students thought that an iron ball would fall faster than a plastic ball: 10% because it weighed more, 15% because of air resistance.

## Apparatus and Materials

- Golf ball
- Ping-Pong ball

## Which Falls Faster?

Ping-Pong ball

Golf ball

### Galileo and the Leaning Tower of Pisa

About 400 years ago, scientists were arguing about whether a heavy object would fall at a different speed than a light one. There is a legend that Galileo and his students took two lead weights of different masses to the top of the Leaning Tower of Pisa in Italy and dropped them off at the same time!

What do you think they would have observed?

### An Experiment

Hold a Ping-Pong ball and a golf ball out in front of you. Drop them at the same time.

### Predict

What do you think will happen? Check one [√]. Don't forget to explain your thinking!

(a) [    ] The Ping-Pong ball will hit the floor first.

(b) [    ] The golf ball will hit the floor first.

(c) [    ] They will both hit the floor at the same time.

_____

_____

_____

### Observe

Describe what you see. _____

_____

### Explain

Can you explain what happened when the two balls were dropped?

_____

_____

### Hey!

Did you observe carefully? Do you think the balls fell at a constant speed, or did they fall faster and faster? _____

Take a second look! What happens?

_____

_____

_____

## Scientific Explanation

Answers to Quick Quiz

(a) When the Ping-Pong ball and the golf ball are dropped from shoulder height, they apparently hit the ground at the same time (see FM8).

(b) When dropped from 5 m, the golf ball hits the ground first.

(c) The book hits the ground first.

(d) The coin hits the ground first.

Take the air away and the coin and feather will fall at the same rate. (Galileo was right!) If you dropped the coin and feather on the Moon, where there is no air, you would see them hit the ground at the same time.

When a piece of paper is put on top of a book, it is shielded from the air resistance and hence falls at the same rate as the book on which it is resting

## Students' Explanations: Field Experience

The responses of 30 grade 7 students to this POE were analyzed. Seventy-three percent (73%) correctly predicted that both the penny and feather would hit the bottom at the same time, and the majority of these students reasoned in terms of air resistance. However some appeared to believe that air resistance only affected the feather:

> *... 'cause there is no air resistance to hold the feather back.*

Two students, predicting correctly reasoned in terms of buoyancy:

> *I think they will both reach at the same time because the feather falls slower.*

> *... (when there is air) because it is so light but it will be heavier.*

Most of those who predicted that either the penny or the feather would hit the bottom first reasoned in terms of the heaviness of objects. After observing, they attempted to reconstruct their thinking in terms of the effects of the air:

> *... because there was no air pressure to stop the penny and the feather.*

## Apparatus and Materials

You can purchase the coin and feather apparatus from a number of scientific supply companies.

## Feather and Coin Mystery

### Quick Quiz
Which hits the ground first?

(a) A Ping-Pong ball or a golf ball, dropped from shoulder height _____

(b) A Ping-Pong ball or a golf ball, dropped from 5 m _____

(c) A book or a piece of paper, dropped from shoulder height _____

(d) A feather or a coin, dropped from shoulder height _____

### An Experiment
Here's a tube about 1 m long. It contains a penny and a feather. All the air has been sucked out. What do you think will happen when the tube is turned upside-down?

(a) The feather will reach the bottom first.

(b) The penny will reach the bottom first.

(c) They will reach the bottom at the same time.

(d) They won't fall and will just float.

Help!
*Gasp*
No air!

1 m long

### Predict
What do you predict: (a), (b), (c), or (d)? Explain your thinking for your prediction.

_____

_____

_____

### Observe
If your school doesn't have this apparatus, your teacher will tell you what happens.

_____

### Explain
How can we explain what actually happens? _____

_____

_____

### What Happens?
Place a piece of paper on top of a book. Which do you think will fall faster, the book or the paper? Let's do it! Try to explain what happens!

_____

_____

_____

_____

# Scientific Explanation

The key to making a correct prediction is to realize that the only force acting on both coins, once they have been launched, is gravity (that is, if one ignores air resistance); hence, both coins accelerate toward the ground at the same rate. Indeed, because the rate of acceleration is independent of mass, coins having different masses would likewise hit the ground at the same time. (This might make an interesting extension to this POE.)

Although the flicked coin launched horizontally had a force applied to it immediately before takeoff, this force stopped once it had left the launcher. According to Newton's first law, it would have continued to move horizontally at constant speed unless acted on by another force.

# Students' Explanations: Field Experience

This POE was used with 25 grade 7 students. Forty-four percent (44%) thought the dropped coin would hit the ground first. Nearly all reasoned in terms of the flicked coin having farther to travel:

> *... because the one flicked will have to go out and down and the other will go straight down.*

> *The dropped coin would hit first because it's going straight down.*

Twenty percent (20%) thought that the flicked coin would hit the ground first. All reasoned in terms of the coin traveling faster:

> *I think the flicked one will hit first because it is going faster.*

> *It will go down faster because more force is applied to the coin.*

Thirty-six percent (36%) predicted correctly that they would hit the ground at the same time. All appeared to appreciate that the horizontal motion had no bearing on the vertical rate of fall and argued in terms of their having the same distance to fall, gravitational force being the same, their mass or weight being the same, or air resistance being the same:

> *They will hit the ground at the same time because they have the same amount of distance to go.*

> *... because the same amount of gravity is pulling on them.*

> *... because they still have the same weight and mass so they fall at the same speed.*

> *They will hit at the same time because they have the same amount of air resistance and mass.*

We don't know if those who said they would hit at the same time because their mass or weight was the same realized that these factors do not determine the rate at which an object falls.

# Students' Explanations: Research Findings

There have been a number of studies of students' thinking about the forces acting on objects in motion. For example, Watts and Zylbersztajn (1981) asked 14-year-old students to identify the forces on a cannonball in mid-flight and on a stone that had been thrown upward.

Eighty-five (85%) thought that there would be a force on the cannonball away from the cannon and an upward force on the stone. In sum, they held the belief that if an object is moving, then there is a force acting on it in the direction of motion. Forces from other directions are not always recognized, as demonstrated in the research by Palmer (2001) in which many students did not believe that gravity does not act on objects that are moving upward.

# Apparatus and Materials

Construct a coin launcher similar to the one in the diagram, or you can practice pushing and flicking the coins off a table at the same time. The coin launcher is made from two pieces of wood (plywood works well). One has a hole drilled in the middle and is mounted on the other piece using a nail or screw.

# Coin Launcher

### At the Pool
Gina and Susan were at the pool. Gina took a running leap off the edge of the pool, and at the same time Susan stepped off the edge and dropped into the pool. Who do you think will hit the water first?

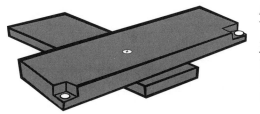

### An Experiment
This simple homemade apparatus is designed to help you launch a coin and drop one at the same time. Place two coins on the apparatus as shown in the diagram. Place the apparatus on the edge of a table and flick one side. Which coin do you think will hit the floor first?

### Predict
Check one [√].

The dropped coin will hit first. **[　]**     The flicked coin will hit first. **[　]**

They will hit at the same time. **[　]**

Please explain your thinking. _____

_____

### Observe
Watch and listen as the two coins hit the floor. What happens? _____

### Explain
Try to explain your observations. _____

_____

_____

_____

### Let's Try This!
What do you think would happen if we used different coins (e.g., a quarter and a nickel) on the launcher. Please explain.

_____

_____

_____

_____

## Scientific Explanation

The wrench will fall to the surface of the Moon. The force of gravitational attraction between the Moon and any object on it is about one-sixth of that on the Earth. On the Moon objects fall (accelerate) at about one-sixth of the rate on Earth.

In general, any two objects attract one another. This is called *gravitational attraction*. The more massive they are or the closer they are, the larger the attraction.

Note: If the flag was a regular flag it would just hang limply. There is no air on the Moon to make it flutter, and gravitational force would take over. Hence, it must be a "fake" flag. Perhaps it has wire along the top, which makes it appear to fly.

## Students' Explanations: Research Findings

Watts and Zylbersztajn (1981) found that 80% of 125 14-year-old students thought the wrench would either move upward or remain stationary at hand height. Their reasons were manifold. Here is a sampling of the answers:

> *There will be no force because there is no gravity or atmosphere.*
>
> *There is no gravity on the Moon so there is no force.*
>
> *On the Moon there is no gravity. Gravity pulls things down to Earth. If there is no gravity the object must go up.*
>
> *It would be pushed up by the force of the Moon air.*
>
> *In space everything is supposed to be lighter, so it will float up like a gas balloon.*

This study was repeated by Berg and Brouwer (1991). They found that the majority of 315 grade 9 students believed that there was no gravity on the Moon because there was no air. Many thought that the wrench would move away from the moon. Galili (1995) similarly found that "students, especially at the lower educational level, tend to associate the *cause* of gravity with air pressure" (p. 63).

## Apparatus and Materials

No materials necessary

## Accident on the Moon

**In the Past ...**

Photo provided by NASA

In 1969, Neil Armstrong became the first person to set foot on the Moon. He left the American flag planted on the Moon's surface for all to see and remember. Armstrong took this photo of fellow astronaut Buzz Aldrin next to the flag.

**In the Future!**

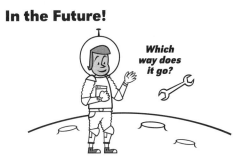

Which way does it go?

Imagine yourself as an astronaut on the Moon. By accident, you let go of a wrench. What do you think will happen to the wrench? Will it move? In which direction?

### Predict
What do you think will happen to the wrench? Please give your reasons!

_____

_____

_____

### Observe
Neil Armstrong would have been able to tell you what would have happened. Your teacher also knows. Write down what you would observe.

_____

### Explain
How would you like to change the reasons for your prediction?

_____

_____

_____

### Check It Out!
Take a close look at the flag in the picture. Is there something strange about it? How would you explain the way it is "fluttering"?

_____

_____

_____

# Scientific Explanation

There are two possible cases that scientists would likely consider: (a) **no air present** in the hole (this is the one students will likely consider), or (b) **air present** in the hole (this might be worth discussing with the students afterward).

(a) **No air present**. Because there is gravitational attraction between the ball and the Earth, *the ball begins to drop into the hole. It drops faster and faster until it reaches the center of the Earth*. Here the Earth pulls on the ball equally in all directions. *After it has passed the center, the ball begins to slow down* because the gravitational force is pulling it back into the hole. *The ball finally stops moving just as it comes out the other side. It is then pulled back into the hole again. It will continue to go backward and forward forever!*

(b) **Air present**. *The ball begins to drop into the hole—but not as fast as before* because of air resistance. *After a few seconds, the ball reaches its terminal velocity:* the gravitational attraction for the Earth being balanced by air resistance. *It then begins to slow down*, because the gravitational attraction becomes progressively weaker. *As it passes the center it is moving quite slowly. It soon turns back* as the gravitational pull toward the center increases. *The ball continues to move backward and forward but less each time. It finally comes to rest in the center of the Earth.* Note: Observations have been italicized.

# Students' Explanations: Field Experience

A similar version of this POE was used with 42 grade 7 students. None of the students considered air resistance. More than 70% thought that the speed of the ball would increase—at least at first—but few appeared to consider what would happen after the ball passed the halfway point:

> **... the ball will get through if the hole is clear. It will increase because if you drop something, it normally gets faster not slower.**

> **I think the ball will increase in speed because the gravity will force it to speed up.**
> **I think the ball will float in the center of the Earth because gravity is equal there.**

Among those who discussed the force of gravitational attraction at the center of the Earth (40%), the overwhelming majority seemed to recognize that gravitational pull is equal there. A number talked in terms of the ball floating in the middle:

> **The ball will get caught because the two gravitational pulls are equal so it will be a big tug of war.**

> **I think there is no gravity in the center of the Earth. Therefore the ball will not make it to the other side because it will just float around.**

Seventy percent (70%) thought the ball would not reach the other side.

# Students' Explanations: Research Findings

Sneider and Pulos (1983) classified students' responses according to their beliefs about gravity. Less than 60% of students in grades 7 and 8 believed that the object would tend to fall toward the center of the Earth. Some thought it would land or float freely at the far edge, some thought it would fly out the other side and go into orbit, and some correctly predicted that it would go back and forth forever if there was no air resistance (see also Nussbaum 1985).

## *A Hole in the Earth*

### A Future Situation
Dr. Y has designed a fantastic drill. He decides to drill a hole in the Earth—all the way through!

### An Experiment
He asks you to help him with the experiment and gives you a heatproof ball to drop into the hole. Now let it go!

### Predict
What do you think will happen? How will the speed of the ball change? Will it get to the other side? Please give your reasons.

_____

_____

_____

_____

### Observe
Using the theories that they have developed, scientists are able to tell you what you would observe. Your teacher can tell you, too.

_____

_____

_____

_____

_____

### Explain
Try to explain these observations.

_____

_____

_____

_____

_____

## Scientific Explanation

The friction between the block lying flat and the block on its side is the same. Strange as it may seem, the surface area in contact does not make a difference. Only the force between the object and the surface (in this case the weight of the block) and the nature of the surfaces touching each other make a difference. This may be represented by the equation $F = \mu N$, where $F$ is the frictional force, $\mu$ is the coefficient of friction between the two surfaces (this varies with the nature of the surfaces), and $N$ is the normal force that the surface exerts vertically on the object (this equals the weight of the object on a horizontal surface).

## Apparatus and Materials

- 2 (or more) wooden blocks (e.g., 25 cm length of 2 × 4)
- Force meter

Note: Before carrying out the experiment, you might first like to compare the forces required to pull on the two blocks. (See left-hand side of illustration at the top of the page.)

## *Reducing Friction?*

### Moving Books

Billy and Jane were helping move the boxes of new books—sliding them over the floor. It was heavy work!

### An Experiment

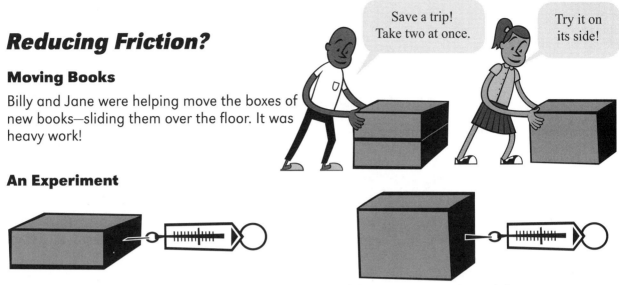

Save a trip! Take two at once.

Try it on its side!

(A) Drag a block at even speed using a force meter

(B) Turn it on its side and drag it again

### Predict

What do you think will happen? Check one [√].

(a) [  ] Friction is greater when the block is flat (Position A).

(b) [  ] Friction is greater when the block is on its side (Position B).

(c) [  ] Friction is the same in both positions.

### Observe

Let's do it! Record the meter readings when you drag the block.

Position A _____          Position B_____

### Explain

Can you make up a rule (hypothesis) that explains what you saw happen? How could you test it?

_____

_____

_____

_____

### *Hey!*

What about Billy's idea? What do you think the reading on the force meter would be? _____
Let's try it. Can you explain what happened?

_____

_____

# References

Berg, T., and W. Brouwer. 1991. Teacher awareness of student alternative conceptions about rotational motion and gravity. *Journal of Research in Science Teaching* 21 (1): 3–18.

Driver, R., A. Squires, P. Rushworth, and V. Wood-Robinson. 1994. *Making sense of secondary science*. London and New York: Routledge.

Galili, I. 1995. Interpretation of students' understanding of the concept of weightlessness. *Research in Science Education* 25 (1): 51–74.

Gunstone, R. F., and D. M. Watts. 1985. Force and motion. In *Children's ideas in science*, ed. R. Driver, E. Guesne, and A. Tiberghien, 85–104. Buckingham, United Kingdom: Open University Press.

Gunstone, R. F., and R. T. White. 1981. Understanding of gravity. *Science Education* 65 (3): 291–299.

Hakkarainen, O., and M. Ahtee. 2005. Pupils' mental models of a pulley in balance. *Journal of Baltic Science Education* 2 (8): 26–34.

Hakkarainen, O., and M. Ahtee. 2006. The durability of conceptual change in learning the concept of weight in the case of a pulley in balance. *International Journal of Science and Mathematics Education* 5: 461–482.

McCloskey, M. 1983. Intuitive physics. *Scientific American* 248 (4): 122–130.

Mildenhall, P. T., and J. S. Williams. 2001. Instability in students' use of intuitive and Newtonian models to predict motion: The critical effect of the parameters involved. *International Journal of Science Education* 23 (6): 643–660.

Nussbaum, J. 1985. The Earth as a cosmic body. In *Children's ideas in science*, ed. R. Driver, E. Guesne, and A. Tiberghien, 170–192. Buckingham, United Kingdom: Open University Press.

Palmer, D. 2001. Students' alternative conceptions and scientifically acceptable conceptions about gravity. *International Journal of Science Education* 23 (7): 691–706.

Sneider, C., and S. Pulos. 1983. Children's cosmographies: Understanding the Earth's shape and gravity. *Science Education* 67: 205–211.

Watts, D. M., and A. Zylbersztajn. 1981. A survey of some children's ideas about force. *Physics Education* 16 (6): 360–365.

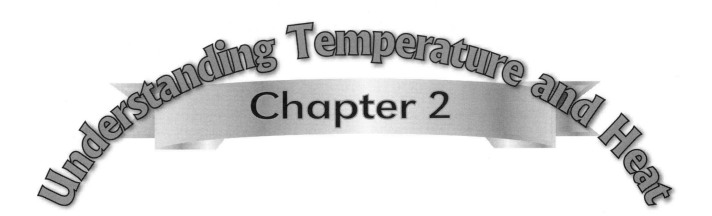

# Chapter 2

## Understanding Temperature and Heat

## Contents

# Scientific Explanation

The temperature of any ice and water mixture is 0°C. If an ice-and-water mixture is heated, the ice melts, and if it is cooled ice forms, but the temperature remains 0°C. Heating ice and water melts the ice but doesn't change the temperature. Ice melts and water freezes at 0°C.

# Students' Explanations: Field Experience

This POE was used with 30 grade 7 students.

Forty-three percent (43%) predicted that the temperature would decrease when ice was added. Some of these students thought that ice was colder than water:

> *I think it will drop because ice is colder than water and the ice will chill the water to a lower temperature than it already is.*

One student perceptively argued for the need for a fixed point in terms of the necessity of having a temperature equilibrium.

> *If the water is the same temperature as the ice cubes, the water will stay the same.*

When asked what would happen if the beaker containing ice and water was heated, nearly all of the students responding predicted that the temperature would increase.

# Students' Explanations: Research Findings

Driver and Russell (1982) found that some students (8- to 14-years-old) suggested that increasing the amount of ice would lower the temperature. Moreover, few students correctly predicted that the temperature of the ice-and-water mixture would stay the same if it was heated for a short time. When looking at a change of state (such as from ice to water), many student ideas are influenced by their seeing warm and cold as two *different* phenomena rather than as a single phenomenon (related to molecular vibration) on a continuum (see De Berg 2008; Paik et al. 2004; Johnson 1998a, 1998b).

# Apparatus and Materials

- Beaker
- Thermometer
- Ice
- Tripod
- Gauze
- Burner or hot plate

NATIONAL SCIENCE TEACHERS ASSOCIATION

## *How Much Ice Do You Want?*

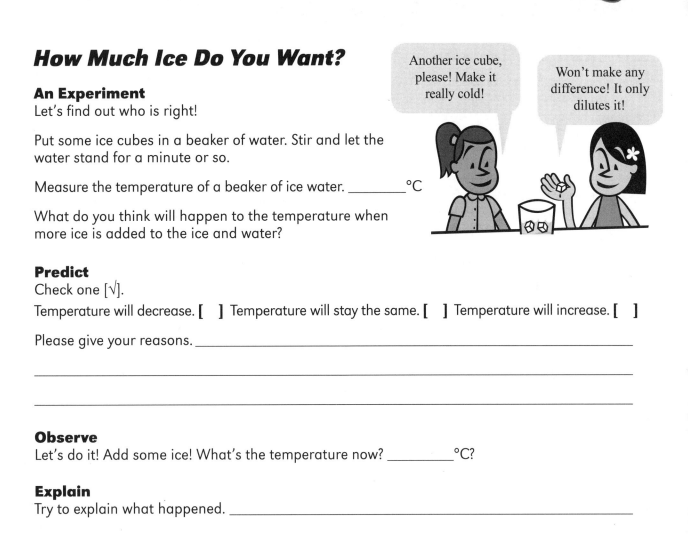

### An Experiment
Let's find out who is right!

Put some ice cubes in a beaker of water. Stir and let the water stand for a minute or so.

Measure the temperature of a beaker of ice water. _____°C

What do you think will happen to the temperature when more ice is added to the ice and water?

### Predict
Check one [√].

Temperature will decrease. **[     ]**     Temperature will stay the same. **[     ]**     Temperature will increase. **[     ]**

Please give your reasons. _____

_____

_____

### Observe
Let's do it! Add some ice! What's the temperature now? _____°C?

### Explain
Try to explain what happened. _____

_____

_____

_____

### *Try This!*
Let's try heating the beaker for a short time to melt some of the ice. What do you think will happen to the temperature? How come?_____

_____

_____

Can you explain that? _____

_____

_____

## Scientific Explanation

Water boils at 100°C. It makes no difference if you boil it quickly or slowly.

Turning water at 100°C into steam at 100°C requires heat energy. Hence, when you increase the heat supplied to boiling water, you do not increase its temperature, but you do produce steam more rapidly.

## Students' Explanations: Field Experience

One teacher has this to say:

> **Good for questioning: "If heat is going into the beaker, why is the temperature not going up? What is the energy (heat) doing?"**

## Students' Explanations: Research Findings

Brook, Briggs, Bell, and Driver (1987) reported that among 15-year-old students, only 37% of responses to the potato question included accepted ideas about heat transfer during change of state.

## Apparatus and Materials

- 2 hot plates
- 2 beakers
- Thermometer

## Boiling Potatoes

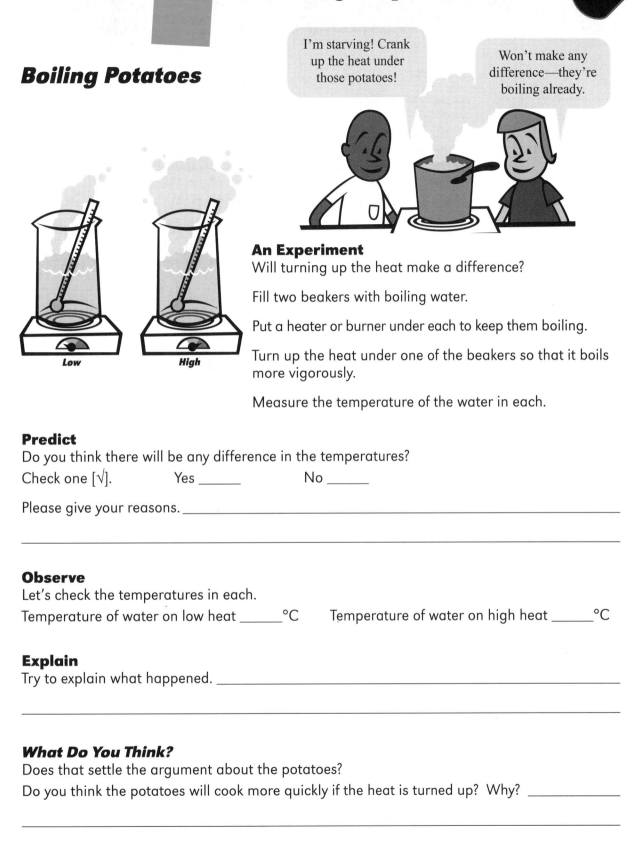

*I'm starving! Crank up the heat under those potatoes!*

*Won't make any difference—they're boiling already.*

**An Experiment**

Will turning up the heat make a difference?

Fill two beakers with boiling water.

Put a heater or burner under each to keep them boiling.

Turn up the heat under one of the beakers so that it boils more vigorously.

Measure the temperature of the water in each.

**Predict**

Do you think there will be any difference in the temperatures?

Check one [√].          Yes _____          No _____

Please give your reasons. _____

_____

**Observe**

Let's check the temperatures in each.

Temperature of water on low heat _____°C          Temperature of water on high heat _____°C

**Explain**

Try to explain what happened. _____

_____

**What Do You Think?**

Does that settle the argument about the potatoes?

Do you think the potatoes will cook more quickly if the heat is turned up?  Why? _____

_____

_____

_____

## Scientific Explanation

When antifreeze or sugar is dissolved in water, the boiling point is raised; the more that is added, the more the boiling point is raised. When dissolved, sugar or antifreeze is attracted to the water particles. This makes it more difficult for the water to change into a gas (steam) and escape.

In general, when you add a solute to a solvent, the boiling point of the resulting solution is greater than that of the pure solvent. The more solute that is added, the greater the elevation of the boiling point.

## Students' Explanations: Research Findings

Horton (2004) reported Thomaz et al.'s (1995) finding that some students believe that the temperature at which water boils is the maximum temperature to which it can be raised.

With this in mind, it may be interesting to do the second part of the experiment *after* your students have had the opportunity to explain the first part.

## Apparatus and Materials

- 2 beakers
- 2 hot plates (or two tripods, gauze, and burners)
- Thermometer.
- 100 ml measuring cylinder
- Antifreeze
- Sugar lumps

## *Overheated*

### Riddle

If antifreeze prevents your car radiator from freezing, can it possibly keep your engine from overheating?

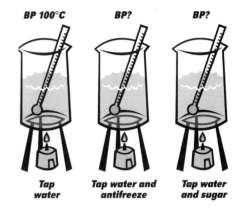

BP 100°C    BP?    BP?

Tap water | Tap water and antifreeze | Tap water and sugar

### Two Experiments

Water boils at 100°C. What do you think would happen to the boiling point if we added

(a) some antifreeze or (b) some sugar? Do you think the boiling point would go up, go down, or stay the same?

### Predict

(a) Adding antifreeze _____ (b) Adding sugar _____

Try to explain your thinking. _____

### Observe

Measure 100 ml of water into each of two beakers. Add increasing amounts of antifreeze to one and sugar to the other. Measure their boiling points.

| Antifreeze Added (ml) | Boiling Point (°C) | | Sugar Lumps Added | Boiling Point (°C) |
|---|---|---|---|---|
| 10 | | | 1 | |
| 20 | | | 2 | |
| 30 | | | 3 | |

### Explain

Can you make up a rule that tells you what happens to the boiling point of a solvent when you add solute?

_____

_____

_____

# Scientific Explanation

The answer to both introductory questions is true.

(i) The air in a tennis ball tries to expand as it heats up. This affects the bounce.

(ii) As you drive, your tires heat up on account of friction. The air tries to expand. The pressure inside the tire rises.

Air expands when it is heated. The balloon inflates a little when the bottle is put in warm water. It inflates more when the bottle is put in hot water. Dr. Y's invention helps you see this expansion clearly. The glass tube records small changes in volume. Dr. Y's invention can be turned into a thermometer by calibrating it.

# Students' Explanations: Field Experience

This POE was used with grade 7 students. A sample of 25 responses was analyzed. Ninety-six percent (96%) predicted correctly that the balloon would increase in size. The teacher remarked, "High success rate—some students felt it was much too easy." However, a close examination of their responses indicated that only 60–70% seemed to directly relate the expansion of air to temperature increase. Some of these students expressed themselves succinctly, some did not. Compare these two examples:

> *The air will expand and fill the balloon because it cannot escape.*

> *I think the balloon will blow up because the hot air pressure will make the balloon expand making it blow up.*

Among the remainder, a variety of scientifically unacceptable reasons for their predictions was evident:

> *Because heat rises so that it will blow up the balloon.*

> *The air will turn into steam.*

> *I think the vapor will blow up the balloon. The vapor has to go up so it will go into the balloon.*

> *... the water will expand and force air into the balloon.*

Forty percent (40%) of students made valuable suggestions for improving Dr. Y's temperature measurer, 24% suggested putting a scale on the glass tubing, and 16% talked in terms of calibrating the tube.

This student even gave details of how he would calibrate the tube.

> *I would put it in freezing water to make the water go to zero and make a mark, then put it in boiling water and make a mark, then divide the rest of the middle up.*

# Students' Explanations: Research Findings

In his study of 25 8- to 11-year-olds (reported in Driver, Squires, Rushworth, and Wood-Robinson 1995), Appleton found that many lacked knowledge of how thermometers worked, possibly related to them seeing heat as a "substance" (see De Berg 2008) rather than being related to the *thermal motion* of particles. When students understand that heat represents the thermal motion of particles, then they have improved understanding of the contraction and expansion of materials when heated or cooled (Ebenezer and Puvirajah 2005).

# Apparatus and Materials

- Soda bottle (glass works best)
- Balloon
- Bucket

Dr. Y's invention: 1 hole stopper, small flask or bottle (about 100 ml), 1 m of glass tubing (if desired, this can be bent in a propane flame), rubber tubing

# Hot Air

### True or False?

At major tennis tournaments, the balls are stored in a cooler before they are used.

True or false? _____

The pressure in your car tires is higher after a drive.

True or false? _____

Do you know why?

### An Experiment

Do you know what happens to air when it is heated?

Stretch a balloon across the top of a soda bottle.

First put the bottle in warm water.

Then put the bottle in hot water.

Warm water

### Predict

What do you think will happen? Please explain. _____

_____

### Observe

Let's do it! What happens? _____

### Explain

Try to explain what happened using the word *expands*.

_____

_____

Dr. Y has invented a *temperature measurer.*

**Rubber tubing**

**Glass tube with a "u" at one end**

**Colored water**

Do you think it will work? What do you think will happen if he puts the bottle into warm water?

_____

_____

_____

Can you improve it? Can you turn it into a thermometer? How?

_____

_____

_____

## Scientific Explanation

When you heat the ball, it expands. The amount of expansion is so small that you can't detect it with your eye. The ball can no longer pass through the ring.

When you heat the ring, this expands. The ball passes through easily.

When you heat the bottle cap, the cap expands more than the bottle and is more easily unscrewed.

## Students' Explanations: Field Experience

This POE was used with grade 7 students. A sample of 25 of their responses was analyzed.

Eighty-eight percent (88%) predicted correctly that the ball would not go through the ring after it was heated. All of these students used the idea of expansion in their reasoning:

> *Because it will expand when it is heated just enough to not go through.*

> *Because when something's heated it expands, so it will make the ball bigger so it can't get through the ring.*

After observing what happened, all of those who predicted incorrectly were able to give reasons in terms of expansion.

The teacher explained that this high success rate was probably due to the fact that the students had already been taught that an increase in temperature results in expansion.

## Students' Explanations: Research Findings

In his study of 25 8- to 11-year-olds (reported in Driver, Squires, Rushworth, and Wood-Robinson 1995), Appleton found that many lacked knowledge of how thermometers worked, possibly related to them seeing heat as a "substance" (see De Berg 2008) rather than being related to the *thermal motion* of particles. When students understand that heat represents the thermal motion of particles, then they have improved understanding of the contraction and expansion of materials when heated or cooled (Ebenezer and Puvirajah 2005).

## Apparatus and Materials

- Ball and ring (available commercially)
- Burner
- Bottle with screw top (optional)

## The Ball and Ring

**Hot water**

Have you ever struggled to unscrew the cap of a soda bottle?
Try warming the cap under hot water!
Do you know why this works?

### An Experiment
Have you seen the ball and ring trick?

The ball just passes through the ring.

*Now* heat the ball and try again.

Do you think it will pass through?

### Predict
Will the ball still pass through? Check one [√].   Yes **[   ]** No **[   ]**

Please give your reasons. _____

_____

### Observe
What happens after you have heated the ball? _____

_____

### Explain
Try to explain what you saw. _____

_____

(a) Cool the ball and ring under the tap. Then heat the ring. What do you think will happen this time? Please explain.

_____

_____

(b) Do you have any ideas about why warming the bottle cap loosens it?

_____

_____

## Scientific Explanation

Metals expand when heated—although it's often impossible to detect this with the eye. When the threaded brass rod is heated, it expands and some of its mass moves away from the balance point. Compare this with what happens as you edge your way toward the end of a teeter-totter.

Some may think that it goes down because heat energy has mass. But heat doesn't have mass! You could demonstrate this by weighing the rod and bolt before and after heating. It will weigh the same.

## Students' Explanations: Research Findings

Schmidt (1997) (reported in Horton [2004]) identified the following alternative conceptions that students have about heat:

(a) Heat can add weight to the object being heated; heated copper is heavier than cold copper.

(b) Heat is like a fluid that can pass from one substance to another.

An analysis of the student discussions reported in Ebenezer and Puvirajah (2005) indicates some success in helping students understand scientific ideas behind thermal expansion, including the idea that particles with a lot of heat energy "push" against one another more than do particles with less heat energy.

## Apparatus and Materials

- Length of threaded brass rod and bolt to fit
- Razor blade
- Lump of modeling clay
- Source of heat

Safety note: It is recommended that a one-sided razor blade, such as those found in utility knives, is used, and that the experiment is demonstrated by the teacher.

## *Hot Rod!*

### Wondering Why?

1. Have you ever wondered why railway engineers leave a small gap between the lengths of rail line?

2. Have you ever wondered why road engineers leave small gaps in the roadway where they build bridges?

### An Experiment

What do you think will happen when you heat the rod?

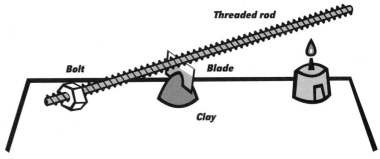

- Screw a bolt to a length of threaded rod. Then balance the rod on a blade (support the blade with a lump of clay or a block of wood).

- Unscrew the bolt until the rod just tilts to touch the tabletop.

- Heat the end of the rod.

### Predict

What do you think will happen? Please give your reasons. _____

_____

_____

### Observe

Let's heat it! Then let it cool! What happens? _____

_____

_____

### Explain

Try to explain what you saw. _____

_____

_____

# Scientific Explanation

Solid materials expand when they are heated, but they don't expand very much and you can't detect this expansion with your eye.

Different materials expand by different amounts. If different materials are stuck together, the laminate curves because one expands more than the other. Your eye can detect this curving.

A thermostat strip often is made from iron and brass stuck together.

# Students' Explanations: Field Experience

This POE was used with grade 7 students. A sample of 25 responses was examined.

Because 72% of the students correctly predicted that the strip made from aluminum foil and clear tape would bend, most of their explanations were the same as their predictions.

A few (20%) provided scientifically acceptable explanations:

> **The aluminum expanded and the tape didn't and it went toward the tape.**

Some explained what they saw in terms of the tape melting:

> **When we put it near the flame, the tape melted and made it curve toward the tape.**

Some hypothesized that the tape contracted:

> **The plastic tape contracted and pulled the aluminum foil to one side.**

Some attributed living qualities to the tape:

> **The tape is trying to protect itself to get away from the heat.**

As a result of this feedback, the explorations at the end of the POE assume importance. We suggest that you try a bimetallic strip of brass and iron, a brass strip, an iron strip, and so on.

# Students' Explanations: Research Findings

An analysis of the student discussions reported in Ebenezer and Puvirajah (2005) indicates some success in helping students understand scientific ideas behind thermal expansion, including the idea that particles with a lot of heat energy "push" against each other more than do particles with less heat energy.

# Apparatus and Materials

- Aluminum foil
- Masking tape
- Clear tape
- Heat source
- Scissors
- A variety of strips (e.g., a bimetallic strip [available from some scientific providers], brass, iron, etc.) The laminate used to vacuum-seal coffee also works well and can provide an interesting puzzle.

## How Does a Thermostat Work?

Do you know how the thermostat in your electric kettle or range works?

When the kettle or range gets too hot, the thermostat strip **bends** and breaks the circuit.

But why does it bend?

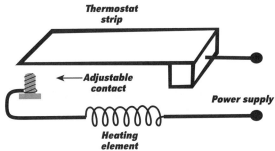

### An Experiment

Could a strip of aluminum foil be used in a thermostat?

Could a strip of aluminum foil with masking tape or clear tape stuck to the back be used?

Warm the strips over a hot plate, Bunsen burner, or candle. (Don't burn the tape or your fingers!)

### Predict
Which strip(s) do you think will bend?        (a) Aluminum **[    ]**        (b) Aluminum + Tape **[    ]**

Please give your reasons. _____

_____

### Observe
Let's do it! What happens? _____

_____

### Explain
Try to explain what happened. _____

_____

### More to Explore!
Try some strips made from other materials.

Which strips bend? _____

Which strips don't bend? _____

What material do you think was used to make the metal strip in the thermostat?

_____

_____

## Scientific Explanation

When the amount of heat energy is doubled, scientists would expect the temperature increase to double. However, because some heat is lost to the surrounding air, there will be some discrepancy.

## Students' Explanations: Field Experience

This POE was used with 52 grade 7 students. The students' predictions were difficult to interpret. And their observations varied. Their explanations were absent more often than not. We surmise that this may be attributed to the students doing this as a lab and because the completion of the POE was not closely supervised. This in turn led us to wonder if learning would have been enhanced if the experience had been more tightly structured.

However, a teacher rated the learning experience as very good:

> *Very straightforward. Students grasp energy input is proportional to temperature rise and it springboards into calorimetry.*

## Students' Explanations: Research Findings

In their summary of research into students' ideas about heat and temperature, Erikson and Tiberghein (1985) noted that many students have difficulty distinguishing between heat and temperature. Some consider temperature to be an extensive property of substances, believing, for example that the temperature of an object is related to its size (such that a large ice cube is colder than a small ice cube).

In addition, De Berg (2008) in his summary of research, identifies five more common student ideas that are not in accord with the current scientific views:

1. Temperature is thought to be a measurement of heat.

2. Heat is opposite of cold (rather than being a phenomenon of the same kind).

3. Students make judgments about the temperature of an object based on the material from which the object is made, rather than on its environment. (This problem is considered in HT4.)

4. Students use addition and subtraction strategies when mixing equal volumes of water at different temperatures. (This problem is the focus of TH10.)

5. The consistency of temperature during boiling and freezing is counterintuitive (see TH1 and TH2).

## Apparatus and Materials

- Boiling tube
- Thermometer
- Measuring cylinder (10 or 25 ml)
- Book of cardboard matches
- Pins (used for holding matches away from fingers) (Instead of lighting the match on the cover, you might find it easier to use a candle or another lighted match.)

Note: It is recommended that this experiment be done as a demonstration, especially as there is the possibility of students burning their fingers. Should you decide that it is desirable for the students to carry out the experiment, then it is recommended that you use tealights as an alternative to matches. Holding a tealight under a boiling tube containing 10 ml of water for 10 sec. will raise the temperature of the water by about 5°C.

# Can You Tell the Difference? I

Do you know the difference between heat and temperature? See if you can fill in the blanks in the sentences below. Try to use the words *heat* or *temperature* as scientists use them.

What is the _____ of tap water?

Two matches give off twice as much _____ as one.

Can you get enough _____ from a burning match to raise the _____ of water to its boiling point?

Now try to write down what you understand by these two words.

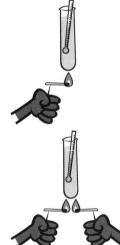

Let's find out how much the temperature of 10 ml of tap water will rise when it is warmed up with the heat from one match.

• Measure the temperature of the tap water at the beginning.      ____ °C

• Now heat the water with a match. Measure the final temperature.   ____ °C

• How much did the temperature rise?                 ____ °C

### An Experiment: Doubling the Heat
Let's find out if there is any difference when we use the heat from two matches?

Put 10 ml of fresh tap water into a cold test tube. How much do you think the temperature will rise?

### Predict
How much do you think the temperature will rise? _____°C

Please give your reasons. _____

_____

### Observe
Beginning temperature _____°C     Final temperature _____°C     Temperature increase _____°C

### Explain
Compare the temperature increase between one and two matches. Try to make sense of your results.

_____

_____

### Hmm ...
Let's try doubling the heat and doubling the volume of water! What do you think will happen?

Try to explain. _____

_____

_____

## Scientific Explanation

The element in the kettle turns electrical energy into *thermal motion* (increased vibration of molecules, which we often call heat energy). The amount of heat produced in 60 seconds is twice that produced in 30 seconds. Doubling the heat or thermal motion doubles the increase in temperature.

When you double the amount of water, you halve the temperature increase because there is twice as much water to heat up (twice as many molecules to vibrate to the same amount).

When you double the amount of water and double the heat provided, you obtain the same temperature increase as before. (Note that the extra energy required to cause a change in state [e.g., from liquid to gas] means that the relationship between energy input and temperature increase is not strictly linear.)

## Students' Explanations: Research Findings

In their summary of research into students' ideas about heat and temperature, Erikson and Tiberghein (1985) noted that many students have difficulty distinguishing between heat and temperature. Some consider temperature to be an extensive property of substances, believing, for example, that the temperature of an object is related to its size (such that a large ice cube is colder than a small ice cube).

In addition, De Berg (2008), in his summary of research, identifies five more common student ideas that are not in accord with the current scientific views:

1.  Temperature is thought to be a measurement of heat.

2.  Heat is opposite of cold (rather than being a phenomena of the same kind).

3.  Students make judgments about the temperature of an object based on the material from which the object is made, rather than on its environment. (This problem is considered in HT4.)

4.  Students use addition and subtraction strategies when mixing equal volumes of water at different temperatures. (This problem is the focus of TH10.)

5.  The consistency of temperature during boiling and freezing is counterintuitive (see TH1 and TH2).

## Apparatus and Materials

- Kettle
- Measuring cylinder (500 ml measure)
- Thermometer

# Can You Tell the Difference? II

## Investigating the Heat From Electricity

The element in a kettle changes electrical energy into heat energy.

Let's find out how much the temperature of the water rises if we heat 500 ml of water for 30 sec.

- Put 500 ml of cold tap water into the empty kettle and take the beginning temperature. _____°C

- Turn on the kettle for 30 sec. and take the final temperature. _____°C

- Calculate the rise in temperature. _____°C

### Experiment 1: Doubling the Heat

Put **500 ml** of cold tap water into the empty kettle and heat for **60 sec**.

### Predict

What do you predict the rise in temperature will be? _____°C  Please explain._____

_____

### Experiment 2: Doubling the Heat and Doubling the Volume of Water

Put **1,000 ml** of cold tap water into the empty kettle and heat for **60 sec**.

### Predict

What do you predict the rise in temperature will be? _____°C  Please explain. _____

_____

### Observe

Record your observations for all of your experiments in the table.

| | First Investigation | Experiment 1: Doubling the Heat | Experiment 2: Doubling Heat and Doubling Volume of Water |
|---|---|---|---|
| Amount of water | 500 ml | 500 ml | 1,000 ml |
| Heating time | 30 s | 60 s | 60 s |
| Final temperature | | | |
| Beginning temperature | | | |
| Rise in temperature | | | |

### Explain

Try to make sense of the way the temperature increase varies depending on the amount of heat and the amount of water._____

_____

_____

## Scientific Explanation

When you mix one cup of hot water with one cup of cold water (or two hot with two cold), the final temperature is halfway between the two temperatures. Hot water has more heat energy than cold water. When you mix it with cold water, this energy is dispersed over the whole volume. Temperature measures *thermal motion* (the random jiggling motion of atoms where increased jiggling indicates greater energy).

## Students' Explanations: Field Experience

Twenty-nine (29) grade 7 students were asked to predict the final temperature when water at 10°C was mixed with an equal quantity of water at 80°C. Here are their predictions:

| Temperature Prediction (°C) | Number of Students Making Prediction |
|:---:|:---:|
| 90 | 4 |
| 80 | 3 |
| 76 | 1 |
| 70 | 4 |
| 65 | 2 |
| 64 | 1 |
| 60 | 2 |
| 50 | 1 |
| 45 | 4 |
| 40 | 6 |
| 39 | 1 |

This was evidently a difficult task for students. Some appeared to struggle to put their ideas into words, and others admitted to guessing:

*I think it is because the more of one kind it will be that, but when even (amount of cups) it will be in the middle. (predicted 60°C)*

*I made my prediction on plain and simple guess and by trying to use the facts. (predicted 45°C)*

Some added temperature together, and some subtracted them:

*I added to total amount to get the prediction. (predicted 90°C)*

*I think it would go to 70°C because 10°C of cool water would cool the 80°C water down. (predicted 70°C)*

On one hand, these students evidently did not recognize temperature as being an intensive property of matter. On the other hand, some did recognize temperature as being an intensive property:

*I made my prediction halfway between the two temperatures. (predicted 45°C)*

*I made my prediction by guessing because if you had one of each it would be luke warm. (predicted 40°C)*

Some of their reasons were difficult to interpret:

*I think the cold water will have no effect. (predicted 80°C)*

Three or four students shared this view, which would seem to be a denial of their everyday experiences.

## Students' Explanations: Research Findings

Children's ideas about mixing hot and cold water have been studied by a number of researchers (see Erikson and Tiberghein [1985] and De Berg [2008] for summaries. They highlighted several problems, including that students often use the terms *temperature* and *heat* interchangeably. Their findings are similar to ours. Both addition and subtraction strategies were evident. Although young students intuitively understand what happens qualitatively, one study indicated that only 10–25% of 13- and 14-year-olds were able to respond correctly to quantitative problems. Some success in helping the students resolve this discrepancy was achieved by deliberately inviting them to juxtapose their qualitative and quantitative thinking.

## Apparatus and Materials

- 5 Styrofoam cups
- Ice cream bucket
- Thermometer

# Mixing Hot and Cold Water

### Just the Right Temperature for Bathing

Have you ever had problems getting the temperature of the bath or shower just right?  What's the secret?

If you mix 1 cup of water at 10°C with 1 cup of water at 50°C, what temperature will you get?

### An Experiment

Try mixing different quantities of hot and cold water.

- Run the tap and then collect 3 cups of cold water and 2 cups of hot water in separate containers.

- Measure their temperatures.

  Cold water _____°C

  Hot water _____°C

### Predict

Try to predict the resulting temperature when you mix different quantities together. Use the table below.

| Number of Cups of Cold Water (___°C) | Number of Cups of Hot Water (___°C) | Predicted Temp. of Mixture (___°C) | Observed Temp. of Mixture (___°C) |
|:---:|:---:|:---:|:---:|
| 1 | 1 | | |
| 1 | 2 | | |
| 2 | 2 | | |
| 3 | 2 | | |

Try to explain how you made your predictions. _____

_____

### Observe

Let's do it! Fill in the last column of the table.

### Explain

How good were your predictions? Can you find a way to calculate the temperature of the mixture?

_____

_____

_____

## Scientific Explanation

Oil heats up more rapidly than water. It takes less heat energy than water to raise its temperature. Oil has a lower heat capacity than water.

If you lower a 100 g weight at 100°C into 100 ml of oil and another into 100ml of water, the temperature of the oil rises more than the temperature of the water. Because the heat capacity of oil is less than that of water, it requires less heat to raise its temperature by a given amount. The same amount of heat will raise its temperature more.

## Students' Explanations: Research Findings

Horton (2004) identified studies that report the following alternative conceptions about heat capacity:

(a) Metals hold heat better then wood.

(b) Metals hold cold.

(c) Metals absorb more cold than plastic

## Apparatus and Materials

- Hot plate
- 2 beakers
- 2 thermometers
- 2 100 g weights (iron or brass)
- Cooking oil

## Heat Capacities of Different Liquids

### Quick Quiz
Do you know which heats up faster on your stove, a pan of cooking oil or a pan of water?

### An Experiment
Put two beakers of the same size on a hot plate.

- Fill the beakers to the same level, one with oil and one with water.

- Which do you think will heat up faster?

### Predict
Check one [√].      (a) Oil **[   ]**      (b) Water **[   ]**      (c) Same **[   ]**

Please give your reasons. _____

_____

### Observe
Turn on the hot plate. Record the time it takes for each liquid to reach 50°C.

Oil _____                    Water _____

### Explain
Try to explain what happened using your ideas about temperature and heat.

_____

_____

### Another Experiment
Heat up two 100 g weights to 100°C in boiling water. Lower one into 100 ml of oil and the other into 100 ml of water.

Oil      Water

Do you think the temperature of one liquid will rise more than the other? Please explain.

_____

_____

_____

## Scientific Explanation

The temperature of the water increases far more when 100 g of water are added than when 100 g of metal weight (iron or brass) are added. The heat capacity of water is about 10 times greater than the heat capacity of metal (the specific heat capacity of water is 4.2 Joules/g°C, whereas that of brass and iron is about 0.4 Joules/g°C).

## Students' Explanations: Field Experience

A sample of 28 responses from grade 7 students was analyzed.

Fifty percent (50%) correctly predicted that the water would hold more heat energy. Some of these students associated this with the fact that water takes a longer time to cool:

> *... because when you boil water it stays hot for a long time but rocks don't stay hot as long.*

Some of those who predicted that the metal would hold more heat associated this with it being a solid, others thought this was because its melting point is greater than 100°C, and others made this prediction because it seems to be hotter on a summer day.

The teacher noted that the students were interested in talking about the length of time it took to warm the local swimming spot.

## Students' Explanations: Research Findings

Horton (2004) identified studies that report the following alternative conceptions about heat capacity:

(a) Metals hold heat better than wood.

(b) Metals hold cold.

(c) Metals absorb more cold than plastic.

## Apparatus and Materials

- 2 or 3 beakers (250 ml)
- 100 g brass or iron weight
- 100 ml measuring cylinder
- Thermometer
- Source of heat
- Electric kettle (optional)

# Which Contains More Heat Energy?

### Did You Know?

In days gone by, before houses had heating systems, people used to warm their beds with hot water bottles or hot rocks. They would have liked to have known what worked best—water, rocks, or something else.

Do you think there is any difference? Which contains more heat energy?

### An Experiment

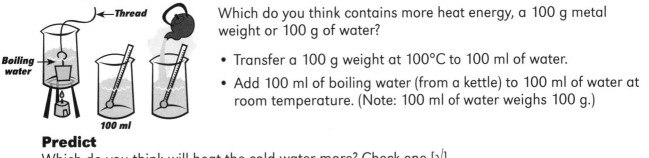

Which do you think contains more heat energy, a 100 g metal weight or 100 g of water?

- Transfer a 100 g weight at 100°C to 100 ml of water.
- Add 100 ml of boiling water (from a kettle) to 100 ml of water at room temperature. (Note: 100 ml of water weighs 100 g.)

### Predict

Which do you think will heat the cold water more? Check one [√].

The metal weight **[    ]**          The boiling water **[    ]**          The same **[    ]**

Please give your reasons for your prediction._____

_____

_____

### Observe

| | |
|---|---|
| Temperature of cold water | _____°C |
| Temperature of cold water + 100 g metal (at 100°C) | _____°C |
| Temperature of cold water + 100 g of boiling water | _____°C |

### Explain

Which contains more heat energy? Does this surprise you?

_____

_____

### *Hold on!*

Back to the bed-warmers!

How would you design an experiment to find out which contains more heat: a rock (the size of a large pebble) or the same mass of water?

_____

_____

# References

Brook, A., H. Briggs, B. Bell, and R. Driver. 1987. *Aspects of secondary students' understanding of heat.* Leeds, United Kingdom: University of Leeds.

De Berg, K. C. 2008. The concepts of heat and temperature: The problem of determining the content for the construction of a historical case study which is sensitive to Nature of Science issues and teaching-learning issues. *Science & Education* 17 (1): 75–114.

Driver, R., and T. Russell. 1982. *An investigation of the ideas of heat, temperature and change of state of children ages 8 and 14 years.* London: University of Leeds and Chelsea College.

Driver, R., A. Squires, P. Rushworth, and V. Wood-Robinson. 1995. Heating. In *Making sense of secondary science*, 138–142. London and New York: Routledge.

Ebenezer, J., and A. Puvirajah. 2005. WebCT dialogues on particle theory of matter: Presumptive reasoning schemes. *Educational Research and Evaluation* 11: 561–589.

Erikson, G., and A. Tiberghein. 1985. Heat and temperature. In *Children's ideas in science*, ed. R. Driver, E. Guesne, and A. Tiberghein, 52–84. Buckingham, United Kingdom: Open University Press.

Horton, C. 2004. Student alternative conceptions in chemistry. Report by the Modeling Instruction in Chemistry action research team, Arizona State University. *http://modeling.asu.edu/modeling/Chem-AltConceptions3-09.doc.*

Johnson, P. 1998a. Children's understanding of changes of state involving the gas state, Part 1: Boiling water and the particle theory. *International Journal of Science Education* 20 (5): 567–583.

Johnson, P. 1998b. Children's understanding of changes of state involving the gas state, Part 2: Evaporation and condensation below boiling point. *International Journal of Science Education* 20 (6): 695–709.

Paik, S-H., H. N. Kim, G. K. Cho, and J. W. Park. 2004. K–8th grade Korean students' conceptions of "changes of state" and "conditions for change of state." *International Journal of Science Education* 26 (2): 207–224.

Schmidt, H-J. 1997. Students' misconceptions: Looking for a pattern. *Science Education* 81 (2): 123–135.

Thomaz, M., M. C. Valente, I. M. Maliquias, and M. Aritanes. 1995. An attempt to overcome alternative conceptions related to heat and temperature. *Physics Education* 30 (1): 19–36.

# Chapter 3

**Contents**

## Scientific Explanation

The rods made from aluminum, brass, and iron feel hot. Those made from glass, wood, and plastic feel cold. Heat travels easily through metals. Metals are good conductors of heat; by comparison, other materials are poor. When your skin is used to detect temperature, you are basing your conclusion about the temperature on the *thermal motion* of the molecules of the materials you are touching—in other words, how fast its atoms are vibrating.

## Students' Explanations: Research Findings

Studies indicate that students use a variety of ideas to explain the thermal conductivity of different materials—for example, some materials attract heat better than others, some materials hold heat better than others, weaker materials transmit heat better, and heat is not strong enough to penetrate some objects (Erikson 1985).

When students were asked to explain why a metal spoon felt hotter than a plastic or wooden spoon when placed in hot water, 64% of 15-year-old students gave acceptable explanations (in terms of conduction). Sixteen percent (16%) provided explanations in terms of other processes, such as metal attracting or absorbing heat better, metal conducting electricity better, or hot water being unable to penetrate the metal (Brook, Briggs, Bell, and Driver 1987).

## Apparatus and Materials

- Rods made of aluminum, brass, iron, plastic, wood, and glass
- Beaker (To cut down on the effects of convection, cover the beaker with a piece of cardboard that has holes pierced in it.)
- Kettle

Safety note: Hot water can scald. Make sure any students participating in the experiment do not knock over the beaker. It is unlikely that students will burn themselves from touching any of the metal rods. However, as a precaution, you might first check the rods yourself and only fill the beaker halfway.

## *Hot Spoons*

If you leave a metal spoon, a plastic spoon, and a wooden spoon in a cup of hot chocolate, which feels hottest? Do you know why?

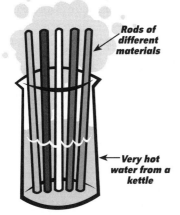

*Rods of different materials*

*Very hot water from a kettle*

### An Experiment

Which materials get hotter the fastest: glass, brass, iron, plastic, wood, aluminum?

Put rods made from these materials in very hot water and leave them there for a few minutes.

### Predict

Which rods do you think will feel hot?  _____

Which rods do you think will feel cool?  _____

Do you have any ideas why?_____

_____

_____

### Observe

These materials felt hot (or very warm).  _____    _____    _____

These materials felt cold (or cool).  _____    _____    _____

### Explain

Which types of materials got hotter more quickly? Do you have any ideas why? _____

_____

_____

_____

## Scientific Explanation

If all containers were identical (in shape, thickness, and color), scientists would expect the metal container to cool fastest, the china next, plastic next, and Styrofoam last. Although we often think that heat travels fastest through iron, it is better to think of iron as a good conductor of *thermal motion* (the vibration of molecules)—which is the transfer of energy through the iron. Thus, iron is a good conductor of energy, and china and plastic are poor conductors of energy. Styrofoam is a poor conductor of energy and is therefore used as an insulator.

The Styrofoam mug will keep a hot drink hot for the longest time, followed by plastic, then china, then metal.

## Students' Explanations: Research Findings

Studies indicate that students use a variety of ideas to explain the thermal conductivity of different materials—for example, some materials attract heat energy better than others, some materials hold heat energy better than others, weaker materials transmit heat better, and heat is not strong enough to penetrate some objects (Erikson 1985).

When asked to explain why a metal spoon felt hotter than a plastic or wooden spoon when placed in hot water, 64% of 15-year-old students gave acceptable explanations (in terms of conduction). Sixteen percent (16%) provided explanations in terms of other processes, such as metal attracting or absorbing heat better, metal conducting electricity better, or hot water being unable to penetrate the metal (Brook, Briggs, Bell, and Driver 1987).

## Apparatus and Materials

- 4 similar mugs or cups (tin, china, plastic, Styrofoam)
- Thermometer
- Kettle
- Cardstock

Note: Styrofoam cups (4) filled 1 cm below the lip provide useful measures. You might need some ice cubes to carry out the follow-up experiment.

# Keeping Coffee Hot

*China*      *Metal*      *Styrofoam*      *Plastic*

Which mug will keep coffee or hot chocolate hot the longest? Do you know why?

## An Experiment

250 ml of water

- To be accurate, choose mugs or cups of similar size and shape.
- Fill each cup with the same quantity of boiling water (about 250 ml).
- Cover each with a piece of cardstock and measure the water temperatures after 10 min.
- While you're waiting for the water to cool, check the temperatures of the outside of the containers. You can use your fingers.

## Predict

Which do you think will remain hottest? _____ Which next? _____

Next? _____ Next? _____

Give your reasons for your predictions. _____

_____

_____

## Observe

While you are waiting, record which mugs or cups feel hottest on the outside.

Hottest   _____   _____   _____   _____   Coldest

| Type of Mug | China | Metal | Styrofoam | Plastic |
|---|---|---|---|---|
| Temperature after 10 min. (°C) | | | | |

## Explain

Try to explain your observations. (Hint: Through which materials does heat travel quickly?)

_____

## Hey!

Which mug do you think will keep a cold drink coolest? _____

Design an experiment to test your prediction.

## Scientific Explanation

Copper conducts heat much better than wood. The temperature of the wood rod (at the joint) increases faster than the copper rod because the heat is conducted away less quickly. Hence, the "scorching temperature" of paper is reached more quickly on the wooden side of the joint.

## Students' Explanations: Research Findings

Studies indicate that students use a variety of ideas to explain the thermal conductivity of different materials—for example, some materials attract heat better than others, some materials hold heat better than others, weaker materials transmit heat better, and heat is not strong enough to penetrate some objects (Erikson 1985).

When students were asked to explain why a metal spoon felt hotter than a plastic or wooden spoon when placed in hot water, 64% of 15-year-old students gave acceptable explanations (in terms of conduction). Sixteen percent (16%) provided explanations in terms of other processes, such as metal attracting or absorbing heat better, metal conducting electricity better, or hot water being unable to penetrate the metal (Brook, Briggs, Bell, and Driver 1987).

This POE invites students to reconsider two alternative conceptions that have been identified by a number of researchers (see Horton 2004).

1.  Conductors (metal) conduct heat more slowly than insulators, so heat builds up in them more quickly.

2.  Metals attract heat better than wood.

## Apparatus and Materials

- 30 cm of 1/2 in. copper pipe
- 30 cm of 1/2 in. wooden dowel (the end of the dowel can be sanded or shaved a little to fit inside the pipe)
- Masking tape
- Heat source (e.g., candle)

## *Scorching Paper*

### True or False?
Check one [√].

(1) Paper scorches when you heat it gently.  True _____  False _____

(2) Copper conducts heat better than wood.  True _____  False _____

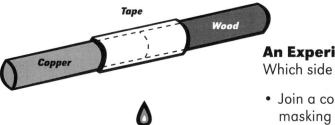

### An Experiment
Which side of the paper will scorch first? _____

- Join a copper rod and a wooden rod with one layer of masking tape.
- Slowly heat the paper over a heat source.

### Predict
Which side of paper will scorch first? Check one [√].

The side covering the copper **[ ]**  The side covering the wood **[ ]**  Both the same **[ ]**

Please give your reasons. _____

_____

_____

### Observe
Let's do it!

Which side of the paper scorches first? _____

### Explain
Try to explain what happened. _____

_____

_____

## Scientific Explanation

All the materials (carpet, wood, and tile) are at the same temperature—room temperature. Tiles feel coldest to your feet. They conduct heat away from your feet faster than wood or carpet. Carpet feels the warmest. It is a poor conductor of heat.

## Students' Explanations: Research Findings

Students suggest a variety of reasons as to why metals feel cold—for example, metals attract cold, metals lose heat to the air, metals have smooth shiny surfaces, and metals are cold by nature (Erikson 1985, p.59).

When asked why, on a cold day, metal handlebars feel colder than plastic hand grips, only 16% of students ages 11 to 15 gave acceptable answers in terms of conduction. Many other explanations of the phenomenon were given in terms of other properties of metals—for example, metals reflect heat, metal attracts heat, metal *is* colder, metal holds coldness, metal absorbs cold air, metal is harder, and metal is more susceptible to the surrounding temperature (Brook, Briggs, Bell, and Driver 1987).

Some students evidently judge the temperature of objects according to how they feel to the touch without considering how well they conduct heat. They think that metals are cold and nonmetals are warm even when both are sitting in a room at the same temperature (see review in De Berg 2008). This perspective may influence their responses in this POE.

This POE also addresses the concept of temperature equilibrium. Many students believe that two objects sitting in the same environment for a long period of time do not necessarily reach the same temperature (see Horton 2004).

## Apparatus and Materials

- Thermometer
- Squares of carpet, tile, and wood.

Note: Other materials (e.g., metal, plastic, paper, glass, Styrofoam) also produce good effects.

# Cold to the Touch

Which feels coldest to your feet:
carpet, tile, or wood?

Do you have any ideas why?

**Carpet**   **Tile**   **Wood**

## An Experiment
Hold different materials against your
cheek. How do they feel? Is one really colder than the other?

Make your predictions about the temperatures of the materials. Then check the
temperatures by laying a thermometer on top.

## Predict
Which materials do you think are hotter than room temperature? _____

Which do you think are colder? _____

Which do you think are room temperature? _____

Do you think your cheek can measure temperature well? Please explain. _____

_____

_____

## Observe
Let's check their temperatures! Room temperature _____ °C

Carpet _____ °C          Tile _____ °C          Wood _____ °C

Material (_____) ___°C   Material (_____) ___°C   Material (_____) ___°C

## Explain
Which material conducts heat best? _____ Worst? _____

Do you have any explanations for the perception that the materials are at different temperatures?

_____

_____

_____

_____

_____

## Scientific Explanation

Hot air rises; it is less dense than cold air.

When the T-piece is in place, the hot air above the candle rises and escapes on one side of the T-piece. Fresh air is drawn in on the other side. When the T-piece is taken out, the hot air above the candle rises and escapes. This prevents the fresh air containing oxygen from being drawn in. The candle goes out.

## Students' Explanations: Research Findings

Students may have difficulty appreciating that the density of a gas varies with temperature. Johnson (1998) suggests, "If we are to develop an understanding of the gas state, the particle theory would appear to be a necessary way in." The higher the temperature, the farther apart the gas particles.

## Apparatus and Materials

- Soda bottle
- T-piece made of aluminum foil
- Candle
- 60 cm wire

## Hurricane Lamp

### Camping Tip
Here's how to make a good hurricane lamp:

Use a piece of wire to lower a lighted candle into a bottle.

Then insert a T-piece made from thick aluminum foil.

The candle won't blow out—even in strong winds.

Try it!

### An Experiment
The design of the lamp is a clever one. How does it work? Let's experiment!

### Predict
What do you think will happen if you take out the T-piece?

_____

Please give your reasons.

_____

_____

### Observe
Let's do it! What did you see? _____

_____

### Explain
Try to explain what happened. (Use the diagram above to show how you think air flows around the T-piece.)

_____

_____

_____

### Hey!
Check those explanations! Light the lamp again and hold a piece of smoking string at the mouth of the bottle to reveal the air currents in the bottle.

## Scientific Explanation

Hot liquids rise, just like air. The hot colored water escapes from one of the glass tubes and is replaced by cold water that enters through the other tube.

The magic trick isn't magic! Little mixing occurs when the hot water is in the top bottle.

## Apparatus and Materials

- Bottle
- 2-hole stoppers fitted with short glass tubes
- Large beaker
- Food coloring (much is needed)
- Optional: 4 bottles, index cards, large bowl

# Do Hot Liquids Rise?

## Quick Quiz

1. In your home, where is the best place for hot-air vents? Circle one.

   (a) near the floor       (b) near the ceiling       (c) halfway up the wall

2. Where is the best place for the heater in a hot water tank? Circle one.

   (a) at the bottom       (b) halfway up       (c) at the top

3. Hot air rises; how about hot water? _____

## An Experiment

How do hot and cold liquids mix?

Fill a bottle with brightly colored hot water.

Insert a 2-hole stopper and cover the tubes with your fingers.

Lower the stopper into a large beaker of cold water and remove your fingers.

### Predict

What do you think will happen? Use arrows in the diagram above to show how you think the water will move in and out of the bottle. Why do you think this will happen?

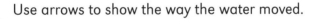

## Observe

Use arrows to show the way the water moved.

### Explain

Try to explain why the water moved this way.

_____

_____

_____

## *Magic or Science?*

All the bottles contain water. The water in the upper bottles is colored.

Look what happens when the cards are slipped out!

Magic? Can you explain how the trick works? Check your explanation—try it out!

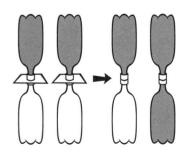

## Scientific Explanation

Warm liquids rise and cool liquids fall. This is called *convection*.

The cold water released by the floating ice cube as it melts naturally falls to the bottom of the beaker. It is replaced by the warmer water. The supply of warmer water melts more ice.

As the sunken ice cube melts, it becomes surrounded with cold water. This tends to stay at the bottom. Hence, the ice cube melts more slowly.

Believe it or not, Dr. Y is probably telling the truth! Hot water rises. The hot water produced by the burner moves away from the ice cube in the bottom of the test tube and moves toward the ice cube at the top. Hence the ice cube at the top probably will melt first.

## Apparatus and Materials

- 2 equal ice cubes (these may be colored with food coloring)
- Length of wire (e.g., copper)

Note: If you wish to perform Dr. Y's experiment, prepare ice cubes in the test tubes (having put a ball of copper wire in the test tube first). When you're ready, add cold water to each test tube to release the ice cubes.

## A Stirring Tale of Ice

### True or False
Stirring the ice in your drink melts the ice more quickly and cools your drink faster.

True **[   ]**   False **[   ]**   Please explain.

_____

_____

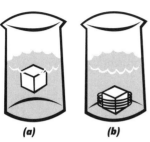

(a)          (b)

### An Experiment
Does ice melt faster if you push it under water?

Make 2 equal ice cubes (coloring the ice cubes with food coloring will help you see what happens).

Wrap wire around one of the ice cubes to make it sink.

Now put the ice cubes in two beakers, each containing the same amount of water.

Try it again using colored ice cubes.

### Predict
Which of the ice cubes do you think will melt first? Check one [√].

(a) Floating ice cube **[   ]**   (b) Ice cube wrapped with wire **[   ]**   (c) Both at the same time **[   ]**

Please explain your prediction. _____

_____

### Observe
Which melted first? _____

If you used colored water to make your ice cubes, describe what you saw.

(a) _____

(b) _____

### Explain
Try to explain what happened. _____

_____

### Believe It or Not!
Dr. Y claims to have made a remarkable discovery! He says the floating ice cube melts first. Do you believe him? Please explain.

_____

_____

_____

## Scientific Explanation

When the air inside a bottle warms up, it expands and fills the balloon. The air inside the black bottle warms fastest because dark colors absorb radiant heat better. The air inside the silver bottle warms slowest because the silver reflects most of the radiant heat.

## Students' Explanations: Research Findings

It is possible that the use of foil might confuse some students on account of their believing that foil is better at keeping things cold than a blanket because metals are cold and blankets are warm (Lewis and Linn 1994).

## Apparatus and Materials

- 3 similar soda bottles: 1 painted black, 1 painted white, 1 covered with aluminum foil
- 3 balloons
- Lamp (100 W) in holder

# What Color to Wear in the Summertime?

### Wonder Why?
Have you ever wondered why

- people wear white clothes in the tropics?
- space suits are shiny?
- tar on the road melts on hot, sunny days?

### An Experiment

Black   White   Shiny

Do some colors absorb radiant heat better than others?

Obtain 3 similar soda bottles. Paint 1 black and 1 white, and cover the third with aluminum foil.

Stretch a balloon over the mouth of each bottle.

Put a bright lamp midway between the bottles or put them outside in the sun. Watch what happens.

### Predict
What do you think will happen to the balloons?

_____

_____

Please give your reasons. _____

_____

### Observe
Record what you see. _____

_____

### Explain
Try to explain what happened. _____

_____

_____

## Scientific Explanation

The black can cools fastest. Dark-colored material radiates heat faster than light-colored or shiny material.

## Apparatus and Materials

- 3 soup cans: 1 painted black, 1 painted white, the third left shiny
- Card
- Thermometer
- Kettle
- Cardstock

# The Color of Woodstoves and Kettles

## Wonder Why?
Have you ever wondered why

- woodstoves and car radiators are usually black?
- kettles and toasters are usually made from materials that are light colored or shiny?

Do you have any ideas why?

## An Experiment

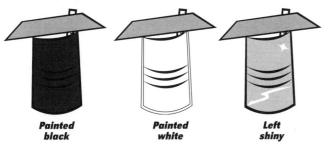

**Painted black**     **Painted white**     **Left shiny**

Which soup can loses heat fastest?

Obtain 3 similar soup cans. Paint 1 black and 1 white, and leave 1 shiny.

Fill each with the same quantity of boiling water and cover each with a piece of cardstock.

After 5 min., record the temperatures of each can of water.

## Predict
Do you expect the water temperature in the cans to be the same or different?

_____

Please give your reasons. _____

_____

## Observe
Record the temperature of the water in the cans.

Black can _____ °C          White can _____ °C          Shiny can _____ °C

## Explain
Try to explain what happened. _____

_____

_____

## Hey!
So why do you think woodstoves are black and kettles are light or shiny?

_____

_____

_____

# References

Brook, A., H. Briggs, B. Bell, and R. Driver. 1987. *Aspects of secondary students' understanding of heat.* Leeds, United Kingdom: University of Leeds.

De Berg, K. C. 2008. The concepts of heat and temperature: The problem of determining the content for the construction of a historical case study which is sensitive to Nature of Science issues and teaching-learning issues. *Science & Education* 17 (1): 75–114.

Erikson, G. 1985. Heat travel: An overview of pupils' ideas. In *Children's ideas in science.* ed. R. Driver, E. Guesne, and A. Tiberghien, 58–59. Buckingham, United Kingdom: Open University Press.

Horton, C. 2004. Student alternative conceptions in chemistry. Report by the Modeling Instruction in Chemistry action research team, Arizona State University. *http://modeling.asu.edu/modeling/Chem-AltConceptions3-09.doc.*

Johnson, P. 1998. Children's understanding of changes of state involving the gas state, Part 1: Boiling water and the particle theory. *International Journal of Science Education* 20 (5): 567–583.

Lewis, E., and M. Linn. 1994. Heat energy and temperature concepts of adolescents, adults and experts: Implications for curriculum developers. *Journal of Research in Science Teaching* 31: 657–77.

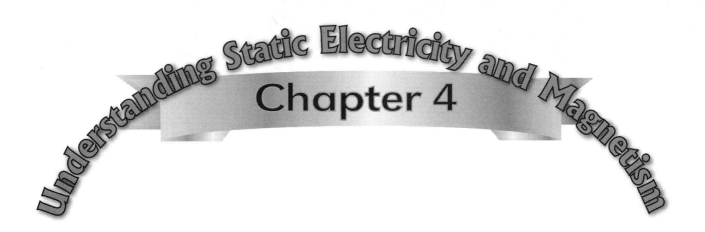

# Chapter 4

## Understanding Static Electricity and Magnetism

## Contents

# Scientific Explanation

A wheat puff is attracted to a charged plastic strip. All uncharged objects are attracted to charged objects.

If you let the charged strip touch the wheat puff, it shares some of its charge with the wheat puff. The puff and the strip now repel one another. Similarly charged objects repel one another. Sometimes your hair refuses to lie down because the separate hairs have become similarly charged.

When you touch the charged puff with your hand, you remove the charge from it (the charge is drained away). The charged strip will again attract the puff (all uncharged objects are attracted to charged objects).

Note: These experiments don't work well on humid days. The water in the air drains away the charge from charged objects.

# Students' Explanations: Research Findings

Students use many commonsense ideas to explain the phenomena associated with static electricity. Some think that static electricity results from friction alone (Siegel and Lee 2001; Baser and Geban 2007).

Guruswarmy, Somars, and Hussey (1997) report a variety of ideas about charge transfer: that there is no transfer between a charged object and a neutral object, and that charge transfer between objects occurs until an object is neutral. These research findings may resonate with some of your students' responses to this POE.

Other ideas about static electricity that students have used include the following: a charged object contains only electrons or protons (Siegel and Lee 2001), an electron is a pure negative charge with no mass, and static electricity is the opposite of current electricity (Baser and Geban 2007).

# Apparatus and Materials

- Styrofoam or wooden block
- Coat hanger wire
- Nylon thread
- Wheat puff
- Plastic strip or ruler

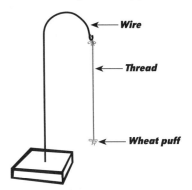

Whoa! Bad hair day!

## Making a Charge Detector

After combing your hair, have you ever tried picking up pieces of paper with your comb? What happens? Do you have any ideas about why this happens?

Do you ever have flyaway hair? Any ideas why?

← **Wire**

← **Thread**

← **Wheat puff**

### An Experiment

The picture shows how to make a charge detector.

Charge a plastic strip such as a ruler by rubbing it on your sweater. See how the wheat puff is attracted to it.

What do you think will happen if you allow the wheat puff to touch the strip?

Will it still work?

### Predict

Check one [√]. Will the plastic ruler

(a) still attract the puff **[   ]**     (b) not attract it anymore **[   ]**     (c) repel it **[   ]**?

Please give your reasons. _____

_____

### Observe

Let's try it! Allow the puff to move along the strip. What happens?

_____

### Explain

Try to use the idea of charge to explain what happens. _____

_____

_____

_____

### Try This!

Now touch the puff with your hand and try again. Can you explain what happens?

_____

_____

_____

## Scientific Explanation

The balloons repel one another. When you charge two balloons by rubbing them on the same materials, you put the same type of charge on both. Like charges repel.

A balloon rubbed on a wool sweater attracts a balloon rubbed with plastic wrap. The type of charge the balloon is given depends on the materials used to rub it. The balloons attract one another because they have different types of charges on them. Unlike charges attract.

## Students' Explanations: Research Findings

The following research findings may help you explain some of your students' responses to this POE:

- Some students think static electricity results from friction alone (Siegel and Lee 2001; Baser and Geban 2007).

- Some students think a charged body contains only electrons or protons (Siegel and Lee 2001).

- Some students think an electron is a pure negative charge with no mass (Baser and Geban 2007).

## Apparatus and Materials

- 3 balloons
- Thread
- Wool cloth
- Plastic wrap

## Charged Balloons

Have you ever tried to stick a balloon to a wall by rubbing the balloon on your sweater?

Do you have any ideas about why it sticks to the wall?

### An Experiment

Let's experiment with two balloons.

"Charge up" two balloons by rubbing them on your shirt or sweater.

Slowly bring them close to one another.

What do you think will happen?

### Predict

Check one [√]. Do you expect the balloons to

(a) attract each other **[   ]**          (b) repel each other **[   ]**          (c) do nothing **[   ]**?

Please give your reasons. _____

_____

_____

### Observe

Let's do it! What do you observe? _____

_____

### Explain

Try to explain what you saw happen. _____

_____

_____

_____

### Try This for Fun!

Rub one balloon against your sweater and rub another with plastic wrap.

Watch what happens when you bring them close.

How can we explain this? _____

_____

_____

## Scientific Explanation

The diagram shows a picture of the way the filings line up around a typical magnet.

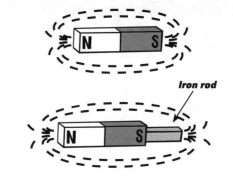

When an iron rod is attached to a magnet, it becomes magnetized. The end farthest from the magnet becomes a pole. Adding the rod apparently makes the magnet longer.

**Iron rod**

Like poles repel one another. The lines of force are bunched closer between the magnets (they don't cross, however). The lines of force appear to push each other away.

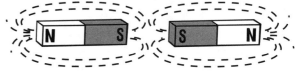

## Students' Explanations: Research Findings

A large number and wide variety of student beliefs about magnetic fields have been reported. Here is a sample:

1. Field lines are real (Galili 1993).

2. Field lines cross each other (Törnkvist, Pettersson, and Tranströmer 1993).

3. Field lines indicate that a magnetic field "flows" (Saglam and Millar 2006).

4. Magnetic fields are two-dimensional rather than three-dimensional (Stephans 1994). (This POE lends itself to consideration and discussion of some of these beliefs.)

5. The north and south poles of a magnet are the equivalent of or even identical to positive and negative electrical charges (Anderson et al. 2000; Maloney et al. 2001; Harlow 2010), suggesting that students also might conclude that electrical charge fields are the same as magnetic fields (Saglam and Millar 2006).

6. Magnetic and gravitational fields are similar or identical (Bradamante and Viennot 2007).

## Apparatus and Materials

- Plotting compass
- 2 magnets
- Iron rod or nail
- Iron filings

### Notes

(a) If you have a limited supply of plotting compasses, you can demonstrate the way the needle is deflected (and plot lines of force) using an overhead projector.

(b) If a glass plate is used to cover the magnet(s), these pictures of magnetic fields show up well on an overhead projector.

(c) To avoid the messiness of iron filings, some teachers sandwich the filings between plastic document covers and seal the edges with tape. (A zip-top bag would work, too.)

## Pictures of Magnetic Fields

You can't see magnetic forces, but you can detect them with a compass.

Try moving a plotting compass around a magnet very slowly. The needle shows the direction of the force—the line of force—in different places.

### An Experiment
Here's how to make a picture of the lines of force around a magnet.

- Cover the magnet with a sheet of paper.
- Sprinkle some iron filings on top.
- Gently tap the sheet.
- Draw a picture of the way the filings line up.

### Predict
How do you think the picture will differ if you

(a) attach a short iron rod or nail to the magnet, and (b) use a second magnet?

### Observe

Let's try it! Draw the pictures you observe.

### Explain
Try to explain why these combinations are different from the single magnet.

_____

_____

### Hey!
Try some other combinations! (Make your predictions first.)

# Scientific Explanation

Magnetic force can attract through card, aluminum, glass, and plastic. It doesn't attract through iron, steel, and nickel. The magnetic field is concentrated within these magnetic materials. It is "shielded" by magnetic materials.

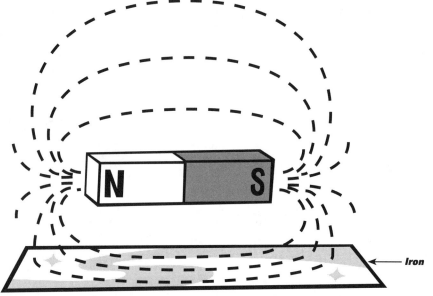

# Students' Explanations: Research Findings

Stephans (1994) has identified a number of student beliefs related to this POE.

1. Magnets are attracted to all metals or silver-color objects.

2. Magnetic fields (and thus attraction) pass through thin objects such as paper, but not through thicker objects such as notebooks, wood, or glass slides.

Hence, this POE could be extended by asking the students to use increasing numbers of pieces of paper or glass slides (while keeping the magnet-to-paper clip distance constant) to see if the attraction changed.

# Apparatus and Materials

- Magnet
- Thread
- Paper clip
- Tape
- Small pieces (about 3 cm x 3 cm) of card

- Aluminum foil
- Glass (slides)
- Iron ("tin can")
- Plastic
- Nickel (try a coin)

Note that the metal composition of pennies and nickels (and other coins) may have changed over time, and how much they interfere with the magnetic field may vary by the coin date.

# Does Magnetic Force Penetrate All Materials?

You can stick notices and other stuff to your fridge with a magnet. Do you know what stuff sticks and what doesn't? Do you have any ideas why?

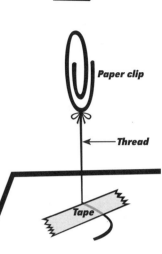

**Magnet**

**Paper clip**

**Thread**

**Tape**

### An Experiment
Which materials let magnetic force pass straight through them? Which don't?

- Set up a magnet so that it holds a paper clip about 1 cm from the magnet.
- Try placing different materials between the magnet and the paper clip.

### Predict
Place a check [√] next to those materials that you think will let the magnetic force pass straight through (the ones you can stick to your fridge).

Card [   ] Aluminum [   ] Glass [   ] Iron [   ] Plastic [   ] Nickel [   ] Your choice _____ [   ]

### Observe
Check it out!

Materials that let magnetic force pass straight through: _____

Materials that don't let it pass straight through: _____

### Explain
What do materials that don't let the magnetic force pass straight through have in common?

_____

_____

### Hey!
Do you have any ideas about why some materials don't let magnetic force pass straight through them?

_____

_____

_____

## Scientific Explanation

The ends (or poles) of the magnet are the strongest parts of the magnet. This is readily explained by thinking of a big magnet as being made from lots of tiny magnets lined up end to end. The tiny magnets in the middle balance one another out, leaving the poles at the ends exposed.

If a magnet is cut in two (or if two magnets lined up end to end are separated), then poles are apparently created in the middle section.

The particulate theory of magnets is considered in SEM6.

## Apparatus and Materials

- Magnet
- Magnetic force detector (pin, thread, coat hanger wire, and Styrofoam or wooden block)
- Coat hanger wire
- Pliers
- Ruler

Note: If it is not possible to provide the students with the apparatus, the experiments may be demonstrated on top of an overhead projector.

# Which Is the Strongest Part of a Magnet?

### An Experiment
The picture shows how you can make a magnetic force detector.

The distance from the magnet to the pin, just when the pin starts to move, gives you a measure of how strong the magnet is.

*Pin on end of thread*

### Predict
Check one [√]. Which do you think is the strongest part of a magnet?

(a) The ends **[    ]**          (b) The middle **[    ]**          (c) They are equally strong. **[    ]**

Please give your reasons. _____

_____

_____

### Observe
Let's do it! (Measure the distance when the pin just starts to move.)

Distance of end of magnet to pin          _____ cm

Distance of middle of magnet to pin          _____ cm

### Explain
Do you have any ideas about why this happened?_____

_____

_____

_____

_____

### Guess What?
You can make a magnet by stroking a thin steel rod with another magnet.

What do you think will happen to its strength if you cut the rod in half with a pair of pliers?

Let's do it! How about that? Any explanations?

_____

_____

## Scientific Explanation

When you stroke a test tube filled with iron filings with a magnet, the iron filings line up. If you then shake up the magnetized test tube of filings, the alignment of the filings breaks down, and the magnet you made loses its strength.

If you hammer a magnet or drop it repeatedly on the floor, it loses some of its strength. If you heat up a magnet, it loses some of its strength. Scientists think a magnet consists of tiny aligned magnetic particles and that dropping or heating the magnet disturbs the alignment.

## Apparatus and Materials

- Test tube of iron filings
- Magnet
- Plotting compass (or magnetic force detector)

# The Particle Theory of Magnetism

You can make a magnet by rubbing an iron bar with a magnet. Scientists think iron is made up of tiny particles and that these particles line themselves up when you rub the bar with the magnet. Do you believe them?

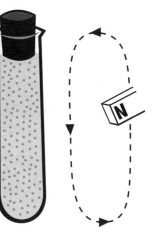

### An Experiment

Try making a magnet from a test tube of iron filings (large particles).

Describe what you think will happen to the filings when you stroke the tube with a magnet.

_____

_____

_____

Use a plotting compass or a magnetic force detector to check out the strength of the magnet you made.

What do you think will happen to the strength of your magnet if you shake up the tube?

### Predict
Check one [√].

The strength of the magnet will remain the **same**.          [   ]

The magnet will lose **some** of its strength.          [   ]

The magnet will lose **all** of its strength.          [   ]

Please give your reasons. _____

_____

_____

### Observe
Compare the strength before and after shaking._____

_____

### Explain
Try to explain what happened. _____

_____

_____

_____

## Scientific Explanation

The iron rod picks up more filings than the steel rod. It is more easily magnetized. Iron is "softer" (more easily bent or shaped) than steel. Perhaps the particles in the iron bar are more easily aligned than in the steel bar.

When the magnet is removed, the iron rod loses most of its filings, whereas only a few fall from the steel rod. Steel magnets hold their strength longer—they are more permanent. Perhaps the particles in the iron rod lose their alignment more easily.

## Apparatus and Materials

- Large magnet (a horseshoe magnet might work well)
- Iron filings
- Iron rod and steel rod (of same size)

## Making Good Magnets

You can make a magnet by stroking a piece of iron or steel.

Do you know which is most easily magnetized, iron or steel? _____

Do you know which holds its strength better, iron or steel? _____

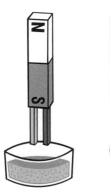

### An Experiment

Attach an iron rod and a steel rod (equal in size) to the end of a bar magnet.

Dip them into a dish of iron filings. The rod that picks up the most filings is the more easily magnetized. Which is it? _____

What do you think will happen when the magnet is removed? Which rod will hold the most filings?

### Predict

Which rod do you think will hold the most filings after the magnet is removed?

_____

Please give your reasons. _____

_____

_____

### Observe

What did you see when the magnet was removed? _____

_____

_____

### Explain

Scientists think all materials are made up of tiny particles. Try to use this idea to help explain which materials are most easily magnetized and which hold their strength longest.

_____

_____

_____

_____

_____

# References

Anderson, D., K. B. Lucas, I. S. Ginns, and L. D. Dierking. 2000. Development of knowledge about electricity and magnetism during a visit to a science museum and related post-visit activities. *Science Education* 84 (5): 658–679.

Baser, M., and O. Geban. 2007. Effect of instruction based on conceptual change activities on students' understanding of static electricity concepts. *Research in Science & Technological Education* 25 (2): 243–267.

Bradamante, F., and L. Viennot. 2007. Mapping gravitational and magnetic fields with children 9–11: Relevance, difficulties and prospects. *International Journal of Science Education* 29 (3): 349–372.

Galili, I. 1993. Perplexity of the field concept in teaching-learning aspect. *Proceedings of the Third International Seminar on Misconceptions and Educational Strategies in Science and Mathematics.* Ithaca, NY: Misconceptions Trust.

Guruswarmy, C., M. D. Somars, and R. G. Hussey. 1997. Students' understanding of the transfer of charge between conductors. *Physics Education* 32 (2): 91–96.

Harlow, D. B. 2010. Structures and improvisation for inquiry-based science instruction: A teacher's adaptation of a model of magnetism activity. *Science Education* 94 (1): 142–163.

Maloney, D. P., T. L. O'Kuma, C. J. Hieggelke, and A. van Heuvelen. 2001. Surveying students' conceptual knowledge of electricity and magnetism. *American Journal of Physics (Physics Education Research Supplement)* 69 (1): S12–S23.

Saglam, M., and R. Millar. 2006. Upper high school students' understanding of electromagnetism. *International Journal of Science Education* 28 (5): 543–566.

Siegel, A. M., and J. A. C. Lee. 2001. "But electricity isn't static": Science discussion, identification of learning issues, and use of resources in a problem-based learning education course. Paper presented at the annual meeting of the National Association for Research in Science Teaching, St. Louis, MO.

Stephans, J. 1994. *Targeting students' science misconceptions.* Riverview, FL: Idea Factory Inc.

Törnkvist, S., K. A. Pettersson, and G. Tranströmer. 1993. Confusion by representation: On students' comprehension of the electric field concept. *American Journal of Physics* 61 (4): 335–338.

# Chapter 5

# Contents

# Scientific Explanation

The four arrangements shown all work.

Electricity (electric charge) flows from the battery, through the filament of the lightbulb, and back to the battery.

# Students' Explanations: Research Findings

The excellent review of children's conceptions of direct current circuits by Shipstone (1985) is worth reading. Children frequently have difficulty understanding the way a flashlight bulb is designed and that it has two connection points (see, for example, Shipstone 1985). Fredette and Clement (1981) report that some university engineering majors were unable to recognize a short circuit. Many children, especially younger ones who have had no formal instruction in electricity, try connecting the top of the battery with the base of the bulb. It's as if they believe the bulb acts as a one-terminal "sink" (Osborne 1983), and such beliefs can persist through older grades (Eylon and Ganiel 1990). Many students may initially believe that only one terminal of the bulb needs to be attached to the battery for the bulb to light—that is, the circuit does not require completion (Gutwill, Fredericksen, and White 1999).

Students portray the current flowing through a bulb in a number of ways (Osborne 1983).

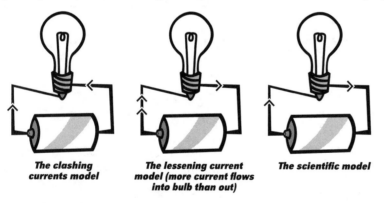

*The clashing currents model*    *The lessening current model (more current flows into bulb than out)*    *The scientific model*

In the next POE, the students are asked to make their model explicit.

# Apparatus and Materials

- D cell battery
- 1.5 V bulb
- 2 lengths of insulated copper wire for each group of students

## Making a Flashlight

Do you know how a flashlight bulb is designed?

Clue! Take a look at the diagram.

Can you get it to work if given a battery and some wire?

**Warning!**
You will quickly run down the battery if you connect the two ends with a piece of wire.

### An Experiment

Which of these combinations do you think will work?

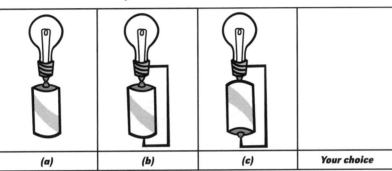

| (a) | (b) | (c) | *Your choice* |
|-----|-----|-----|---------------|

### Predict

Which circuit(s) do you think will work? _____

Please give your reasons. _____

_____

### Observe

Let's experiment! Which circuit(s) worked? _____

Draw any other circuits that worked.

### Explain

Try to explain what you need to do to get a lightbulb to light.

_____

_____

_____

## Scientific Explanation

The arrangement that best represents the way the electric charge flows is (d). However, strictly speaking, negative charge flows from the flat end of the battery. When an extra bulb is put in the circuit, both bulbs light up. They are equally bright but dimmer than when there is only a single bulb in the circuit. The quantity of electric charge flowing through each bulb every second (the current) is the same. However, because the extra bulb makes it more difficult for the charge to flow, the current is less than with one bulb. The brightness of a bulb depends on the amount of charge flowing through it every second (the current).

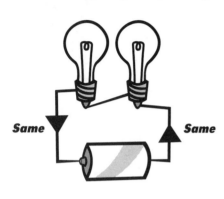

Same    Same

At every point in the circuit the current is the same (see diagram).

A number of analogies have been used to help us understand the flow of electrical charge. The most popular is probably the analogy of the battery to a water pump. Another is the train analogy (see Dupin and Johsua 1989). Here workers (power supply) push cars (electric charge) around a track containing obstacles (resistance). Dupin and Johsua provide a diagram in their article.

## Students' Explanations: Research Findings

Many researchers have reported the difficulties that students experience with the concept of current: Many students confuse current with electrical energy; many think that current is "used up" as it flows through a bulb (so that in a series circuit one bulb would be brighter than another); many believe that the current supplied by a battery is the same regardless of the circuit; and many don't perceive that all the parts of a circuit influence one another and believe that current decreases as it flows "downstream" through the different circuit components (see, for example, Shipstone 1985; Borges and Gilbert 1999). One reason that some of these may occur is that students often conceptualize current as something physical that flows through a circuit (Borges and Gilbert 1999). Gauld (1988) reported that some students he interviewed claimed that the meter readings were helpful. Students often initially believe that bulbs in parallel would shine less than a single bulb, and that there would be no reduction in brightness in bulbs placed in series (Chang, Liu, and Chen 1998).

## Apparatus and Materials

- D cell battery
- 4 1.5 V bulbs
- 4 bulb holders
- 6 short lengths of insulated copper wire
- Ammeter

Note: This might make a valuable laboratory activity for students, in which case each group will require a set of the apparatus (with the exception of the ammeter).

# Circuits With Two Bulbs

When you connect a battery to a bulb, which arrangement do you think best represents the way the electric charge flows?

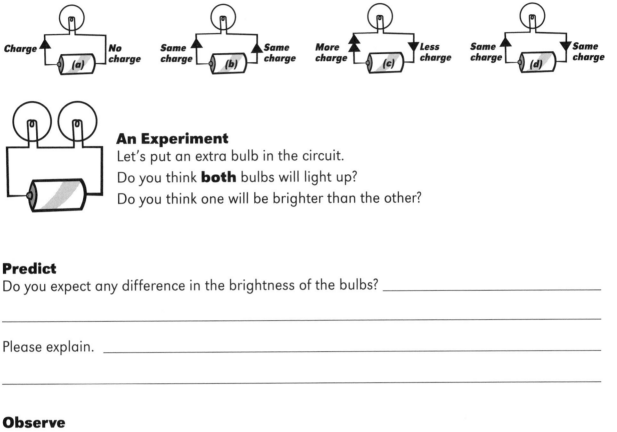

### An Experiment
Let's put an extra bulb in the circuit.

Do you think **both** bulbs will light up?

Do you think one will be brighter than the other?

## Predict
Do you expect any difference in the brightness of the bulbs? _____

_____

Please explain. _____

_____

## Observe
What happens? _____

_____

## Explain
Try to explain what happened. Use the picture above to show how you think electrical charge flows. Use arrows to show the direction and amount of charge flowing.

_____

_____

### Try This for Fun!
What do you think will happen if we put another bulb in the circuit? And another?

_____

_____

We can check out your explanation by putting a current meter (ammeter) in each part of the circuit.

## Scientific Explanation

Comparing A with B and C (lightbulbs in series): Bulb A will burn more brightly. The addition of more bulbs in a series circuit results in a greater series resistance. This decreases the current in the circuit and therefore in each bulb so they are not as bright. Note the brightness of bulbs B and C are the same.

Comparing A with D and E (lightbulbs in parallel): All bulbs will burn with the same brightness. This happens because as more bulbs are added, more paths are made available between the battery terminals. This decreases the circuit resistance. With two paths instead of one, the cell has half the resistance between its terminals. The battery is putting out twice as much energy as when lighting one bulb, so it will wear down twice as fast!

When they added an extra light to the room, the electricians might well have replaced the existing socket with a junction box. They would have taken two sets of wires in parallel from the junction box.

## Students' Explanations: Research Findings

Students often initially believe that bulbs in parallel would shine less than a single bulb and that there would be no reduction of the brightness of the single bulb when another is placed in series (Chang, Liu, and Chen 1998).

They might think that the electric current can be "used up" (Borges and Gilbert 1999) and thus expect lights in series to be of different brightness levels.

Shipstone (1985) reported researchers' findings that some experienced students think the current flowing from a battery is independent of what items are in the circuit, an idea also discussed by Liegeois and Mullet (2002).

## Apparatus and Materials

- 2 D cell batteries
- 4 1.5 V bulbs and bulb holders
- About 10 lengths of insulated copper wire

Note: A circuit board would be valuable for making the wiring arrangements clear.

# How Bright Is the Light?

The electricians came yesterday! They took out the middle light in the sitting room and put in one at each end. It took them 20 minutes and they charged $100!

How did they do it? Did it make the room a lot brighter?

A — Single lightbulb

B C — Lightbulbs in series

D E — Lightbulbs in parallel

## An Experiment

There seem to be two possible ways to connect two lights.

Let's compare them for brightness with the original single light.

## Predict

How do you think the brightness of A will compare with B or C? Please give your reasons.

_____

_____

How do you think A will compare with D or E? Please give your reasons.

_____

_____

## Observe

Let's check! What did you find out? _____

_____

## Explain

Can you come up with some rules that will help you explain how electricity flows through different arrangements of bulbs?

_____

_____

_____

*Help with your explanations: Imagine the cell to be like a water pump, the connectors as wide tubing and the bulbs as narrow tubing. Compare the amount of water flowing through each section of narrow tubing (the bulbs).*

## Scientific Explanation

Bulbs A and B will be less bright than bulbs C and D because less current (electrical charge per second) is flowing through them. In the parallel circuit, there are two paths for the electrical charge to take between the battery terminals, and therefore there is less resistance to the passage of electricity.

When bulb C is unscrewed, the brightness of bulb D doesn't change. The number of paths has been halved, but so has the resistance. When there are two bulbs in parallel, the battery is putting out twice as much energy as with one bulb; therefore twice the amount of charge flows. It will run down twice as fast.

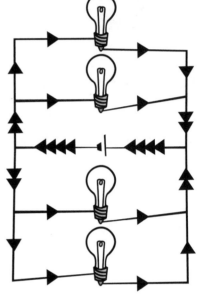

Four bulbs in parallel will be as bright as two bulbs in parallel.

When electricians wire a house, they take wires in parallel from the main supply (fuse box) to junction boxes. These junction boxes then act as secondary suppliers. More wires in parallel are taken off each junction box.

## Students' Explanations: Research Findings

Students often initially believe that bulbs in parallel would shine less than a single bulb and that there would be no reduction of the brightness of the single bulb when another is placed in series (Chang, Liu, and Chen 1998).

They might think that the electric current can be "used up" and thus expect lights in series to be of different brightness (Borges and Gilbert 1999).

A number of researchers have found that many experienced students (grade 9–12) think that the current flowing from a battery did not change when the external circuit was altered (e.g., Cohen, Eylon, and Ganiel [1982]).

Shipstone (1985) similarly reported that researchers have found that some experienced students think the current flowing from a battery is independent of what items are in the circuit, an idea also discussed by Liegeois and Mullet (2002).

Viard and Khantine-Langlois (2001) reported that they and other researchers have found that many students think the total resistance of a circuit decreases if one removes a resistance connected in parallel to another one and that 15–20% of third-year university students hold this belief.

## Apparatus and Materials

- 2 D cell batteries
- 4 1.5 V bulbs and bulb holders
- 10 lengths of insulated copper wire

Note: A circuit board would be valuable for making the wiring arrangements clear. This might make a valuable laboratory exercise.

# How Do They Wire a House?

**Power supply**

Do you know how electricians wire a house? One problem is to get all the lights to burn at full brightness. How would you wire a model house? Let's make the problem simpler: How would you connect just two lights, in series or in parallel?

## An Experiment

Let's compare these two arrangements. How do you think the brightness of the bulbs compare?

A   B

D

C

**Series circuit**

**Parallel circuit**

## Predict

1. Which bulbs will burn brightest?
   Circle your choice.   A   B   C   D

Please explain. _____

_____

2. If bulb C is unscrewed, will the brightness of bulb D change?      Yes ____      No ____

Please explain. _____

_____

_____

## Observe

Let's try it. What happened? _____

_____

## Explain

Can you explain why the two circuits behaved differently? _____

_____

_____

How would you wire a model house with three lights or four lights? Any ideas? Try drawing a circuit diagram! Let's check it out!

## Interesting ...

Finally, if the batteries in both circuits started with the same amount of charge, which one would last longest? Circle one.

Series          Parallel          Why? _____

_____

## Scientific Explanation

Batteries in series have to be aligned so that the positive pole of one is in contact with the negative pole of another (i.e., combinations (a) and (c) both light the bulb). In this way, electrical charge from one battery flows in the same direction as electrical charge from the other.

When two batteries are in series, then the combination is twice as powerful as one, and the bulb will burn twice as brightly. Similarly, two train engines, often used to pull the train up inclines, are twice as powerful as one.

When two batteries are in parallel, they are only as powerful as one but will last twice as long. We connect our car batteries this way when jump-starting a car.

## Apparatus and Materials

- Flashlight with 2 D cell batteries
- 1.5 V bulb in bulb holder
- 4 lengths of insulated copper wire

## *Flashlight Problem*

Which way around do these flashlight batteries go?

Does it matter?

### An Experiment
Will the bulb light? Try these combinations!

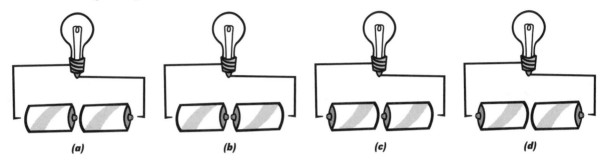

(a)          (b)          (c)          (d)

### Predict
Which combinations do you think will light the bulb?_____

Please explain your answer. _____

_____

### Observe
Let's try it! What happens? _____

### Explain
Try to explain what happened. _____

_____

_____

### *Hey!*
Wonder what will happen if we try it this way?
Why do they use two batteries anyway? Let's try it with one!

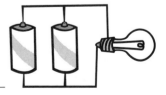

What do you think will happen? _____

_____

## Scientific Explanation

Copper, iron, and aluminum conduct electricity. Metals are *conductors*. Wood, glass, plastic, and rubber do not conduct electricity. They are *insulators*.

Fresh water does not conduct electricity. Saltwater, potato, and fruit juices contain charged particles in solution. These particles transport electricity.

## Apparatus and Materials

- Circuit center (D cell battery, 1.5 V bulb, 2 alligator clamps, 2 lengths of wire)
- Iron nail
- Aluminum pie plate
- Plastic pen
- Copper pipe
- Piece of wood
- Piece of rubber
- Saltwater
- Fruit juice
- Piece of potato
- Glass rod

# Will the Electricity Flow?

**Accidental Death (from our news reporter)**
George Pace, a 20-year-old house painter, was killed when his extension ladder came in contact with power lines.

In court today, the coroner passed the verdict of accidental death. "People should know that ladders conduct electricity," he said.

### An Experiment

Here's a single circuit tester. You can attach the clips to anything you want to test. If the bulb lights, that shows it conducts electricity.

Tape →

### Predict

Please check [√] all the things you think will conduct electricity:

Copper pipe [    ]    Piece of wood [    ]    Iron nail [    ]    Aluminum pie plate [    ]
Glass rod [    ]    Plastic pen [    ]    Rubber [    ]

Try to explain the reasons for your choices. _____

_____

### Observe

Let's check it out!

Things that conduct electricity: _____

Things that don't conduct electricity: _____

### Explain

What do the items that conduct electricity have in common? Try to make a rule that helps you remember what they have in common.

_____

_____

### Wow!

Do you think any of these will conduct electricity? Please check [√].

Fresh water [    ]          Saltwater [    ]          Piece of potato [    ]          Fruit juice [    ]

What happened? Does this make sense to you? Should you write a new rule?

_____

_____

_____

## Scientific Explanation

The bulb burns dimmer and dimmer as one goes from copper to aluminum to iron to nichrome.

The resistance of nichrome is greater than that of iron, which is greater than that of aluminum, which is greater than that of copper. Copper is used to wire houses because it is the best conductor (twice as good as aluminum, 8 times as good as iron, and 60 times as good as nichrome).

## Students' Explanations: Research Findings

Shipstone (1985) reported researchers' findings that some experienced students think the current flowing from a battery is independent of what items are in the circuit. None of the research we found explored students' understanding of the conductivity of different metals.

## Apparatus and Materials

- D cell battery
- 1.5 V bulb
- 2 alligator clips
- Copper wire (to make circuit dowel rods)
- 4 equal lengths of thin (but equally thick) copper, aluminum, nichrome, and iron wire

## Do Some Metals Conduct Better Than Others?

### Quick Quiz
1. Why do we use copper wires when wiring our houses?
2. If you run out of copper wire, can you use another type of wire?
3. Do some metals conduct better than others?

### An Experiment
Let's compare copper wire, iron wire, nichrome wire, and aluminum wire.

Cut off equal lengths of wire and wrap them around a dowel rod. To be fair, the wires should have the same thickness.

Test each with a circuit tester.

### Predict
What do you think will happen to the bulb brightness when you replace copper wire with

• Iron wire: _____

  Please explain. _____

• Nichrome wire: _____

  Please explain. _____

• Aluminum wire: _____

  Please explain. _____

### Observe
Try each type of wire, one at a time, and write down your observations. Does the bulb light? Is it brighter or dimmer?

Iron wire: _____

Nichrome wire: _____

Aluminum wire: _____

### Explain
Try to explain what happened. _____

_____

_____

Teacher's Notes: Does the Length of the Wire Affect the Current?    CE8I

**Topic:** Current Electricity    **Concept:** Variation of the resistance with length of a wire

## Scientific Explanation

The longer the wire, the greater the resistance, the less the current (charge per second) flowing through the circuit, and therefore the dimmer the lamp will be. Similarly, less water per second will flow through a long pipe than through a short one.

## Students' Explanations: Research Findings

Shipstone (1985) reported researchers' findings that some experienced students think the current flowing from a battery is independent of what items are in the circuit. None of the research we found explored students' understanding of the conductivity of different metals.

## Apparatus and Materials

- 2 or 3 D cell batteries
- 1.5 V bulb and bulb holder
- Length of thin nichrome wire
- Dowel rod

## Does the Length of the Wire Affect the Current?

### Riddle
Does electricity flow through a wire like water through a pipe?

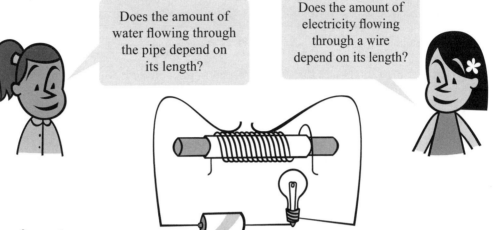

Does the amount of water flowing through the pipe depend on its length?

Does the amount of electricity flowing through a wire depend on its length?

### An Experiment
Vary the length of the thin nichrome wire in the circuit by placing the contact wires at different points along the wire. What do you think will happen to the brightness of the lamp?

### Predict
What do you think will happen?

_____

_____

### Observe
Let's try it. What happens?_____

_____

### Explain
Try to explain your observations. _____

_____

_____

### Hey!
Can you design an experiment to find out what happens when water flows through different lengths of pipe?

_____

_____

_____

**Topic:** Current Electricity    **Concepts:** Variation of resistance with wire thickness
Analogy between electricity flow and water flow

## Scientific Explanation

The thinner the wire (i.e., the smaller the area of cross-section), the greater the resistance, the less the current (charge per second) flowing through the circuit, and therefore the dimmer the lamp will be. Similarly, less water per second flows through a narrow pipe than through a wide one.

## Students' Explanations: Research Findings

Viard and Khantine-Langlois (2001) say that many researchers, including themselves, found that students often think the resistance of a conductor increases with its size, in particular in relation to its thickness. This thinking is shared by many university students.

Although some students say they find the analogy between the flow of water and the flow of electricity useful, many encountered difficulty. For example, Wilkinson (reported in Shipstone 1985) found that 60% of students ages 12 and 13 believed that the rate of flow through a constriction in a pipe would be less than the flow in the wider pipe on either side of it, even though the majority recognized that the speed of the flow would be greater through the constriction.

## Apparatus and Materials

- Dowel rod
- 2 D cell batteries
- 1.5 V bulb and holder
- Thin and thick nichrome wires (same length)

## Does the Thickness of the Wire Affect the Current?

### Riddle
Does electricity flow through a wire like water through a pipe?

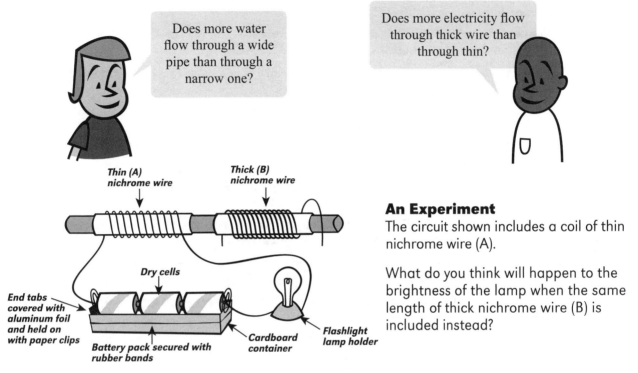

Does more water flow through a wide pipe than through a narrow one?

Does more electricity flow through thick wire than through thin?

Thin (A) nichrome wire

Thick (B) nichrome wire

Dry cells

End tabs covered with aluminum foil and held on with paper clips

Battery pack secured with rubber bands

Cardboard container

Flashlight lamp holder

### An Experiment
The circuit shown includes a coil of thin nichrome wire (A).

What do you think will happen to the brightness of the lamp when the same length of thick nichrome wire (B) is included instead?

### Predict
Check one [√].    The light will be brighter with the thin wire. **[  ]**

The light will be brighter with the thick wire. **[  ]**      The brightness will stay the same. **[  ]**

Please explain your thinking. _____

_____

### Observe
Let's check it. What happens? _____

_____

### Explain
Try to explain what happened. _____

_____

_____

### Hey!
How do you think the diameter of a pipe affects the flow of water through it?

The quantity of water passing through? _____

The speed of the flow? _____

# References

Borges, A. T., and J. K. Gilbert. 1999. Mental models of electricity. *International Journal of Science Education* 21 (1): 95–117.

Chang, K.-E., S.-H. Liu, and S.-W. Chen. 1998. A testing system for diagnosing misconceptions in DC electric circuits. *Computers & Education* 31 (2): 195–210.

Cohen, R., B. Eylon, and U. Ganiel. 1982. Potential differences and current in simple electric circuits: A study of students' concepts. *American Journal of Physics* 51: 407–412.

Dupin, J. J., and S. Johsua. 1989. Analogies and "modeling analogies" in teaching: Some examples in basic electricity. *Science Education* 73 (2): 207–224.

Eylon, B. S., and U. Ganiel. 1990. Macro-micro relationships: The missing link between electrostatics and electrodynamics in students' reasoning. *International Journal of Science Education* 12 (1): 79–94.

Fredette. N., and J. J. Clement. 1981. Student misconceptions of an electric current: What do they mean? *Journal of College Science Teaching* 10 (5): 280–285.

Gauld, C. F. 1988. The cognitive contexts of pupils' alternative frameworks. *International Journal of Science Educators* 10 (3): 267–274.

Gutwill, J. P., J. R. Fredericksen, and B. Y. White. 1999. Making their own connections: Students' understanding of multiple models in basic electricity. *Cognition and Instruction* 17 (3): 249–282.

Liegeois, L., and E. Mullet. 2002. High school students' understanding of resistance in simple series electrical circuits. *International Journal of Science Education* 24 (6): 551–564.

Osborne, R. J. 1983. Towards modifying children's ideas about electric current. *Journal of Research in Science and Technological Education* 1 (1): 73–81.

Shipstone, D. 1985. Electricity in simple circuits. In *Children's ideas in science*, ed. R. Driver, E. Guesne, and A. Tiberghein, 33–51. Buckingham, United Kingdom: Open University Press.

Viard, J., and F. Khantine-Langlois. 2001. The concept of electrical resistance: How Cassirer's philosophy, and the early developments of electric circuit theory allow a better understanding of students' learning difficulties. *Science and Education* 10 (3): 267–286.

# Chapter 6

## Contents

## Scientific Explanation

If you pour the water slowly into the funnel, some may trickle down the side into the flask or bottle. However, sooner or later a "plug" of water will form in the stem of the funnel. This effectively seals the flask or bottle. No more water can enter because the pressure of the air inside the bottle balances the pressure of the column of water together with the pressure of the air outside the flask or bottle (atmospheric pressure).

As you add more water to the funnel, the water level will slowly move down the stem. However, when it does, it compresses the air inside the flask or bottle until a balance is reached between the pressure of air inside the bottle and the pressure of the column of water plus the pressure of the atmosphere.

Putting a second hole in the stopper enables the air inside the bottle to escape. The pressure of air inside the bottle (atmospheric pressure) will be less than the pressure of the column of water plus the pressure of the atmosphere. Hence the bottle can be filled without any difficulty.

## Students' Explanations: Research Findings

When students are asked to predict how much water will enter the flask, Biro and Zwolanski-Morovic (1992) suggest that student predictions will "range from up to the level to the end of the funnel to full. A few wonder if the water would block the funnel" (p. 26).

This POE—together with PR2, PR3, PR4, and eight other activities—was used in an interesting study by Tytler (1998). His findings include the following:

- Very few children ages 11 and 12 seemed to have access to the notion of the interplay between atmospheric pressure and the pressure inside the container.

- Very few children used the idea of outside air pressing. However, by the age of 11 and 12, they proved more willing to accept the idea.

- Atmospheric pressure is a difficult concept on account of (a) children ages 11 and 12 not having sufficient prerequisite knowledge about air, and (b) our being unaware of air's existence in our everyday lives.

## Apparatus and Materials

- Conical flask or glass bottle
- Funnel
- 1-hole stopper and a 2-hole stopper
- Beaker
- Food coloring (to color the water)

## *Using a Funnel*

Funnels are very useful. They reduce the risk of a spill when you fill cans or bottles.

Your classmate Rick wonders if funnels would be even better if you fitted them with a cork or stopper.

What do you think? Let's experiment!

### Predict
What do you think will happen as you pour in water? Please give your reasons.

_____

_____

_____

### Observe
Start by pouring very slowly. Then pour faster. What happens? Look carefully!

_____

_____

_____

### Explain
Try to explain what happens.

_____

_____

_____

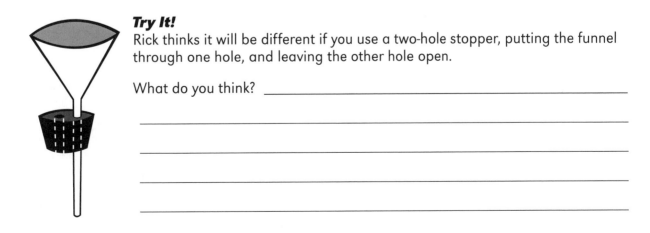

***Try It!***
Rick thinks it will be different if you use a two-hole stopper, putting the funnel through one hole, and leaving the other hole open.

What do you think? _____

_____

_____

_____

# Scientific Explanation

**Experiment 1:** Sucking removes some air from the straw—the air pressure inside the straw drops. The air pressure inside the flask is now higher than that inside the straw and pushes the water up the straw until the pressures are balanced. A little water may enter your mouth but not very much.

**Experiment 2:** Blowing into the straw increases the air pressure in the straw. The water level inside the straw drops and bubbles of air escape into the flask. This increases the air pressure in the flask. The bubbles stop when the pressure inside the flask is the same as the pressure inside your mouth. When you stop blowing, the air pressure inside the flask (greater than atmospheric pressure) pushes the water up the tube and a little jet of water escapes.

# Students' Explanations: Field Experience

This POE was used with 25 grade 9 students.

**Experiment 1:** The majority (64%) predicted incorrectly that nothing would happen. Most of these students reasoned that for the liquid to rise, air would need to flow into the bottle:

> ***Because the bottle is airtight and for air to go out air has to go in.***

One-third of the students predicted (again incorrectly) that the drinking bottle would work, and most appeared not to recognize the consequences of the bottle being sealed:

> ***The liquid will go upward because of pressure.***

It may be significant that only 20% of the students used the word *pressure* in their reasoning. Overall, this part of the POE proved to be difficult for this group of students. Indeed, after watching the experiment, none were able to provide a satisfactory scientific explanation of their observations.

**Experiment 2:** This part of the POE appeared to be far more accessible to the students. Although only 2 students (8%) made completely correct predictions, 44% were able to give scientifically acceptable explanations, many in terms of pressure, after they had observed the experiment:

> ***The air pressure pushed the liquid back up the tube.***

# Students' Explanations: Research Findings

Engel, Clough, and Driver found in their sample of 12- to 16-year-olds that many students referred to air or a vacuum sucking and few explained changes in terms of balancing pressures (reported in Driver et al. 1994, p. 152). This kind of reasoning was evident in this POE. To help students look at changes in terms of balancing pressure would appear to be a major challenge that teachers face. The second part of this POE may help in this respect.

# Apparatus and Materials

- Flat-bottom flask (500 ml) or soda bottle
- Rubber stopper fitted with glass tube

Note: For best effects in Experiment 2, slightly taper the end of the tube by drawing it out in a flame.

## *Perfect Drinking Bottle?*

"I've made myself a new drinking bottle. No more leaks! Perfectly sealed!" Bill said as he displayed his masterpiece.

"Won't work!" said Tony.

"Gimme a break! It will work perfectly," Bill argued.

What would you say? Let's investigate.

← *Perfect seal*

*Colored water*

### Experiment 1
Do you think you will be able to drink from the bottle?

### Predict
What do you think will happen when you suck? _____

_____

Please give your reasons. _____

_____

### Observe
Let's try it! What did you see? _____

_____

### Explain
Try to explain what you saw. _____

_____

### Experiment 2
Just for fun, let's try blowing!

### Predict
What do you think will happen? _____

Please give your reasons. _____

_____

### Observe
Let's try it! Watch very carefully. _____

_____

### Explain
Try to explain what you saw using the idea of pressure. _____

_____

_____

# Scientific Explanation

**Experiment 1:** As the balloon begins to expand, the air pressure inside the bottle increases (air cannot escape through tube B). The balloon stops expanding when the air pressure in the bottle balances the pressure of blowing.

**Experiment 2:** Sucking on tube B decreases the air pressure inside the bottle. The pressure of the atmosphere then blows up the balloon.

# Students' Explanations: Field Experience

This POE was used with a sample of 25 grade 9 students.

**Experiment 1:** Thirty-two percent (32%) predicted incorrectly that it would be possible to blow up the balloon. The most common reason given was somewhat tautological. Many thought that you could blow up the balloon because you are blowing into the balloon:

> **[You can blow up the balloon] because you're still putting air into the balloon.**

Sixty-eight percent (68%) predicted correctly that it would not be possible to blow up the balloon. However, many of these students gave explanations in terms of there being no "room" for the balloon to expand:

> **... because there is not enough room to expand.**

Overall, only 20% used the idea of pressure to explain their predictions:

> **[You can't blow up the balloon because] air pressure will get too high and unable to expand any farther.**

Indeed, it was difficult to interpret many of the students' reasons. It was as if they lacked the language to express themselves clearly:

> **The balloon will not blow up because the air gets blocked off by the stopper and the elastic.**

**Experiment 2:** Sixty percent (60%) thought the balloon would blow up, but only a quarter of these were able to articulate scientifically acceptable (or at least partially acceptable) answers:

> **It's the same as blowing into tube A ...**

> **The balloon would fill with air because the air pressure isn't hard and is being sucked out.**

Forty percent (40%) thought the balloon would shrivel or shrink or that nothing would happen. They apparently did not take into consideration the fact that tube A was open to the atmosphere or that the atmosphere exerts pressure, e.g.,

> **It will shrink because no air can get in to blow it up.**

# Students' Explanations: Research Findings

In their review of the research, Basca and Grotzer (2001) report that students frequently do not consider the air pressure both inside and outside the balloon. They do not consider the system as a whole; they have a one-way focus rather than a two-way focus.

# Apparatus and Materials

- Large soda bottle with wide mouth
- 2-hole stopper to fit
- L-shape and straight glass tubes
- Balloon
- Tape or elastic

# How Do Your Lungs Work?

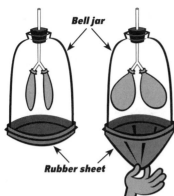

*Bell jar*

*Rubber sheet*

Do you know how your lungs work? In some ways, they are like balloons. They inflate and deflate inside your chest cavity. But what makes them inflate and deflate? You could explore this question by making a model of your chest like the one in the diagram (on the left).

Let's try some experiments! First try blowing up the balloon using tube A. Did it work?

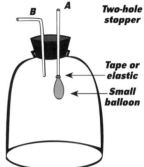

*B* *A* **Two-hole stopper**

**Tape or elastic**

**Small balloon**

## Experiment 1
Now put your finger over B. Do you think you can blow up the balloon?

## Predict

_____

Please give your reasons. _____

_____

## Observe
What did you observe? _____

_____

## Explain
Try to explain your observations. (Use the word *pressure* if you can.) _____

_____

_____

## Experiment 2
What do you think would happen if you sucked on tube B?

## Predict

_____

Please give your reasons. _____

## Observe
Let's try it! _____

## Explain
Try to explain what you saw happen. (Use the word *pressure* if you can.)

_____

## Hey!
Neat experiment! But what does it have to do with how lungs work? _____

_____

# Scientific Explanation

When heated, 1 ml of water will produce about 1,000 ml of steam. This effect can be demonstrated by boiling a few drops of water in a test tube and then inverting the test tube in water. The steam condenses and the water fills the test tube.

In the fountain experiment, the steam from the boiling water drives out the air. After the tube is inserted, the steam begins to condense and the pressure inside the flask drops. The atmospheric pressure drives the (colored) water up the tube and creates a fountain.

# Students' Explanations: Field Experience

This POE was used with a sample of 33 grade 9 students.

Sixty-seven percent (67%) correctly predicted that the colored water would enter the straw or the flask:

> *I think the colored water will go up the straw.*

> *I think the water will get sucked up through the straw.*

> *I think the flask will get water into it.*

Some of these students reasoned in terms of "pressure":

> *I think that the air pressure will force the colored water up the straw.*

> *The air pressure is sealed in and when hung upside down makes a vacuum.*

Others reasoned in terms of "heat." We were unable to interpret their thinking.

> *The hot water will make the water go up the tube.*

> *Heat makes the colored water rise.*

> *Because of the hot air.*

# Students' Explanations: Research Findings

Engel, Clough, and Driver found in their sample of 12- to 16-year-olds that many students referred to air or a vacuum sucking and few explained changes in terms of balancing pressures (reported in Driver et al. 1994, p. 152). This kind of reasoning was evident in this POE. To help students look at changes in terms of balancing pressure would appear to be a major challenge that teachers face.

# Apparatus and Materials

- Round-bottom flask
- 1-hole stopper
- Length of glass tubing (tapered at one end)
- Heat source
- Test tube

# *Fountain*

### Amazing Fact

If you turn 1 ml of water into steam, do you know what volume of steam will be produced?
Check one [√].　　10 ml **[  ]**　　　100 ml **[  ]**　　　1,000 ml **[  ]**

### An Experiment

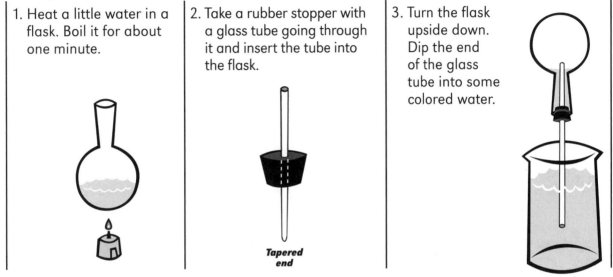

1. Heat a little water in a flask. Boil it for about one minute.

2. Take a rubber stopper with a glass tube going through it and insert the tube into the flask.

   *Tapered end*

3. Turn the flask upside down. Dip the end of the glass tube into some colored water.

### Predict

What do you think will happen? _____

_____

Please give your reasons.  _____

_____

_____

### Observe

Let's do it! What did you observe? _____

_____

### Explain

Try to explain what you saw happen. _____

_____

_____

_____

_____

## Scientific Explanation

The steam drives the air out of the can. After the can is taken off the heat and sealed, it begins to cool. The steam inside the can begins to condense and the pressure begins to drop.

Atmospheric pressure is very large: 100,000 N/m² (100 kiloPascals). A 4 L can would have a surface area of about 0.1 m². When there is no air pressure inside, the force the can is subjected to would be similar to that exerted by 10 football players standing on it. It crumples.

## Students' Explanations: Field Experience

This POE was used with a sample of 33 grade 9 students early in their study of pressure.

Only one student correctly predicted what would happen. After seeing the can collapse, only 18% of the students were able to move toward an acceptable scientific explanation. It was evidently difficult for them to understand:

> *It's going to steam up inside the bottle. The can will suck in.*

> *The hot air expanded and when it cooled it had to contract.*

> *The pressure is sucking in the bottle, causing a suction.*

In retrospect, this is not surprising. The students were being asked to bring to bear a wide range of scientific understanding on the problem in order to predict or explain. They would need to understand that water expands about 1,000 times when it turns into steam. They would need to understand that a very low pressure is produced when water condenses. And they would need to know that a can is relatively flimsy. This POE might therefore be used more profitably toward the end of a study of pressure.

## Students' Explanations: Research Findings

Engel, Clough, and Driver found in their sample of 12- to 16-year-olds that many students referred to air or a vacuum sucking and few explained changes in terms of balancing pressures (reported in Driver et al. 1994, p. 152). This kind of reasoning was evident in this POE.

In his review, Horton (2004) reported Schmidt's (1997) finding that some students think air has no mass, and others think it has negative weight.

## Apparatus and Materials

- Can with screw cap or rubber stopper to fit
- Source of heat

Note: An airtight cardboard milk container fitted with a straw might be useful to show what happens when you suck on the straw.

## *Preserving Fruit*

### Preserving Fruit and Vegetables

Every fall, Jane's dad would go on a fruit preserving binge. She would help him. After they had filled the preserving jars with fruit, they would put them in a pot of boiling water for about 15 minutes. This heated the fruit to boiling, killed off the bacteria, and drove out the air. They then carefully removed the jars and clamped the lids tight before they could cool down. Jane wondered if they could use tin cans with screw caps instead.

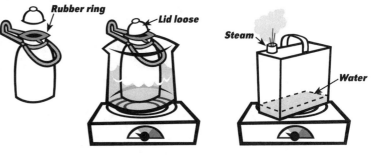

What do you think?

### An Experiment

Just cover the bottom of a can with water. Boil the water for about two minutes. Take the can off the heat (mind your fingers!) and close it with its cap or a stopper.

### Predict

Do you think anything will happen? If so, what? _____

_____

Please give your reasons. _____

_____

### Observe

Let's try! _____

_____

### Explain

_____

_____

### *Let's Think About It!*

I guess preserving jars must be special, right? _____

_____

I wonder why they hiss when you open them. _____

_____

# Scientific Explanation

The pressure exerted by a column of liquid is proportional to its height. Hence, the jets from the lower holes go farther. The paths of the jets cross, provided, of course, that the bottle is a sufficient height above the ground.

The pressure doesn't depend on how much liquid there is. Hence, the size of the bottle doesn't affect the shape of the jets. Note, however, the smaller bottle will empty faster, so the shape of the jets will change faster.

# Students' Explanations: Field Experience

The record sheets of a sample of 29 grade 9 students were analyzed.

Twenty-eight percent (28%) of students predicted correctly. They appeared to recognize that the pressure at the bottom of the bottle was greater than the pressure at the top.

Some of the students predicting incorrectly reasoned the other way:

> **There is more pressure on hole A so the water will go farther.**

After watching the experiment, 30% of the students predicting incorrectly were able to formulate scientifically acceptable explanations.

Because many students appeared to have difficulty drawing the paths of the water jets both before and even after the experiment, the picture of the apparatus was redrawn and the students were invited to think about whether the jets will cross.

# Students' Explanations: Research Findings

In their sample, Clough and Driver (1986) found that 67% of 12-year-olds, 80% of 14-year-olds, and 87% of 16-year-olds thought pressure increased with depth.

# Apparatus and Materials

- Masking tape
- Large bowl to catch water (Practice beforehand!)
- For the first experiment, 2 L plastic bottle with 3 small holes drilled in the side
- For the second experiment, 2 L bottle and a bottle of another size. Drill a small hole in the side, at the same height above the bottom of each.

Note: Fitting the bottles with a cap or stopper can help reduce the risk of a major spill when you are setting up the experiment.

# *Water Jets*

Jeannette is watering the garden. She asks her brother to turn up the water pressure. What do you think will happen to the jet of water? (You can draw it if you like.)

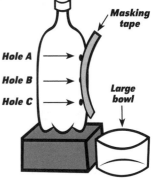

Masking tape

Hole A →

Hole B →

Hole C →

Large bowl

## An Experiment

Drill three small holes in a 2 L soda bottle. Cover the holes with a strip of masking tape and fill the bottle with water. When you are ready, take out the stopper and tear off the masking tape.

What paths do you think the three water jets will take?

## Predict

Draw the path you think the water jets will take (in the diagram above).

Please give your reasons. _____

_____

## Observe

Compare the shapes of the different paths.

Draw what you see.

## Explain

(Use the phrase *water pressure* if you can.)_____

_____

## *Awesome!*

I wonder what would happen to the water jets if you changed the size of the bottles. What do you think?

_____

_____

_____

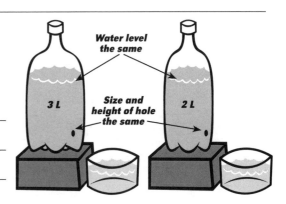

Water level the same

3 L

Size and height of hole the same

2 L

**Teacher's Notes:** *Ten Meters of Water*

**Topic:** Pressure          **Concepts:** The atmosphere exerts a pressure.
The pressure in a gas or a liquid acts equally in all directions.
Unequal pressures try to balance each other.

PR7T

## Scientific Explanation

When you suck on a straw, you take out some of the air and lower the pressure inside the straw. The atmosphere, which is pressing down on the liquid, pushes some of liquid up the straw until it is balanced by the pressure inside the straw plus the pressure of the column of liquid that you have drawn up.

The wider straw has a greater cross-sectional area than the narrow one. The upward force from atmospheric pressure increases with the area of the bottom of the straw.

### *Force = pressure × area*

The downward force of the liquid increases with area, too—the wider the straw, the greater the weight of water it contains. Hence, the area of the bottom of the straw doesn't affect how high the liquid rises.

The atmosphere can support a column of water approximately 10 m long, regardless of the width of the column. This is the maximum height to which a pump can draw water. Because humans cannot remove as much air as a pump, they cannot draw water as high.

Dr. Y cannot beat atmospheric pressure. The water level in the tube will drop to about 10 m. This is all atmospheric pressure can balance. Apart from some water vapor, a vacuum will be left in the closed end of the tube.

## Students' Explanations: Research Findings

Clough and Driver (1985, 1986) have had an experience similar to many science teachers, finding that many students thought in terms of air or a vacuum sucking. In their sample of 84 students, only 13% of 12-year-olds, 19% of 14-year-olds, and 34% of 16-year-olds thought pressure acted in all directions in air or water. The existence of air pressure isn't obvious! De Berg (1995) found that 70% of high school students did not think the air inside a syringe had any pressure, even though they could feel the effects of pushing in and pulling out the plunger. Moreover, it wasn't until 1630 that Torricelli used the idea of air pressure to explain why a water pump could not draw water up a mine shaft more than 10 m.

## Apparatus and Materials

- Wide glass tube and narrower glass tube
- Rubber 1-hole stopper to fit wide glass tube, plus short length of glass tubing to fit inside
- Rubber tubing
- Dish or wide container

## *Ten Meters of Water*

### Interesting Facts

First, measure how high you think you can suck through a soda straw. _____ cm

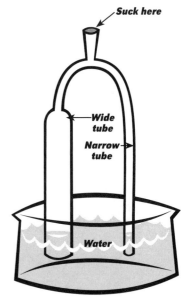

(When you suck, you reduce the pressure inside the soda straw by taking out some of the air. The atmosphere pushes the liquid up until its pressure balances that inside the straw plus that of the column of liquid.)

Do you know the maximum height a water pump can draw water? _____ m

Do you know the length of a column of water that can be balanced by the atmosphere? _____ m

### An Experiment

You go to the supermarket to buy some soda straws.

Which should you buy—the wide straws or the narrow ones?

Does your drink rise higher in a wide soda straw or a narrow one?

In which tube do you think the water will rise more?

### Predict

Circle one.     Wide tube   /   Narrow tube   /   The same

Please give your reason. _____

_____

### Observe

Let's try it. What happens?_____

_____

### Explain

Try to explain. Use the idea of pressure if you can. _____

_____

_____

### *How About This?*

Dr. Y has a plan to beat atmospheric pressure. He has filled a tube 20 m long with water. He plans to raise it vertically!

What do you think will happen? Please explain.

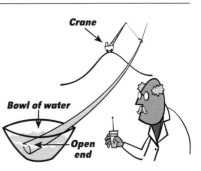

_____

_____

## Scientific Explanation

It may be worth discussing the three ways of emptying a plastic bottle in terms of atmospheric pressure, the pressure inside the bottle, and the pressure of the column of water.

(a) When you turn the bottle upside down, a small amount of water is released until atmospheric pressure balances the pressure of the column of water plus the air pressure inside the bottle. When these pressures are in balance, you would expect nothing more to happen. However, air leaks in around the opening and the process begins again.

(b) When you tilt the bottle, the pressure inside the bottle remains at atmospheric pressure. It is the pressure of the column of water that causes the bottle to empty.

(c) When you squeeze the bottle, you increase the pressure inside the bottle. This pressure plus that of the column of water is greater than atmospheric pressure, and the bottle begins to empty. As the bottle empties, the balance between the atmospheric pressure and the pressure inside the bottle plus that of the column of water is restored.

A. Squeezing the bottle at Point A has the opposite effect of sucking or reducing the pressure above the water. When you squeeze the bottle at Position A, you increase the pressure of the air inside the bottle. The water level drops until atmospheric pressure balances the pressure inside the bottle and that of the column of water.

B. When you squeeze the bottle at Position B, the level does not change. The air pressure in the bottle does not change. The atmospheric pressure continues to balance the air pressure in the bottle plus the pressure of the column of liquid.

Dr. Y's idea is a good one. This is the fastest way to empty the bottle. The height of the column of water is greater than when you tilt the bottle, so it empties faster.

## Students' Explanations: Field Experience

Squeezing the bottle at A: In an earlier version of this POE, 52% of a sample of 25 grade 9 students predicted correctly that the level would go down. However, although none were able to give scientifically complete explanations, a few were on the right track:

> *It will go down because of the pressure pushing it down.*

> *Because you are using air pressure and it forces the water out.*

Many appeared to be struggling with their ideas:

> *Because the pressure squeeze in the water, so all the water comes out.*

Squeezing the bottle at B: None of the students predicted correctly, and only half gave reasons for their predictions. These were unacceptable scientifically.

In neither of the experiments did the students refer to atmospheric pressure, the pressure of the column of water, or the idea of balancing pressures. On this account, it would appear to be important to spend time on the preliminary discussion of the different ways to empty the bottle.

## Apparatus and Materials

- 2 L plastic bottle
- Trough or bucket
- Marker
- 2 L plastic bottle with a small hole in the bottom

## *Emptying a Plastic Soda Bottle*

What's the quickest way to empty a plastic soda bottle filled halfway with soda?

(a) Turn it upside down.    (b) Tilt it.    (c) Squeeze it.

### An Experiment

Fill a 2 L plastic soda bottle halfway with water and turn it upside down in a bowl of water.

Mark the water level in the bottle.

What do you think will happen to the water level if you squeeze the bottle at A? At B?

*Squeeze A*

*Squeeze B*

### Prediction A

Check one [√].    The level will    Go up [  ]    Go down [  ]    Stay the same [  ]

Please give your reasons. _____

### Prediction B

Check one [√].    The level will    Go up [  ]    Go down [  ]    Stay the same [  ]

Please give your reasons. _____

### Observe

Let's do it! What actually happened?

Squeezing at A _____

Squeezing at B _____

### Explain

Try to explain what happens.

A _____

B_____

### *Seriously?*

Dr. Y says the quickest way to empty a soda bottle is to make a small hole in the bottom.

*Small hole*

What do you think? _____

_____

## Scientific Explanation

The water will flow (this is demonstrated vividly if you add colored water). When you add water to one side, the water pressure on that side increases. The water flows until the heights of the water levels are the same.

If you lower one of the beakers, the water begins to flow again because the pressure on the higher side is greater. If you take one of the beakers away, the water flows—this is called *siphoning*.

## Students' Explanations: Field Experience

In a sample of 25 grade 9 students, 84% of students made correct predictions. Two-thirds of those predicting correctly used the word *pressure* to explain their thinking, but only half gave scientifically acceptable explanations:

*Because there is a pressure build-up, causing it to have to flow up.*

## Apparatus and Materials

- 2 straight drying tubes
- 2 pieces of glass tubing (about 40 cm long)
- Length of rubber tubing (about 20 cm long)
- 2 beakers
- Food coloring (optional)

## *Can Water Flow Uphill?*

### Riddle
Can water flow uphill? Here's one way to make it happen!
Amazing!

Do you think this will work?

How come? _____

_____

### An Experiment
Let's try another way!

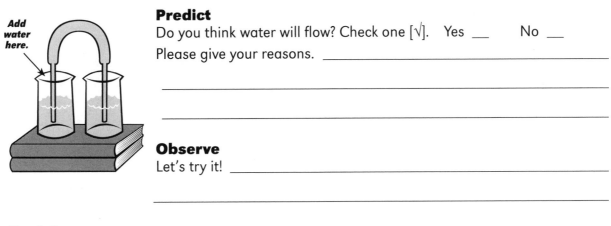

Add water here.

### Predict
Do you think water will flow? Check one [√].   Yes __   No __
Please give your reasons. _____

_____

_____

### Observe
Let's try it! _____

_____

### Explain
Try to explain what happens. _____

_____

_____

### *Try This!*
What do you think would happen if you lowered one of the beakers or even took it away?

_____

_____

_____

_____

_____

## Scientific Explanation

The siphon will stop flowing when there is no pressure difference on the water in the siphon tube. This will happen when the water levels in the jars are the same.

Dr. Y's invention does indeed work. When you turn the flask upside down, the rubber tube leading to the empty jar fills with water. This draws water into the flask in the form of a little jet. The process continues until the bottle or beaker on the right-hand side is empty.

## Apparatus and Materials

- 2 large bottles or beakers
- 2 lengths of rubber tubing (about 50 cm long)
- Flask
- 2-hole stopper
- Short length of glass tubing
- Longer length of glass tubing (with one end drawn to a jet)

## *Siphon*

### Let's Make a Siphon

All you need is a length of rubber or plastic tubing. Fill the tubing with water and pinch the ends shut. Put the ends in the jars and let go!

Any ideas how the siphon works?

When do you think the siphon will stop?

When will the water stop flowing?

### Predict

Predict the final water levels in each of the jars. (Draw your predictions in the diagram.)

Please give your reasons. _____

_____

### Observe

Let's do it! What happens?

_____

_____

### Explain

Try to explain what you observed, using the idea of pressure.

_____

_____

_____

### *Awesome!*

Dr. Y thinks he has invented a spectacular siphon. Dr. Y invites you to turn the bottle in the middle upside down. Will it work? Give your reasons.

_____

_____

_____

_____

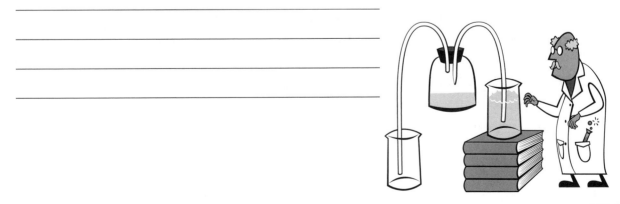

## Scientific Explanation

The paper strip lifts up. This is because the pressure on the top surface is lower than on the bottom. The reason the pressure is lower is on account of the air moving faster on the side of the strip being blown across. With airplanes, the curved shape of the wing means that air travels farther, and therefore faster, over the top of the wing than the bottom. Although this explanation is found in many science textbooks, it has been strongly disputed. For an excellent discussion, see William Beaty (1996).

The two empty soda cans surprisingly move together. When you blow, the pressure between them is lower than the atmospheric pressure.

## Students' Explanations: Field Experience

A sample of 25 POEs from grade 9 students was analyzed.

**Experiment 1:** The majority (56%) predicted correctly that the strip of paper would go up. Here are some of their reasons:

> *It will go up because the wind will blow it up.*

> *The paper will come up and go with the flow of the air.*

> *It will move upward because of the air waves.*

Most of the others thought the strip would move erratically: "flip all over the place," "shake and rattle," "wiggle," "ripple."

Very few students from the sample accounted for their predictions in terms of pressure. Although this student predicted incorrectly, he did associate movement with pressure in a scientifically acceptable way:

> *Flip all over the place because air pressure is making it do that.*

When invited to explain what they had observed in terms of air pressure and speed of the air, few students were able to formulate scientifically acceptable explanations. Here is a sample:

> *The speed of the air was up too strong and caused the wind pressure to blow it up.*

> *The speed of the air made enough pressure to pull the paper up.*

> *The speed of the air creates an upward pressure, then lifting the paper.*

**Experiment 2:** Forty-four percent (44%) of students predicted that the cans would move apart, 40% that they would move together, and 16% that they would stay the same. When students were invited to explain what they had observed, a variety of alternative frameworks was evident.

Although about 20% of students attributed the cans' moving together to the reduction of pressure between them, some conceptualized this in terms of pressure or the air being blown away:

> *The pressure gets blown away, so they stay together.*

> *The air between them will leave and there will be no pressure to keep them apart.*

A significant number of students, about 40%, attributed the cans moving together to the wind, some on account of the wind pushing them together, some because the wind spun them around:

> *The wind went around the cans and pushed them together.*

> *The wind went through the cans, surrounded them, and made them spin.*

## Apparatus and Materials

- Strip of paper, about 20 × 3 cm, for each student
- 2 empty soda cans
- Length of string
- Retort stand and clamps

# Airplane Wings

Do you know why an airplane wing is shaped the way it is? Why do you think it is flat on the bottom and curved on top? As you might expect, scientists and engineers have spent years doing experiments to find out the best shape.

**Blow**

**Paper strip**

### Experiment 1
Hold a strip of paper to your chin. Blow over the top of it, slowly increasing how hard you blow.

### Predict
What do you think will happen? Please explain.

_____

_____

### Observe
What happened? _____

_____

### Explain
(Try to use the terms *speed of the air* and *pressure* in your explanation.)

_____

_____

### Experiment 2
Hang two empty soda cans fairly close together. Blow between them.

### Predict
Do you think they will move apart, move together, or stay the same distance apart?

Please give your reasons. _____

_____

### Observe
What happened? _____

### Explain
(Try to use the word *pressure* in your answer.)

_____

_____

**Blow**

# References

Basca, B. B., and T. A. Grotzer. 2001. Focusing on the nature of causality in a unit on pressure: How does it affect student understanding? Paper presented at the American Educational Research Association, Seattle, WA.

Beaty, W. 1996. Airfoil lifting force misconception widespread in K–6 textbooks, *www.eskimo.com/~billb/ wing/airfoil.html.*

Biro, P., and S. Zwolanski-Morovic. 1992. *Predict, observe, explain: A children's science teaching approach.* Victoria, Australia: Monash Children's Science Group, Faculty of Education, Monash University. Booklet.

Clough, E., and R. Driver. 1985. What do children understand about pressure in fluids? *Research in Science and Technology Education* 3 (2): 133–145.

Clough, E., and R. Driver. 1986. A study of consistency in the use of students' conceptual frameworks across different task contexts. *Science Education* 70 (4): 473–486.

De Berg, K. C. 1995. Student understanding of the volume, mass, and pressure of air within a syringe in different states of compression. *Journal of Research in Science Teaching* 32 (8): 871–884.

Driver, R., A. Squires, P. Rushworth, and V. Wood-Robinson. 1994. *Making sense of secondary science.* London and New York: Routledge.

Horton, C. 2004. Student alternative conceptions in chemistry. Report by the Modeling Instruction in Chemistry action research team, Arizona State University. *http://modeling.asu.edu/modeling/Chem-AltConceptions3-09.doc.*

Schmidt, H-J. 1997. Students' misconceptions: Looking for a pattern. *Science Education* 81: 123–135.

Tytler, R. 1998. Children's conceptions of air pressure: Exploring the nature of conceptual change. *International Journal of Science Education* 20 (8): 929–958.

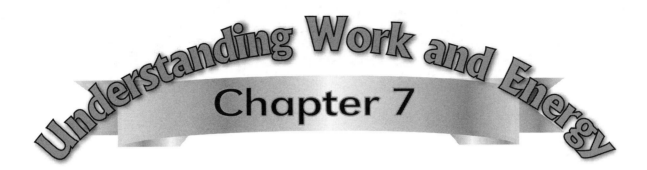

# Chapter 7

# Contents

## Scientific Explanation

Force required: In arrangement A, the pulley simply changes the direction of the force. Hence, if friction is ignored, the force is the same as the direct force. In arrangement B, however, there are two equal upward forces that balance the downward force of the mass. Hence, the force meter reading in arrangement B is half that of A.

Distance moved: In arrangement B, the free end of the string moves twice as far as in arrangement A.

Work done: Work = force × distance. Hence, the work done in both arrangements is the same.

## Students' Explanations: Field Experience

This POE was used with 29 grade 8 students. In the first experiment, all except one made incorrect predictions.

Although pulleys may be outside the everyday experience for the majority, 21% of students nevertheless mentioned that pulleys help:

*I think pulley helps you so there is less force.*

*I think the pulley will decrease the amount of force needed by half and they will be the same because only one pulley was used.*

Some students (10%) recognized that the tree might have a part to play:

*... for in A the tree is helping out but not in B.*

A substantial number of students (24%) thought it would require the same force to lift the weight, regardless of the arrangement:

*... you are still pulling the 10 N. Nothing really changes.*

A few students (10%) appeared to be influenced by the way the experiment was represented in the diagram:

*It seems to me that it would be easiest to pull down on it.*

In the second experiment, most students recognized that the free end would move a different distance in each arrangement, but only 10% predicted correctly.

## Students' Explanations: Research Findings

In a small-scale interview study, Driver and Warrington (1985) asked the 28 academically able students to compare the amount of work a man did when he lifted a load with and without a pulley system. Ten out of twelve 13-year-olds and three out of eight 16-year-olds thought the man would do less work with the pulley system. They reported much confusion between the ideas of work and effort.

## Apparatus and Materials

- Retort stand
- Pulley
- Weight (e.g., 1 kg)
- Spring scale
- String
- Meter rule

## Use a Pulley?

**Pulley fastened to tree**

**Pulley fastened to car**

Their car had slipped off the very icy road. Kim and Lee wondered if the pulley and rope their dad had put in the trunk would be of any use.

Kim wanted to tie the pulley to a tree (A). Lee wanted to tie the pulley to the fender (B). What do you think?

**Direct force**   **A**   **B**

**Experiment 1:** Record the reading on the force meter with the direct force (*N*). Then set up the two pulley arrangements, A and B. Direct force = _____ Newtons

### Predict
What do you think the readings on the force meters will be?

A = _____ Newtons        B = _____ Newtons

Please give your reasons. _____

_____

### Observe
Arrangement A = _____ Newtons        Arrangement B = _____ Newtons

### Explain
Can you explain the force meter readings? _____

_____

**Experiment 2:** Try raising the load 10 cm. Compare how far the free end of the string moves each time.

### Predict
How far do you think the free end will move in each arrangement?  A = ____ cm        B = ____ cm

Please explain. _____

_____

### Observe
Let's do it!   Arrangement A = _____cm        Arrangement B = _____ cm

### Explain
_____

### Hey! Does This Make Sense?
Let's compare the amount of work you do to raise each block 1 m.

Arrangement A = _____ Joules        Arrangement B = _____ Joules

Please explain. _____

_____

## Scientific Explanation

In the one-pulley system, the downward force is balanced by two equal forces: the upward force of the string attached to the clamp and the upward force of the string attached to the force meter. Hence, the force meter will read 5 N.

In the two-pulley system, the downward force is balanced by three equal upward forces. Hence, if the mass of the pulley and friction are ignored, the force on the spring scale would be 3 ⅓ N.

Michelle's idea is indeed a brainwave! In this arrangement, the downward force on each pulley is shared by two strings. Hence, the force on the spring scale would be 2 ½ N.)

In the one-pulley system, the free end of the string will move twice the distance the weight rises. In the two-pulley system, the distance moved by the three strings equals the distance moved by the mass. However, because the string is continuous, the end moves three times as far as the mass when pulled.

## Students' Explanations: Field Experience

An earlier version of this POE was used with 33 grade 8 students. They had already used the previous POE. Only 22 completed their predictions. Moreover, only one successfully predicted what would happen when two pulleys were used.

> **There are three ropes sharing the load on B.**

Eighty percent (80%) predicted that the reading on the force meter in B would be less and apparently realized that pulleys help:

> **One pulley cuts the work in half and with 2 pulleys it will take one quarter of the work.**

The way pulleys work seemed to have been difficult for these students to understand, and from our point of view, their performance in this and the previous POE makes a strong case for hands-on, loosely structured exploration—"messing about," as David Hawkins (1965) called it—prior to these structured demonstrations.

## Apparatus and Materials

- Weight (1 kg)
- 2 (or 3) pulleys
- Spring scale
- String
- Retort stand and clamp
- Meter rule

## *Two Pulleys?*

Mike and Michelle were lifting their dinghy onto the wharf. "If we only had another pulley," Michelle said with a gasp. "How could that help?" Mike grunted.

### An Experiment
Compare the one-pulley system with the two-pulley system.

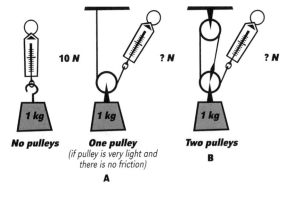

No pulleys

One pulley
*(if pulley is very light and there is no friction)*
**A**

Two pulleys
**B**

### Predict
What do you think the readings on the force meter will be?   A = _____ N      B = _____ N

Please give your reasons. _____

_____

### Observe
In addition to checking the reading on the force meter, examine how far you have to pull the rope to raise the mass 10 cm.

| Number of Pulleys | Force Required (*N*) | Distance Pulled (cm) to Raise Mass 10 cm |
|---|---|---|
| No pulleys | 10 | 10 |
| One pulley | | |
| Two pulleys | | |

### Explain
Try to explain your results.

(a) Force required: _____

_____

(b) Distance pulled: _____

_____

### *How About This?*
Michelle had a brainwave. "We could hook up the pulleys like this."

What do you think?

Mike wanted to try a three-pulley system!

How would they do it? Would it work?

## Scientific Explanation

Every turn of the rope around a broomstick increases your advantage, and it becomes easier to pull the broom handles together. For every extra turn you take, you move farther than before. If you use pulleys instead of broom handles, friction is reduced and the relationship *work = force × distance* becomes more apparent. There is a close parallel between these systems and those using a block and tackle.

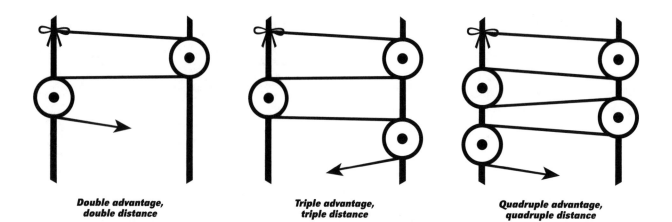

*Double advantage,
double distance*  *Triple advantage,
triple distance*  *Quadruple advantage,
quadruple distance*

## Apparatus and Materials

- 2 broom handles (as thick as possible)
- About 8 m of rope

# Stronger Than the Strongest!

**Party Trick**
Challenge the two strongest people in the room to keep you from pulling the two broom handles together. Can you see how it works? The diagram shows how the broom handles act like a series of pulleys.

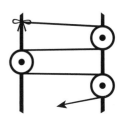

**An Experiment**
Try wrapping the rope around both of the broom handles one more time. Do you think this will make any difference?

**Predict**
How much effort do you think you will use? Check one [√].

More [   ]     Less [   ]     Same [   ]

Please give your reasons below.

_____

_____

_____

**Observe**
In addition to checking the force you need, check out how far you pull the rope.

One turn around each broomstick: _____

As in the diagram above (three turns total): _____

Two turns around each broomstick: _____

**Explain**
Try to use a pulley diagram to explain what happens.




*This Is Fun!*
Why not give the rope another turn around the broom handles?

**Predict** _____

**Observe** _____

**Explain** _____

_____

# Scientific Explanation

If the experiment worked perfectly, you would expect two marbles and one book to move the crash barrier the same distance as one marble and two books. At the top of the track, the marble has potential energy. As it rolls down the track, potential energy is converted into kinetic energy. This kinetic energy is converted into the work done to move the crash barrier against the force of friction. (But there are many imperfections. For example, when two marbles roll down together, they lose some energy by rubbing against each other.)

# Students' Explanations: Field Experience

This POE was used with 27 grade 8 students.

Seventy percent (70%) chose alternative C, in which the track was supported by two books. They often articulated their reasons in terms of height:

> *I think C will push the barrier farthest because the height will give the marble more force.*

> *I think that having two marbles and one book will go farther because of the height. Two marbles will get in the way of each other.*

In contrast, only 11% chose alternative B, in which two marbles are used. As one might expect, all of these students reasoned in terms of mass or weight:

> *I think the two marbles will go farther because of the mass [exerting] more force.*

Nineteen percent (19%) of the students predicted correctly and recognized that both the mass and height would contribute to the distance moved:

> *I think two marbles and one book will move the barrier as far as one marble and two books because speed and mass affect how far the barriers move.*

One-third of the class used the concepts of force, potential energy, or momentum in their explanations (force predominating).

# Students' Explanations: Research Findings

Driver and Warrington (1985) reported that secondary students (ages 13 to 18) rarely used ideas of energy conservation in exploring the functioning of four simple machines (inclined plane, pulley system, lever, water turbine). The concepts of work and energy were referred to by less than 10% of students.

# Apparatus and Materials

- Length of corrugated cardboard (about 70 × 10 cm) *or* length of Hot Wheels track *or* ruler with a central groove
- Barrier made from length of cardboard (about 15 × 3 cm) *or* plastic cup with a "doorway" cut in the lip
- 2 or 3 marbles
- Books
- Ruler or measuring tape

Note: Some teachers chose to do this POE as a class demonstration.

# Crash Barriers

Air bags are a common safety feature in cars. Do you know how they protect you? How do they absorb your energy if you crash?

At the speedway or racetrack, bales of straw are often used as crash barriers. Do you know how these work?

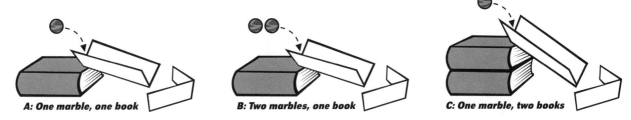

**A: One marble, one book**   **B: Two marbles, one book**   **C: One marble, two books**

## An Experiment
Make a track from a piece of cardboard raised on books. Make a crash barrier from another piece of bent cardboard. Let's investigate. Which crash barrier do you think will be pushed the farthest?

## Predict
Which do you think will be pushed farthest? Please give your reasons.

_____

_____

_____

## Observe
Measure the distance the crash barrier is pushed. (Take the average of three tests.)

A. One marble, one book         _____ cm     _____ cm     _____ cm     Average = _____ cm

B. Two marbles, one book        _____ cm     _____ cm     _____ cm     Average = _____ cm

C. One marble, two books        _____ cm     _____ cm     _____ cm     Average = _____ cm

D. Your choice

_____         _____ cm     _____ cm     _____ cm     Average = _____ cm

## Explain
Can you explain your results using your ideas about energy?

_____

_____

_____

_____

## Scientific Explanation

At the top of the hill, you have potential energy. As you freewheel, this is converted into kinetic energy. Friction slows you down and your kinetic energy is turned into heat energy. In sum, your potential energy equals the work done against friction

**Potential energy = kinetic energy + heat energy**

Because the distance to school is the same by both routes, the friction you encounter will be the same, too. Hence, it shouldn't make any difference which way you go.

Both routes would require the same amount of work (use the same amount of potential energy). Those who prefer to spread this out would choose the gentler slope.

## Apparatus and Materials

- Hot Wheels track
- Toy car
- Ruler or measuring tape
- Books

# Steep and Gentle Slopes

### Coasting to School
You live on top of a hill. There are two routes to school. Both routes are the same distance. One slopes gently down the hill; the other is steep at first, then flattens out.

If you freewheel on your bike down the gentle slope, you can just make it to school, but just barely.

Do you think you will make it to school down the steep route?

### An Experiment

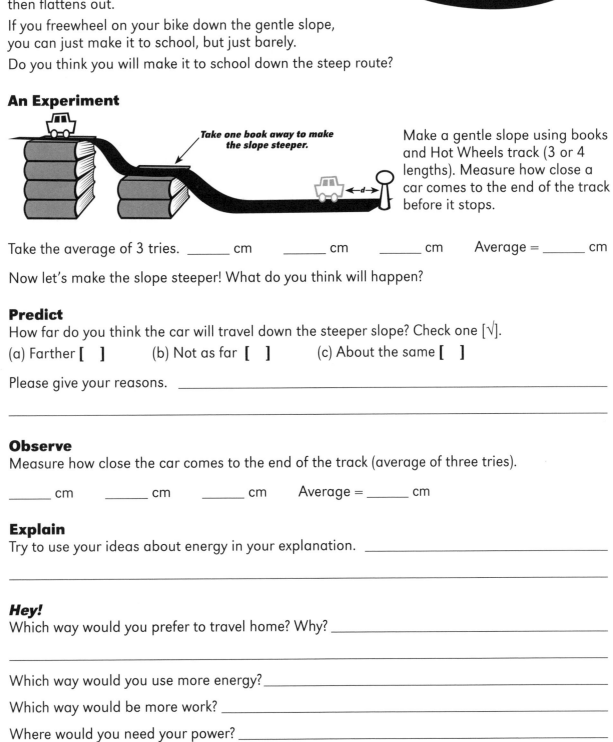

**Take one book away to make the slope steeper.**

Make a gentle slope using books and Hot Wheels track (3 or 4 lengths). Measure how close a car comes to the end of the track before it stops.

Take the average of 3 tries. _____ cm    _____ cm    _____ cm    Average = _____ cm

Now let's make the slope steeper! What do you think will happen?

### Predict
How far do you think the car will travel down the steeper slope? Check one [√].

(a) Farther **[   ]**          (b) Not as far **[   ]**          (c) About the same **[   ]**

Please give your reasons. _____

_____

### Observe
Measure how close the car comes to the end of the track (average of three tries).

_____ cm        _____ cm        _____ cm      Average = _____ cm

### Explain
Try to use your ideas about energy in your explanation. _____

_____

### *Hey!*
Which way would you prefer to travel home? Why? _____

_____

Which way would you use more energy? _____

Which way would be more work? _____

Where would you need your power? _____

## Scientific Explanation

This is an energy problem! The car's potential energy is changed into the work that is done in overcoming friction.

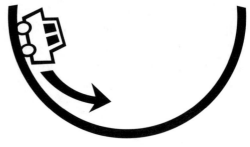

You can see the effects of friction by running a car down a U-shaped track. If there were no friction, the car would travel all the way from one peak to the other. As it is, some of the car's potential energy is used to overcome frictional resistance (try it with a marble, where the frictional resistance is lower). And it wouldn't make any difference if there was a small hill in the middle. There shouldn't be any difference between route A and route B. Indeed, Dr. Y is right!

## Apparatus and Materials

- Hot Wheels track
- Toy car
- Marble

## *Coasting Home*

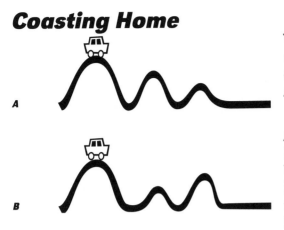

A

B

You run out of gas on top of a steep hill. Home is not far away, but the road is hilly. Do you think the chances of coasting home would be better by Route A or Route B (the distance is the same)?

### An Experiment

Let's investigate the problem above using some Hot Wheels track supported on three piles of books or blocks. First, check to see if the apparatus works well—the car should go the same distance every time you test it. Use the same length of track for each experiment and measure how close the car gets to home.

### Predict

Which route do you think will get you closer to home? Check one [√].

Route A [   ]          Route B [   ]          No significant difference [   ]

Please give your reasons. _____

_____

_____

### Observe

Measure the distance from home. Take the average of three readings for each route.

Route A        _____ cm        _____ cm        _____ cm        Average = _____ cm

Route B        _____ cm        _____ cm        _____ cm        Average = _____ cm

### Explain

Try to explain your results. _____

_____

_____

Dr. Y says the hills don't make any difference—just the length of the track.

Can he really be right?

Would the car still finish the same distance from home if you took the hills away? Please explain.

_____

_____

_____

# References

Driver, R., and L. Warrington. 1985. Students' use of the principle of energy conservation in problem situations. *Physics Education* 20 (4): 171–176.

Hawkins, D. 1965. Messing about in science. *Science and Children* 2 (5): 5–9.

# Chapter 8

## Contents

## Scientific Explanation

The white paper reflects (scatters) light in all directions. It absorbs a small proportion. The black paper absorbs most of the light. A little of the light is scattered—if it wasn't, you couldn't see it. The mirror reflects most of the light but only does so in one direction—just a little is scattered.

Hence, most students in the audience will see the white paper as the brightest. Neither the mirror nor the black paper will appear at all bright. One or two students will see the mirror as being very bright indeed—they will be in the line of the reflected ray. If the mirror is slowly rotated, all the students will be able to see this effect as the reflected ray passes them. High-quality screens reflect in all directions because they are coated with a reflective material. They are thus superior to white paper.

## Students' Explanations: Research Findings

Guesne (1985) reported that most children ages 10 and 11 do not perceive light as being something that moves in space and have no idea of what is involved in reflection. At ages 13 and 14, however, most children recognize that a mirror reflects light but think that when it falls on a paper screen it "stays there." Only 30% thought that when a flashlight shone on a white wall, the light would be reflected and illuminate an object behind the flashlight.

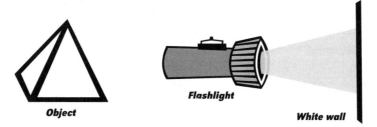

*Object*  *Flashlight*  *White wall*

Dedes and Ravanis (2009) found that when considering light coming from a point source (such as a lightbulb), students can have three conceptions of how light is emitted:

(a) Light goes in a preferential direction toward the viewer.

(b) Light is emitted as if from a spherical object equally in all directions.

(c) A combination of (a) and (b).

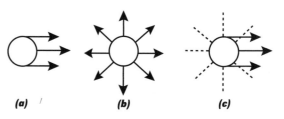

*(a)*  *(b)*  *(c)*

## Apparatus and Materials

- Sheet of white paper
- Sheet of black paper
- Mirror (about the size of a sheet of paper)
- Overhead projector and screen
- Cardstock

## *Overhead Trouble*

The screen of the overhead projector is broken. What could you use instead?
White paper? Black paper? A mirror? Which would work best?

**An Experiment**
Make a narrow slit of light by laying two pieces of cardstock close together on an overhead projector.
Cover the bright slit on the screen with

(a) white paper
(b) black paper
(c) a mirror

### Predict
Which do you think will appear brightest? _____ Second brightest? _____

_____

Please give your reasons. _____

_____

_____

### Observe
Let's do it!   Brightest _____          Second brightest _____

### Explain
Can you explain what you saw? _____

_____

_____

### *Try This!*
What do you think you would see if the mirror is slowly turned from right to left and back?

_____

_____

High-quality projector screens are better than white paper. Do you have any idea why?

_____

_____

**Teacher's Notes: *Shadow Play***

**Topic:** Light          **Concepts:** Light (rays) travel(s) in straight lines.
Each point of a light source emits light in all directions.

LIG2T

## Scientific Explanation

Light radiates in all directions from a light source. It travels in straight paths. A small bulb behaves as if it is a single point of light, whereas a larger bulb behaves as if it contains many point sources.

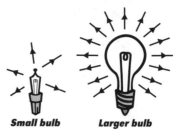

*Small bulb        Larger bulb*

An opaque object placed in the path of light rays from a source prevents the light rays from passing through it and produces a shadow. We can predict where the shadow will be by drawing rays from the point sources that touch each side of the object.

In the experiments shown, the shadow of the rod will be larger than the rod and will be at the bottom of the screen. If the screen is moved away, the shadow becomes larger. If the bulb is moved away, the shadow becomes smaller. The luminous patch is larger than the hole and falls in the middle of the screen.

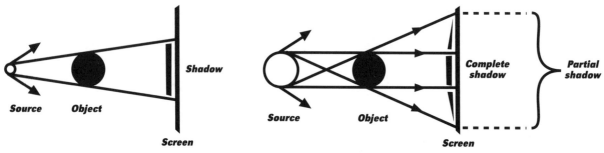

In the follow-up experiments, the flashlight bulb produces a shadow of the tennis ball, which is larger than the ball. The large lamp produces a shadow of the Ping-Pong ball, which is a lot larger than the ball; however, the shadow is only partial at the periphery. In the setup illustrated, there is not much difference between the shadows' sizes. This can be shown by drawing the light rays from each.

## Students' Explanations: Research Findings

About one-third of a group of children ages 13 and 14 used the idea that light rays travel in straight lines when they predicted correctly the size and position of the shadow of the stick and the patch of light. Some children thought that light would only pass through the hole when it was aligned horizontally with the bulb (Guesne 1985).

Galili and Hazan (2000) reported that some students may believe that shadows are actually "cast by an object," a feature of the object itself that light then allows us to observe. Furthermore, some authors report that students may not see a relationship between the propagation of light (i.e., light rays) and the formation of shadows (Eshach 2003).

## Apparatus and Materials

- 2 small bulbs in bulb holders
- 2 batteries
- 2 switches
- 2 screens
- Rod and modeling clay

- Screen with a hole in the middle
- Ping-Pong ball
- Tennis ball
- 2 hollow tubes
- Large lamp (pearl glass)

## Shadow Play

Have you ever tried to make a shadow of a rabbit or a fox with your fist?
How do you do it? What's the secret?

### Some Experiments

(a) What will the shadow of the rod look like? Its size? Where will it be on the screen?

(b) What will the lighted patch look like? Its size? Its position on the screen?

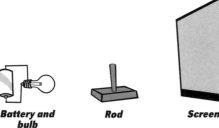

**Battery and bulb**          **Rod**          **Screen**

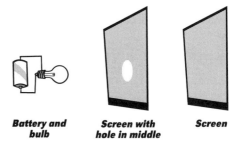

**Battery and bulb**     **Screen with hole in middle**     **Screen**

### Predict

Try drawing carefully (with a ruler, if you like) your predictions on the diagram above.

Pay attention to (a) the size and position of the rod and (b) the size and position of the lighted patch.

### Observe

What happened when we turned on the light? Were you surprised? Check one [√].

Size: Was the shadow of the rod    Bigger **[   ]**     Smaller **[   ]**     Same size **[   ]**?

Position: Where was the shadow of the rod? _____

Where was the lighted patch? _____

### Explain

How can we predict the size and position of a shadow? _____

_____

_____

### Hmm ...

1. How do you think the size of the shadow of the rod in the diagram above will change if

(a) we move the screen farther away?_____

(b) we move the lamp farther away?_____

2. Look at the diagrams below. Which do you think will make the larger shadow, the tennis ball or the Ping-Pong ball? _____

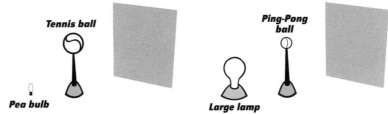

**Tennis ball**          **Ping-Pong ball**

**Pea bulb**          **Large lamp**

## Scientific Explanation

When light rays from a source fall on an object, the object scatters (reflects) the light. We can see the object if some of the scattered rays enter our eyes (see diagram [a]).

Light rays travel in straight lines (you can't see around corners). Hence, the light from the top of the tree travels through the pinhole to the bottom of the waxed paper and light from the right side of the window travels through the pinhole to the left side of the paper. We say the image is inverted.

The same applies to the letter *F*. As you increase the distance between the object (the letter *F*) and the viewer, the image gets smaller.

## Students' Explanations: Research Findings

Andersson and Karrqvist (1983) asked Swedish students in grade 9 to explain how they saw an object. Less than 20% were able to give scientifically acceptable answers in terms of rays going from the object to the eye, even though they had taken a course in optics the previous year. The idea of a visual ray, a ray from the eye to the object, was common.

Galili and Hazan (2000) report that students may believe that light travels from the light source to both the object and the eye; some also may believe that a light ray is a material part of light rather than a tool for representing its path.

Dedes and Ravanis (2009) found that when considering light coming from a point source (such as a lightbulb), students can have three conceptions of how light is emitted:

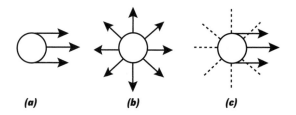

(a) Light goes in a preferential direction toward the viewer.
(b) Light is emitted as if from a spherical object equally in all directions.
(c) A combination of (a) and (b).

*(a)*   *(b)*   *(c)*

Rice and Feher (1987) indicated that children might have difficulty appreciating that each part of the light source radiates light and that the light rays from the object pass through the pinhole in straight lines.

## Apparatus and Materials

- Can with pinhole punched in base
- Wax paper
- Elastic band  (you might require multiple sets depending on how you organize the class)
- Flashlight
- Cutout letter *F* (or a marker to write the letter onto the flashlight)

## *Pinhole Viewer*

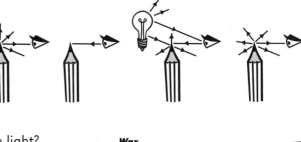

### Riddle

How do you see the tip of your pencil?

Which ray diagram shows the path the light rays take?

Answer: _____

Hint 1: Can you see the pencil if you turn off the light?

Hint 2: Can you see the pencil if you shield the light from your eyes?

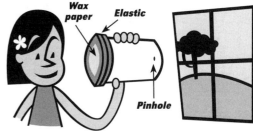

### An Experiment

Make a pinhole viewer by punching a hole the size of a pin or thin nail in the bottom of a can. Cover the open end with wax paper.

In a darkened room, look out a window or at a TV screen.

You could turn this viewer into a pinhole camera if you replaced the wax paper with photographic paper or blueprint paper.

### Predict

Draw what you think the girl in the illustration above will see on the wax paper when she looks at the tree through the window.

### Observe

Take a look through your own pinhole viewer. How is the image on the wax paper different from the real thing?

_____

### Explain

Try drawing a ray diagram that explains your observations.

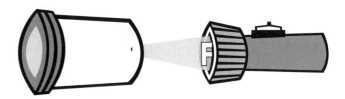

### *OK, But What About This?*

What do you think would happen if you cut out a letter *F*, stuck it on a flashlight, and viewed it through a pinhole viewer?

_____

What do you think it would look like? _____

What would happen to the image if you moved the flashlight farther away? _____

_____

## Scientific Explanation

A fluorescent tube emits light in all directions. Each tube provides millions of point sources.

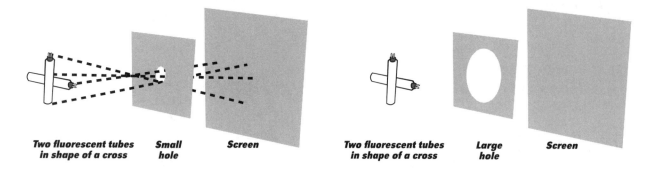

**Two fluorescent tubes      Small          Screen**
**in shape of a cross        hole**

**Two fluorescent tubes      Large          Screen**
**in shape of a cross        hole**

Experiment 1: Rays from each point source travel through the small hole. This happens for each point of the cross. Hence, we see an image of a cross on the screen. The ray diagram shows rays emitted at the four ends of the cross.

Experiment 2: When the rays travel through the large hole, the image is large and circular. Imagine the rays emitted from just one point source. The hole allows a cone of light to pass through, and we see a circular patch on the screen. The rays from other point sources pass through the hole in a similar way.

When half of the small hole is covered, we still see the cross, even though fewer rays pass through. When the top half of the fluorescent cross is covered, giving a *T*, we see an inverted *T* on the screen.

## Students' Explanations: Research Findings

This POE is based on research done by Rice and Feher (1987) with children ages 9 to 13 at the Science Center in San Diego. In making their predictions, about half of the children attributed the shape of the image to the hole, while the others attributed it to the light source. A small number of the children were able to use ray diagrams successfully to explain the observed effects. This would be surprising unless they had already been taught about the diagrams. For example, some children did not portray light rays traveling in straight lines and thought they diverged on passing through the hole. The majority had not understood the concept that each element of a source emits light equally in all directions. They also may believe that light from a light source travels in parallel lines from a point source, and that screen placement does not affect clarity when going through a pinhole (Tao 2004).

## Apparatus and Materials

- 2 fluorescent tubes, each about 20 cm long, mounted in the shape of a cross
- Sheet of bristol board with a 20 cm hole in the middle
- Sheet of bristol board with a 1 cm hole in the middle
- Screen (placed about 2 m from the light source)

# Images: Does the Size of the Hole Make a Difference?

Can you draw a picture to show how light rays are emitted from a fluorescent tube?

## Two Experiments

When we turn on the tubes, what do you think we will see on the screens?

**Experiment 1**                                         **Experiment 2**

                    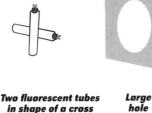 

*Two fluorescent tubes*   *Small*   *Screen*         *Two fluorescent tubes*   *Large*   *Screen*
*in shape of a cross*    *hole*                *in shape of a cross*    *hole*

## Predict

Draw what you think you will see on the screens in the diagram above.

## Observe

What did you see when the fluorescent tubes were turned on?

Experiment 1: _____

Experiment 2: _____

## Explain

Try to draw ray diagrams to explain what happened.

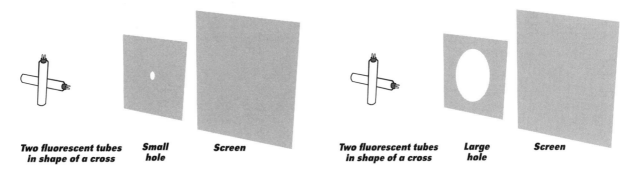

*Two fluorescent tubes*   *Small*   *Screen*         *Two fluorescent tubes*   *Large*   *Screen*
*in shape of a cross*    *hole*                *in shape of a cross*    *hole*

(a) In experiment 1, what do you think would happen if we covered up half of the small hole?

_____

_____

(b) In experiment 1, what do you think would happen if we covered up the top half of the cross, leaving a T-shaped light?

_____

_____

## Scientific Explanation

First position (mirror opposite C):      A will see E.     B will see D.     C will see C.
Second position (mirror opposite D):   A will see G.     B will see F.     C will see E.

Light rays are reflected from a mirror at the same angle as they hit the mirror. They behave in a similar way to billiard balls hitting a cushion. The angle of incidence equals the angle of reflection.

When the mirror (Position 1) is slowly rotated counterclockwise, A will see F first, then G. When it is rotated clockwise, A will see F, then E, then D, then C, then B, then himself or herself.

The shape of a mirror that would enable D to see everyone is convex. Look at how the angle of incidence always equals the angle of reflection.

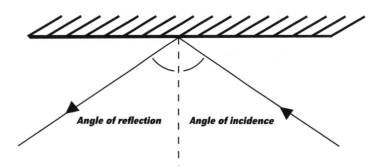

## Students' Explanations: Research Experience

Although 200 East Indian students (ages 15 and 16) were able to remember (if not understand) the second law of reflection, more than 80% thought it only applied to a plane mirror (Mohapatra 1988). One issue that may influence student responses is that the role of the observer in optics often is ignored and light must enter the eye for vision to take place (Galili and Hazan 2000).

## Apparatus and Materials

- Mirror (about 30 cm wide)

## Who Can See Whom?

At the hair salon, where could you and your friend sit so that you could see each other while you were having your hair cut?

### An Experiment

Seven students line up facing a mirror.
Who can see whom?

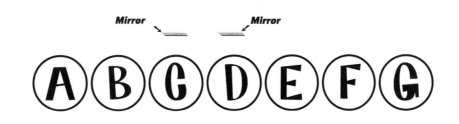

Mirror    Mirror

### Predict

First position (mirror opposite **C**)    **A** will see _____.    **B** will see _____.    **C** will see _____.

Second position (mirror opposite **D**)    **A** will see _____.    **B** will see _____.    **C** will see _____.

### Observe

First position (mirror opposite **C**)    **A** sees _____.    **B** sees _____.    **C** sees _____.

Second position (mirror opposite **D**)    **A** sees _____.    **B** sees _____.    **C** sees _____.

### Explain

Can you make up a rule that tells you who can see whom? (Hint: Use ray diagrams to show how light travels from *X* to you.)

_____

_____

### Hey!

What will A see if the first mirror is slowly rotated counterclockwise? Clockwise?

_____

_____

What shape of mirror would help D see everyone in the lineup? Perhaps this would be perfect security for a convenience store? Try to draw it below.

_____

_____

## Scientific Explanation

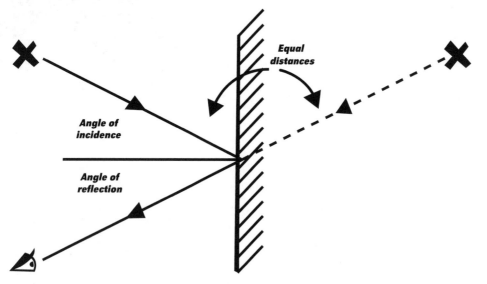

Light from the letter X is reflected off the mirror at the same angle as it hits it (second law of reflection). Your eye does not detect that the ray has been bent and you perceive the letter X the same distance behind the mirror as it is in front. The letter X appears to be in the same position in the mirror, wherever your viewing position.

## Students' Explanations: Research Findings

Most authors report that students do not have difficulty with the idea that light travels in a straight line.

## Apparatus and Materials

- Smoked-glass mirror for each student

## *Coded Messages*

If you had a mirror, you could decode this message. Any ideas what it says?

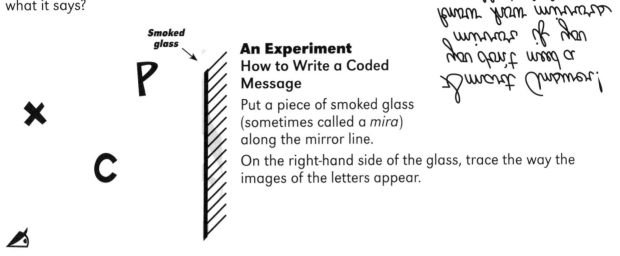

**Smoked glass**

**An Experiment**
**How to Write a Coded Message**

Put a piece of smoked glass (sometimes called a *mira*) along the mirror line.

On the right-hand side of the glass, trace the way the images of the letters appear.

### Predict
Use a *pencil* to draw the way you think you will see the letters in the smoked-glass mirror.

### Observe
Use a *pen* to trace what you actually see. How do your observations differ from your predictions?

_____

### Explain
Can you make up a rule that tells you where your letter will be in the mirror?

_____

Try to draw a ray diagram that shows how light travels from the letter *X* to your eye (use the diagram above).

### *Cool!*
Does the position of the image depend on where you stand?

_____

Try drawing another ray diagram with your eye in another place.

## Scientific Explanation

You need a half-length mirror to see all of yourself. If you look about halfway down you can see your toes because the angle of reflection equals the angle of incidence. (Similarly, if you look at a line halfway between your ears and the top of your head, you will indeed see the top of your head!)

It doesn't matter how far you stand away from the mirror—you still need a half-length mirror. This is because both the angle of incidence and the angle of reflection change.

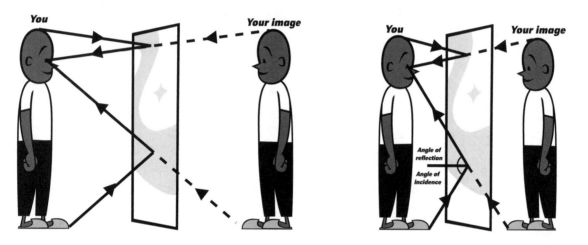

In a flat mirror, the image appears to be the same distance behind the mirror as the object in front; your eye thinks light travels in straight lines and, hence, the light from your toe comes from the position shown in the diagram.

Paul Hewitt's book *Conceptual Physics* contains many interesting problems, such as this question about mirrors, that lend themselves to being turned into POEs.

## Students' Explanations: Research Findings

Ramadas and Driver (1989) reported that students attribute the formation of images in a mirror to a property of mirrors themselves rather than to the propagation of light. Students may believe that the image is always present in the mirror, regardless of whether or not it is observed (Galili and Hazan 2000).

## Apparatus and Materials

- Mirror (about 1 m long)
- Marker
- Meterstick

## *Looking at Yourself in a Mirror*

You need a mirror for your bedroom, one long enough to give you a full view of yourself from head to toe! Which one should you buy?

| **Special Offer** | |
|---|---|
| **Full-length mirror** | **$49.99** |
| **Half-length mirror** | **$29.99** |
| **Quarter-length mirror** | **$19.99** |

### An Experiment

Stand 1 m away from a long mirror. Where do you see the top of your head and the top of your toes in the mirror? Mark the positions with a felt pen.

1 m

### Predict

What length will enable you to see your whole body? Check one [√].

Full **[ ]**          Half **[ ]**          Quarter **[ ]**

Please explain your thinking. _____

_____

### Observe

Let's do it!   Height of first student _____ cm      Length of mirror required _____ cm

Height of second student _____ cm      Length of mirror required _____ cm

Height of third student _____ cm      Length of mirror required _____ cm

### Explain

Can you draw a ray diagram that shows the way light travels from your toe to your eye? Fill in the picture above if you like.

### *Interesting!*

I wonder if it makes a difference how far away from the mirror you are standing.

_____

How come? _____

_____

_____

# Scientific Explanation

Without water in the cup, you cannot see the penny.

When the water is added, the penny moves into view. The light ray appears to come from Position B along the dotted line.

But the penny is really still at A. Hence, the light ray must travel along the heavy line and bend at the surface of the water (W).

And what would the fish see? If the fish's eye is at Position A, the light ray would appear to come from an extension of the line *AW*. The trapper would appear to be almost overhead.

## Students' Explanations: Research Findings

Many students may initially have difficulty with the idea of light changing direction when it enters a new medium (Langley, Ronen, and Eylon 1997). This difficulty might occur because many hold the idea that light (or light rays) only travels in a straight line.

## Apparatus and Materials

- Yogurt pot
- Penny
- Supply of water for each student

## *Spearing Fish*

Although he's very quick and accurate, the young hunter misses the fish completely.

Somehow his sharp eyes are fooled. What advice would you give him?

Eye

### An Experiment

The penny in the middle of the bottom of a cup or yogurt container represents the fish.

Move your head so that the penny just disappears from sight behind the lip. Then ...

Very slowly, fill the cup with water.

Any ideas what will happen?

?

### Predict

Do you think you will be able to see the penny? Check one [√].   Yes **[   ]**   Maybe **[   ]**   No **[   ]**

Give your reasons for your answer. _____

### Observe

Very carefully, observe as you add the water. List what you see happen.

_____

### Explain

Try to explain what you saw. _____

_____

_____

Can you draw a ray diagram that shows how light from the penny travels toward your eye? Fill in the diagram above on the right.

### *So ...*

What advice would you give the young hunter?_____

I wonder what the fish sees.

_____

_____

# Scientific Explanation

Filters allow only light of their own color to pass through (e.g., a red filter will allow red light through but not blue. Hence, the blue light will appear black through a red filter.).

The question arises as to why white light appears red through a red filter and blue through a blue one. Could it be that white light is made up of many colors? (Scientists believe this to be the case—see next POE.)

If you put a red transparency on the overhead projector and then cover this with a blue one, most of the light is cut out. The red light from the first filter cannot pass through the blue filter. (Note: The quality of filters can really affect the outcome. We recommend testing this first.)

The same ideas apply when you look at a printed picture. A printed color (e.g., red) simply reflects light of its own color—it acts as if it was a (red) light source. When white light shines onto a color, all except that color are absorbed by the paint pigment.

Strangely enough, black is not a color. It is the absence of color.

# Students' Explanations: Research Findings

Galili and Hazan (2000) discuss the difficulties that students may encounter in developing their understanding of color. These include

- the color of an object being subjective, based on individual perception and their optical processing;
- background colors; and
- degree of illumination.

# Apparatus and Materials

- Overhead projector
- Large acetate filters: red, blue, green (check quality of filters before using) for overhead projector; small (5 cm squares) of red and blue filters for each student
- Colored pictures from magazines for students

# Watching TV Through Colored Glasses

Things look different through colored glasses. What do you think you would see if you looked at a TV screen through red glasses, blue glasses, or green glasses? What would the picture opposite look like? What color would the little red schoolhouse be? How about the white cloud?

### An Experiment

Use an overhead projector to reflect lights of different colors. What colors do you think you will see when you look at these lights through different-color filters?

### Predict

Use the table below to make your predictions.

| Color of Light | Color of Filter | |
|---|---|---|
| | **Red** | **Blue** |
| **Red** | | |
| **Blue** | | |
| **Green** | | |
| **White** | | |

Can you explain your predictions? How do you think filters work? _____

_____

### Observe

Let's check your predictions. What did you see?

| Color of Light | Color of Filter | |
|---|---|---|
| | **Red** | **Blue** |
| **Red** | | |
| **Blue** | | |
| **Green** | | |
| **White** | | |

### Explain

Can you make up a rule that tells you how filters work?_____

_____

### Hey!

What do you think you would see if you put a red transparency on the overhead projector and then covered it with a blue one? _____

What do you think you would see if you looked at a printed picture of the little red schoolhouse through red glasses? _____

Is black a color?_____

## Scientific Explanation

(a) A raindrop and a prism can each split light into the colors from which it is made.

(b) Filters take out from white light all the colors but their own. A perfect filter lets only its own color through. For example, a green filter lets only the green light through.

Hence, if the filter is placed on the far side of the prism (position A), you will only see the green band of the spectrum because it takes out the other bands. On the near side (position B), it takes out the other colors before the light is split. Thus, you see the same thing regardless of whether the filter is placed before or after the prism.

## Students' Explanations: Research Findings

Research indicates that there often is confusion between light as a physical entity and light as sense perception. The "role of the observer" (which often is central to understanding many topics) is ignored. This might result in difficulty understanding phenomena such as color. Many students believe that color and light are different phenomena (Galili and Hazan 2000).

## Apparatus and Materials

- Flashlight (or beam from an overhead projector). You can use masking tape to make a slit.
- White card (or screen)
- Acetate filters (green, yellow)
- Prism

# *Rainbow*

The storm was over. The sun came out. Spike put on her new green-tinted sunglasses. She looked at the rainbow. What do you think she saw?

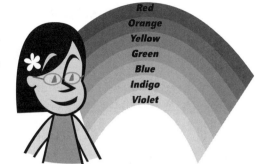

## An Experiment

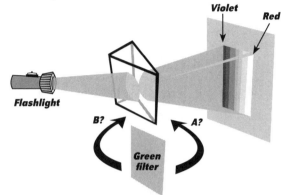

Use a prism to make a rainbow.

Try putting a green filter in the light path

(a) between the prism and the screen

(b) between the flashlight slit and the prism

## Predict

Position A: What will the rainbow look like?_____

Please give your reasons. _____

_____

Position B: What will the rainbow look like?_____

Please give your reasons. _____

## Observe

Let's check it out!

Position A: _____

Position B: _____

## Explain

How do you explain what you observed?_____

_____

## *Hey!*

What do you think Spike saw? _____

Sam has yellow sunglasses. What would he have seen?

_____

Do you have any ideas about how a prism works? Any ideas about what filters do?

_____

## Scientific Explanation

White light is made up of all the colors of the spectrum: red, orange, yellow, green, blue, indigo, violet. If you mix two (spectral) colors together, you are beginning to put the spectrum back together and the mixture will be whiter.

Each of the colors on the spinning top acts as a source of light because it is reflecting its own color. Hence, when you spin it, you get the same effect as if you had mixed all the colors of the spectrum—white light.

## Students' Explanations: Research Findings

Research indicates that there often is confusion between light as a physical entity and light as sense perception. The "role of the observer" (which is often central to understanding many topics) is ignored. This might result in difficulty understanding phenomena such as color. Many students believe that color and light are different phenomena (Galili and Hazan 2000).

## Apparatus and Materials

- 2 flashlights or 2 overhead projectors
- Acetate filters: yellow, blue, red, and green

# In the Spotlight: Mixing Colored Lights

The end-of-term dance was bound to be a success. Spike and Sam were in charge of special effects.

"Let's use colored spotlights!" Spike exclaimed.

"Yeah! Yellow, blue, red, green ..."

"What happens if you mix yellow and blue *or* red and green *or* ... ?"

## An Experiment

Cover two flashlights with different-color filters. Mix the colored lights on a white wall or screen.

For large-scale effects, use two overhead projectors!

*Yellow*          *Blue*

## Predict

What color do you think you will see when you mix

(a) Yellow and blue _____ Please give your reasons. _____

_____

(b) Red and green _____ Please give your reasons. _____

_____

## Observe

Let's experiment!

(a) Yellow light and blue light create _____

(b) Red light and green light create _____

## Explain

Try to explain what you saw. _____

_____

## Try This!

What do you think you would see if you spun a top colored like a rainbow?

_____

Can you explain why?_____

_____

_____

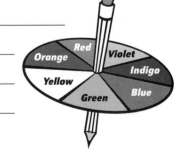

## Scientific Explanation

In white light, yellow paint reflects yellow light. However, it's not pure yellow light because it also reflects a small amount of other colors (e.g., orange and green). The eye doesn't pick these up because yellow dominates. Colors apart from yellow, green, and orange are absorbed by the paint.

In white light, blue paint absorbs all the colors except blue, green and indigo. Hence, when blue and yellow paints are mixed, the only color not absorbed is green. Therefore, we see green.

In general, the color you see is the color(s) not absorbed by the paint.

Printers (and computer printer ribbons) use three colors: red, blue, and yellow. These three mixed in different proportions can give all the colors; when mixed together, they give black because together they absorb all the colors of light.

## Approaches and Materials

Each student will need a set of markers or crayons.

# *Mixing Colored Paints*

## Quick Quiz

What colors make up white light? _____

What colors do you get if you mix blue and yellow lights? _____

_____

Why does paper painted blue look blue in white light? _____

_____

Why does paper painted blue look black through a yellow filter? _____

_____

What color do you get if you mix blue and yellow paints? _____

_____

## An Experiment

Try your hand at mixing different color paints or markers.

## Predict

What color do you think you will get if you mix the following paints?

(a) Red and yellow _____          (b) Yellow and blue _____

(c) Red and blue _____          (d) Green and orange _____

Choose any one and give your reason. _____

_____

## Observe

Let's check it out!

(a) Red and yellow _____

(b) Any surprises? _____

## Explain

Try to explain what happens using the answers to the questions in the quick quiz.

_____

_____

## *Guess What!*

When they print colored books, printers need only three colors. Take a guess at what they are!

_____     _____     _____

Can you explain?

_____

## Scientific Explanation

White light consists of red, orange, yellow, green, blue, indigo, and violet lights. Blue light is scattered more by milk and dust particles than red light. Hence, when you look directly into the beam, it appears orange-red because the blue light has been scattered. From the side, the beam appears blue because you are seeing the scattered light.

As the sun sets, its light passes through a thick layer of atmosphere. It appears red because the blue light is scattered. The sky is blue because you see the scattered light. In space, there is no atmosphere and no particles to scatter light. Hence, the "sky" is black.

## Apparatus and Materials

- Flashlight
- Large bottle
- Milk or milk crystals

## *Blue Sky—Red Sunset*

### Three Riddles
Why does the sun appear red when it sets?
Why is the sky blue?
Why is the sky black in outer space?
(Hint: The atmosphere contains many tiny dust particles that scatter the light.)

### An Experiment
Make an artificial atmosphere by adding a drop or two of milk (or two or three skim milk crystals) to a bottle of water. Use a strong flashlight as the sun.

*Look through the bottle.*

### Predict
What color do you think you will see if you look straight through the bottle at the artificial sun (A)? _____

What color do you think you will see if you look at the light beam from the side (B)? _____

Please explain your answers. _____

_____

### Observe
Color seen at A _____      Color seen at B _____

### Explain
Try to explain what you saw using the idea that milk particles scatter light.

_____

_____

### *How About Those Riddles?*
How come the sky is black in outer space?

_____

_____

_____

# References

Andersson, B., and C. Karrqvist. 1983. How Swedish people, aged 12–15 years, understand light and its properties. *European Journal of Science Education* 5 (4): 387–401.

Dedes, C., and K. Ravanis. 2009. Teaching image formation by extended light sources: The use of a model derived from the history of science. *Research in Science Education* 39 (1): 57–73.

Eshach, H. 2003. Small-group interview-based discussions about diffused shadow. *Journal of Science Education and Technology* 12 (3): 261–275.

Galili, I., and A. Hazan. 2000. Learners' knowledge in optics: Interpretation, structure and analysis. *International Journal of Science Education* 22 (1): 57–88.

Guesne, E. 1985. Light. In *Children's ideas in science.* ed. R. Driver, E. Guesne, and A. Tiberghein, 10–32. Buckingham, United Kingdom: Open University Press.

Langley, D., M. Ronen, and B. S. Eylon. 1997. Light propagation and visual patterns: Preinstruction learners' conceptions. *Journal of Research in Science Teaching* 34 (4): 399–424.

Mohapatra, J. K. 1988. Induced incorrect generalizations leading to misconceptions—An exploratory investigation about the laws of reflection of light. *Journal of Research in Science Teaching* 25 (9): 777–784.

Ramadas, J., and R. Driver. 1989. *Aspects of secondary students' ideas about light.* Leeds, United Kingdom: University of Leeds.

Rice, K., and E. Feher. 1987. Pinholes and images: Children's conceptions of light and vision. *Science Education* 71 (4): 629–639.

Tao, P.-K. 2004. Developing understanding of image formation by lenses through collaborative learning mediated by multimedia computer-assisted learning programs. *International Journal of Science Education* 26 (10): 1171–1197.

# Chapter 9

## Understanding Sound

## Contents

## Scientific Explanation

When you tap the empty can, it vibrates. These vibrations create sound waves. The full can doesn't ring as well as the empty can. The liquid in the full can "damps" down the vibrations.

When you tap a glass with a thin piece of wire laid across the top, the glass vibrates but the vibrations make the piece of wire vibrate, move up and down, as well. You no longer hear the glass ringing with such a clear note.

## Students' Explanations: Research Findings

Research into children's conceptions of sound has been limited. Asoko and her colleagues reported that the majority of children ages 4 to 16 seemed to readily associate the production of sound with the vibration of objects (see Driver et al. 1994). Students, however, also often believe that sound is a material or a substance (Eshach and Schwartz 2006; Mazens and Lautrey 2003; Houle and Barnett 2008).

It may be noted here that in a study about how pupils think sound travels from a radio to the ear, Boyes and Stannisstreet (1991) reported that a small percentage of students believed that sound traveled from the ear to the object and back again, or that the ear was a passive receptor. In their study, 40% of a group of 11- and 12-year-olds and 80% of a group of 15- and 16-year-olds gave scientifically acceptable answers.

## Apparatus and Materials

- 2 juice or soda cans
- 2 wine glasses
- Short length of wire (about 10 cm)

# Empty Vessels Make the Most Noise

### Riddle
One can is empty, the other is full.

Without opening or lifting them, how could you tell the empty can from the full can?

### An Experiment
(A) Tap a glass with a pencil. Listen to the way it rings.

(B) Lay a thin piece of wire across the top. Do you think the way it rings will change when you try it?

*Piece of thin wire*

*A*          *B*

### Predict
How do you think the sound produced by B will differ from A?

_____

Please give your reasons. _____

_____

### Observe
Let's try it!_____

### Explain
Try to explain why the sounds are different. _____

_____

_____

### Try This!
What do you think will happen when the glass is filled with water?

_____

_____

What happens? Try to explain why. _____

_____

_____

## Scientific Explanation

Sound is caused by matter (solids, liquids, or gases) vibrating. When you blow into a bottle, the air vibrates: The shorter the column of air, the higher the note.

When you tap a bottle, the glass (above the water) vibrates: The shorter the length of the glass, the higher the note.

## Students' Explanations: Research Findings

Asoko, Leach, and Scott (1991) report that younger children often believe that sound is part of the object from which the sound is coming.

It may be noted here that in a study about how pupils think sound travels from a radio to the ear, Boyes and Stannisstreet (1991) reported that a small percentage of students believed that sound traveled from the ear to the object and back again, or that the ear was a passive receptor. In their study, 40% of a group of 11- and 12-year-olds and 80% of a group of 15- and 16-year-olds gave scientifically acceptable answers.

## Apparatus and Materials

- 3 glass bottles

## Bottle Sounds

### Everyday Puzzle

Have you ever stopped to wonder why the sound produced by a bottle goes up the scale as you fill it?

Check out the sound produced by a bottle as you empty it.

### An Experiment

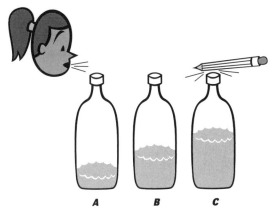

A          B          C

Fill these glass soda bottles with different amounts of water.

Let's blow into them! Which do you think will produce the higher note?

Now let's tap them! Now which one produces the higher note?

### Predict

Which bottle do you think will produce the higher note?

(a) Blowing _____     (b) Tapping _____

Please give your reasons. _____

_____

### Observe

Let's do it!

(a) Blowing _____

(b) Tapping _____

### Explain

Try to explain what you observed (use the word *vibrate* if you can). Clue: Ask yourself what vibrates when you blow and what vibrates when you tap.

_____

_____

_____

## Scientific Explanation

As the flask cools down, the steam condenses and leaves less and less water vapor in its atmosphere (at room temperature there is almost a vacuum in the flask).

As the flask cools down, the sound of the bell decreases. If you listen carefully, you can just hear it at room temperature.

Sound is audible vibration. Vibration cannot pass through a vacuum because there is nothing there to vibrate.

## Students' Explanations: Research Findings

Researchers have found that although younger children readily associate sound with an object vibrating, they less readily perceive that air or another medium is required to transmit these vibrations. By age 16, however, three-quarters of students appear to understand that air is needed (Asoko, Leach, and Scott 1991).

## Apparatus and Materials

- Flask
- 1-hole stopper with small stopper to fit
- Length of copper wire
- Small bell

## *Air to Hear?*

### Riddle
You need air to breathe, but do you need air to hear? There's no air on the Moon—could you hear anything there?

### An Experiment

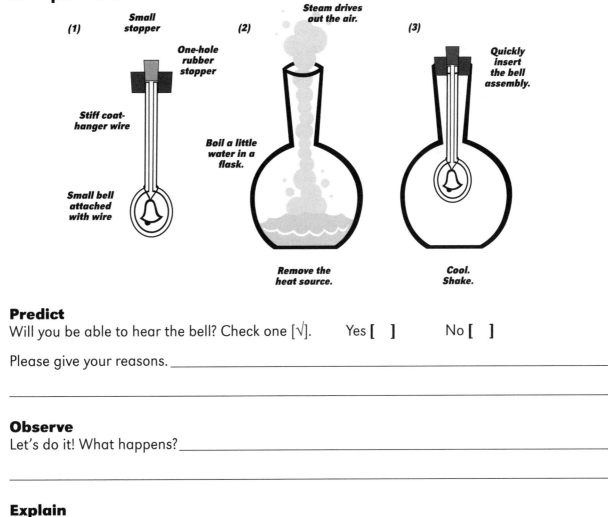

(1) **Small stopper**

**One-hole rubber stopper**

**Stiff coat-hanger wire**

**Small bell attached with wire**

(2) **Steam drives out the air.**

**Boil a little water in a flask.**

**Remove the heat source.**

(3) **Quickly insert the bell assembly.**

**Cool. Shake.**

### Predict
Will you be able to hear the bell? Check one [√].        Yes [ ]        No [ ]

Please give your reasons. _____

_____

### Observe
Let's do it! What happens?_____

_____

### Explain
Can you explain your observations? _____

_____

### *Hey!*
What do you think will happen if you remove the small stopper and allow air to enter the flask? Try to explain your answer.

_____

_____

_____

## Scientific Explanation

Scratching (or a tuning fork) produces vibrations. These vibrations travel better through solids than through air because air is quite compressible and solids are less so. Hence sound travels better through solids. (See SND5T for further discussion of this topic.)

## Students' Explanations: Research Findings

In their study of students in grades 8 and 9, Houle and Barnett (2008) found three types of models that students use to picture the movement of sound.

(a) A sinusoidal "wave" model. Here the students view transmission as a sinusoidal transverse wave (possibly derived from textbooks) rather than a compression wave, which is the scientific view.

(b) A "material" model. Here the students view sound as a substance. One student described sound waves as being "like little molecules that travel from one place to another."

(c) A "shaking" model (Hrepic, Zollman, and Rebello 2002). Here the students perceive sound being transmitted by particles vibrating.

## Apparatus and Materials

- Tuning fork
- Lengths of wood, plastic, metal, etc.

Note: If this POE is done as a laboratory experiment, then class quantities of the apparatus will be required.

## Ear to the Ground

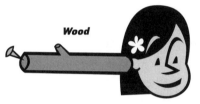

### Science or Folklore?
Native people used to put their ears to the ground to hear if horses were approaching.

Do you think this works?

### An Experiment

Do you think sound travels better through a solid than it does through air?

Hold a length of wood close to (but not touching) your ear. Scratch it with a pin.

Now touch your ear with the wood. Does the sound get any louder?

### Predict
Do you think you will be able to hear better through air or through wood? Try to explain your answer.

_____

_____

### Observe
Check it out! What happens? _____

_____

### Explain
Sound comes from vibration. Can you use the word *vibrate* to explain what you heard? _____

_____

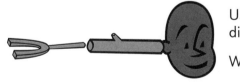

Use a tuning fork to test how well sound travels through different materials (wood, plastic, metal, etc.).

Which works best?

1. _____  2. _____  3. _____  4. _____

Try to explain why. _____

_____

_____

## Scientific Explanation

When you tap two spoons together underwater, they produce vibrations (pulses or pushes). This is how sound vibrations travel. Imagine a crowded room. Someone at one end of the room begins pushing. The push is transmitted to the next person, who in turn bumps into the next one. The push travels across the room, even though the people stay in their original places.

Now water vibrates better than air. Hence, the sound underwater is louder.

## Students' Explanations: Research Findings

In their study of students in grades 8 and 9, Houle and Barnett (2008) found three types of models that students use to picture the movement of sound.

(a) A sinusoidal "wave" model. Here the students view transmission as a sinusoidal transverse wave (possibly derived from textbooks) rather than a compression wave, which is the scientific view.

(b) A "material" model. Here the students view sound as a substance. One student described sound waves as being "like little molecules that travel from one place to another."

(c) A "shaking" model (after Hrepic, Zollman, and Rebello 2002). Here the students perceive sound being transmitted by particles vibrating.

## Apparatus and Materials

- Bucket (or tank)
- 2 spoons
- Homemade stethoscope (2 funnels connected by a length of rubber tubing; one funnel has a balloon stretched over the open end)

## *Listening Underwater*

Have you ever wondered if you can hear underwater? Next time you go to the swimming pool, put your head underwater and listen.

Do you think you would be able to hear your friend humming? How well does sound travel in the water?

### An Experiment

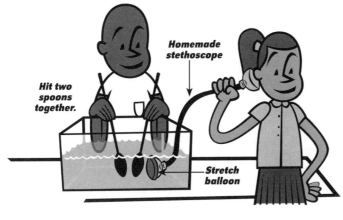

*Hit two spoons together.*

*Homemade stethoscope*

*Stretch balloon*

Do you think the sound of the spoons will be louder in air or when you listen through the stethoscope? Confirm it by pressing your ear against the tank.

### Predict
Check one [√].      Louder in air **[   ]**      Louder in water **[   ]**      No real difference **[   ]**

Please give your reasons. _____

_____

### Observe
Let's check it out. What do you observe?_____

_____

### Explain
Try to explain what you observed (use the word *vibrate* if you can).

_____

### *Hey!*
Try these experiments in your bathtub at home or the next time you go swimming.

A sound underwater:     (a) ears in air      (b) ears in water

A sound in the air:     (c) ears in air      (d) ears in water

Which sound do you think will be the loudest (a, b, c, or d)? _____

Can you explain why? _____

## Scientific Explanation

The notes produced by the wide tube and the narrow tube have the same pitch. The compressions have the same distance to travel in each case.

## Apparatus and Materials

- 2 test tubes of the same length but different diameters

## *Pipes of Pan*

Have you ever produced a clear sound by blowing across the top of a bottle or tube? Did you notice that short tubes give you high-pitched notes and long tubes give low-pitched notes? Have you ever wondered why?

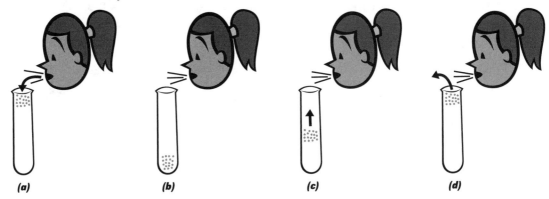

(a)          (b)          (c)          (d)

When you blow across the top of a tube, you send a little puff, or compression of air, rushing down the tube (a). It bounces off the bottom (b). It rushes back up the tube (c). It escapes (d). Another little puff or compression enters, and the process continues. The air in the tube begins to vibrate. You hear the sound.

Why does the length of the tube make a difference? Any ideas?

The longer the tube, the more time it takes for each compression to travel to the end of the tube and back. Hence the vibrations will be slower and the pitch of the note lower.

Do you think the width of the tube will make a difference? Let's find out.

### An Experiment
Obtain a narrow test tube and a wide test tube (sometimes called a *boiling tube*).

Blow across the top of each. Do you think the pitch of the notes produced will be the same or different?

### Predict
Check one [√].      Same [   ]      Different [   ]

Please give your reasons. _____

_____

### Observe
Let's try it! What do you observe? _____

_____

### Explain
Try to explain what happens. _____

_____

## Scientific Explanation

As it vibrates, the tuning fork sends out compression waves. These waves echo from the bottom of the bottle. If they echo back in time with the tuning fork, the sound is amplified. The air in the bottle vibrates at the same speed as the tuning fork. The bottle appears to "sing."

When you pluck a string on a guitar, compression waves travel through the hole and cause the air inside the guitar to resonate.

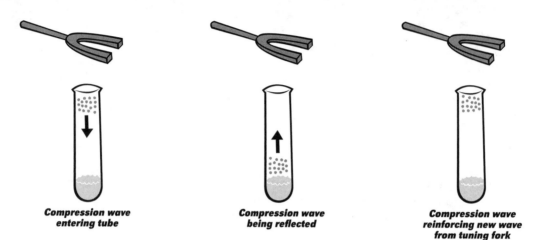

*Compression wave entering tube*          *Compression wave being reflected*          *Compression wave reinforcing new wave from tuning fork*

## Students' Explanations: Research Findings

Eshach and Schwartz (2006) are among a number of researchers who revealed two major difficulties that students have with understanding the transmission of sound:

1. Viewing sound as a substance that can move or be moved

2. Adopting the vernacular image of waves, which supports the notion that sound is a transverse sinusoidal wave rather than a compression wave

Indeed, it was reported that university students can have difficulty with the idea that waves can be additive (Wittman, Steinberg, and Redish 1999).

## Apparatus and Materials

- Tuning fork(s)
- 4 bottles or measuring cylinders
- Wide glass tube (about 2 cm)
- Beaker

## *Resonance*

### Know Your Guitar

1. Does anything vibrate, apart from the strings, when you play a guitar?

2. Why does a guitar have a hole in it?

### An Experiment

Fill a bottle with water so that it makes the same note (when you blow across the top) as a tuning fork.

Fill three other bottles with different amounts of water.

Strike the tuning fork and hold it over each of the bottles for about one second.

### Predict
Which bottle will "sing" the loudest?_____

Please give your reasons. _____

_____

### Observe
Let's do it! What happens?_____

_____

### Explain
Can you explain what you observed, using the idea that the prongs of a tuning fork send compression waves into the bottles?

_____

_____

_____

### *Hey!*
What do you think will happen as you move the tube slowly up and down in the water? Can you explain?

_____

Do you have any thoughts about the hole in the guitar? How about its shape?

_____

_____

# References

Asoko, H. M., J. Leach, and P. H. Scott. 1991. A study of students' understanding of sound 5–16 as an example of action research. Paper presented at the annual conference of the British Educational Research Association, London.

Boyes, E., and M. Stanisstreet. 1991. Development of pupils' ideas about seeing and hearing—The path of light and sound. *Research in Science and Technology Education* 9 (2): 223–251.

Driver, R., A. Squires, P. Rushworth, and V. Wood-Robinson. 1994. *Making sense of secondary science: Research in children's ideas*. New York and London: Routledge.

Eshach, H., and J. L. Schwartz. 2006. Sound stuff? Naive materialism in middle-school students' conceptions of sound. *International Journal of Science Education* 28 (7): 733–764.

Houle, M. E., and G. M. Barnett. 2008. Students' conceptions of sound waves resulting from the enactment of a new technology-enhanced inquiry-based curriculum on urban bird communication. *Journal of Science Education and Technology* 17 (3): 242–251.

Hrepic, Z., D. Zollman, and S. Rebello 2002. Identifying students' models of sound propagation. Paper presented at the Physics Education Conference, Boise, ID.

Mazens, K., and J. Lautrey. 2003. Conceptual change in physics: Children's naive representations of sound. *Cognitive Development* 18 (2): 159–176.

Wittman, M. C., R. N. Steinberg, and E. F. Redish. 1999. Making sense of how students make sense of mechanical waves. *The Physics Teacher* 37 (1): 15–21.

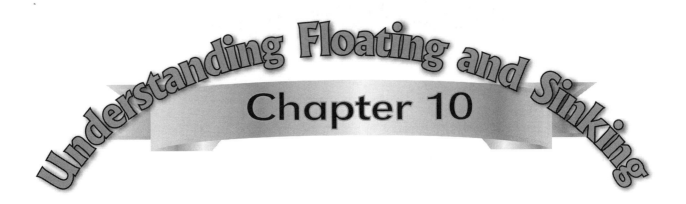

# Understanding Floating and Sinking
# Chapter 10

## Contents

## Scientific Explanation

The aluminum nail sinks because its density is greater than that of water.

The piece of aluminum foil floats because it cannot puncture the surface "skin" on the water. However, if it is pushed under or if the "skin" is cut by dropping the foil edgewise, it will sink. You can also help the foil sink if you wipe it with liquid detergent. This reduces the surface tension and makes the skin more flimsy.

The crumpled ball of aluminum foil floats because it is buoyed up by the trapped air. The tighter the ball is crumpled, the less air is trapped and the more it sinks in the water.

You can make a lump of clay float by shaping it into a boat. This gives it buoyancy. It is also possible to make it float by taking a very small piece of clay, flattening it, then placing it gently on the water so as not to break the surface skin.

## Students' Explanations: Field Experience

This POE was used with 25 grade 9 students.

Most (72%) of students' predictions were completely correct, and the remainder were partially correct. However, only a few students (16%) gave scientifically acceptable reasons:

> **The nail was too small for its weight to float.**

> **I think the ball will float because of the air spaces.**

> **... because the surface tension of the water will float it [the foil].**

The other students gave a variety of reasons.
Some (28%) associated the nail's sinking with its weight:

> **Foil is lighter than the nail. Weight of the nail caused it to sink.**

Some (16%) ascribed the nail's sinking to its density:

> **The aluminum is less dense than the nail.**

Others (24%) considered either the shape and/or the flatness of the object to be important:

> **The shape of an object matters. A flat bottom allows it to float.**

## Students' Explanations: Research Experience

One study found that 75% of a group of ninth graders felt that a crumpled piece of aluminum foil weighed more than an uncrumpled one. The same researchers also found that a large number of college students said that when you crumple an aluminum sheet, you have made it heavier (Stepans, Beiswenger, and Dyche 1986). Any concept involving ratio and proportion (which includes the concept of density) can be difficult for students to understand (Smith et al. 1997; Hitt 2005). Common student ideas about floating and sinking include mixing up size and density such that "big things sink, small things float"; hollow objects (or objects with air in them) float; objects with holes will sink; surface area of flat objects affects floating ability; sharp edges make objects sink; how well a rectangular block floats or sinks is related to which surface is in contact with the water (liquid); hard objects sink and soft objects float; objects "in" a vessel help the vessel float; a large amount of water makes objects float; and "sticky" liquids help objects float (Bloom 2001; Yin, Tomita, and Shavelson 2008).

## Apparatus and Materials

- Aluminum foil
- Aluminum nail
- Basin
- Water
- Piece of clay or plasticene

## Float a Boat!

### Riddle
How can you make a lump of clay float in water (without attaching anything to it)?

### An Experiment

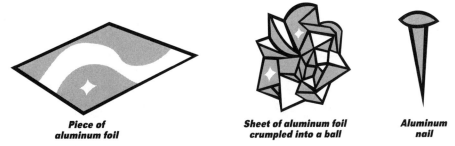

*Piece of
aluminum foil*

*Sheet of aluminum foil
crumpled into a ball*

*Aluminum
nail*

Here are three pieces of aluminum. Which do you think will float on water?

### Predict
Put a check [√] by the picture of those you think will float. Try to explain your answers.

_____

_____

_____

### Observe
Let's try it. What happens?

_____

_____

_____

### Explain
Try to explain what happened. _____

_____

_____

### *Did You Solve the Riddle?*
*Hint:* How could you give a lump of clay buoyancy? _____

_____

How could you prevent the surface skin of the water from being punctured?

_____

# Scientific Explanation

When objects denser than water are submerged, they displace a volume of water equal to the volume of the submerged object. Therefore, because the aluminum and brass objects are the same size and shape (same volume), they will displace the same amount of water and the water levels will be the same.

We use the idea of **density** to measure how heavy something is for its size or, more precisely, the mass of a material per unit volume.

# Students' Explanations: Field Experience

This POE was used with 15 grade 9 students.

A small majority of students (53%) correctly predicted that the rise in water level would be the same for both the brass and aluminum balls. They all reasoned that the two balls had the same volume:

> *They both have the same size, take up the same space.*

Most of the other students did indeed confuse mass with volume and thought that the brass ball would cause the water level to rise more because it was heavier or more dense:

> *I think it will go higher because it is heavier.*

> *I think the water level will go up because it is more dense and takes up more space.*

# Students' Explanations: Research Findings

Many students predict that "the heavier object will displace more water because heavier means bigger, and bigger takes up more space, so the heavier object will make the water level rise more" (Saunders 1992).

Biddulph and Osborne (1984) wondered if the **shape** of a piece of clay would influence students' thinking about the amount of water it would displace. They found that only one-third of their sample of children ages 11 to 14 correctly predicted that the same amount of water would be displaced regardless of shape.

It is not uncommon for students to mix up the ideas of mass and density. Keeping the two ideas separate is related to students understanding that weight is a fundamental additive property of matter (an extensive property) and density is an intensive property (the same for different objects made from the same material) (Smith et al. 1997).

# Apparatus and Materials

- Graduated cylinder (2 if possible)
- Aluminum and brass objects of equal size and shape (It doesn't matter if you substitute different metals, so long as their weights are obviously different. You can purchase balls or cubes of differing materials from most scientific suppliers.)
- Clay

# Don't Confuse Mass and Volume!

### Two Riddles
Which weighs more, 10 kg of lead or 10 kg of feathers?

Which takes up more space, 10 L of gold or 10 L of wood?

### An Experiment
Here are two metal objects that are the same size and shape, one brass and one aluminum. Pick one up in each hand and compare their weights.

Put the aluminum object in a graduated cylinder filled halfway with water. Make a note of how high the water rose.

### Predict
What will happen to the water level if you put in the brass object instead? Check one [√].

Will the level be  Higher **[    ]**    Same **[    ]**    Lower **[    ]**?

Try to explain your thinking.

_____

_____

_____

### Observe
Put in the brass object and see what happens.

_____

_____

### Explain
Can you explain the change in water level when the brass object was put in the graduated cylinder?

_____

_____

_____

### Try This!
If you roll a clay ball into the shape of a sausage, will it still displace the same amount of water?

What do you think? _____

_____

_____

## Scientific Explanation

(a) Size doesn't make a difference.

(b) Shape can make a difference. You can make something float by hollowing it out. The hollow gives it added buoyancy.

(c) Some big items don't weigh very much. Some small items weigh a lot. Small items that weigh a lot often sink.

## Students' Explanations: Research Findings

Common student ideas about floating and sinking include mixing up size and density such that "big things sink, small things float"; hollow objects (or objects with air in them) float; objects with holes will sink; surface area of flat objects affects floating ability; sharp edges make objects sink; how well a rectangular block floats or sinks is related to which surface is in contact with the water (liquid); hard objects sink and soft objects float; objects "in" a vessel help the vessel float; a large amount of water makes objects float; and "sticky" liquids helps objects float (Bloom 2001; Yin, Tomita, and Shavelson 2008).

## Apparatus and Materials

- 1 L ice cream container or beaker.

- Small and large candles

- Small and large pieces of wood

- Piece of modeling clay (plasticene)

- Selection of 4 different substances (e.g., stone, pumice stone, rubber eraser, rubber bouncing ball, metal ball or weight, coal, piece of wood, piece of bone). Write your selections on the activity record sheet.

Note: We tried to include items that encouraged students to compare the denser objects (e.g., a stone) with the less dense objects (e.g., pumice).

# Why Does It Float?

### Common Sense and Science Sense

You know lots of stuff about floating. Some things float. Some things don't! It's *common sense!*

It floats because …

Scientists try to improve on common sense.

They try to sort out the things that float from those that don't.

They want to know what makes the difference. They try to make *science sense!*

I can float!

I sink!

### Predict

How good is your common sense?

Write **F** if you think an object will float.

Write **S** if you think an object will sink.

| Different Sizes of Objects | | Different Shapes of Objects | | Different Substances (Choose from those provided.) | |
|---|---|---|---|---|---|
| _____ | Small candle | _____ | Clay ball | _____ | |
| _____ | Large candle | _____ | Clay sausage | _____ | |
| _____ | Small piece of wood | _____ | Clay boat | _____ | |
| _____ | Large piece of wood | _____ | Another clay shape (your choice) | _____ | |

Do you have any ideas why some things will float and others will not?

_____

_____

### Observe

Let's try them! Put a check [√] beside each correct prediction.

### Explain

Be a scientist! Can you make up some rules about the characteristics of things that might make a difference?

(a)_____

(b)_____

(c)_____

## Scientific Explanation

All the blocks are the same size, but some are heavier than others. These blocks are denser. The greater the density, the less well an object floats. Density is a measure of how heavy something is for its size.

## Students' Explanations: Research Findings

It is not uncommon for students to mix up the ideas of mass and density. Keeping the two ideas separate is related to students understanding that weight is a fundamental additive property of matter (an extensive property) and density is the same for different objects made from the same material (an intensive property) (Smith et al. 1997).

## Apparatus and Materials

- Large beaker
- Ruler
- Try to obtain samples of 5 of the following woods: balsa* (used for model airplanes), pine **, spruce**, birch***, maple***, oak***, beech****, mahogany****, teak****, ebony***** (* = least dense   ***** = most dense).  Prepare equal size blocks, about 3 cm x 4 cm x 4 cm. (Your industrial arts teacher might help you.)  Label them with the wood types.

## *Building a Raft*

Do railway ties float?

Are some kinds of wood better floaters than others?

Spruce? Maple?

What is the best wood to use?

### An Experiment

Try to find out which block floats best.

Measure how much stays above the water surface.

**Pine** **Oak** **Spruce**

### Predict

Which wooden blocks do you think will float best? Have a look at the sample blocks (they are all the same size) and arrange them in order.

Best floaters _____ _____ _____ _____ _____ Worst floaters

Do you have any ideas why some will float more easily than others? _____

_____

_____

### Observe

Let's measure how much stays above the surface of the water! _____

_____  _____  _____  _____

### Explain

Try to explain why some floated better! _____

_____

### *Hey!*

Let's arrange them in order of density (least to most dense).

_____

_____

## Scientific Explanation

One milliliter (1 ml) of salty water has a greater mass than 1 ml of tap water. Salty water is denser than tap water (so is fruit juice concentrate). Salty water sinks in tap water.

If you gently pour tap water on top of salty water (or pour salty water underneath tap water), they tend to remain separate. Tap water floats on salty water. We see this in river estuaries. On the other hand, if you pour salty water on top of tap water, the salty water tries to sink and mixes itself as it passes through.

## Apparatus and Materials

- Water
- Saltwater
- 2 different food colorings
- Funnel with long stem (long enough to reach bottom of containers)
- Clear containers

## Mix Me a Drink

I think it's best to add water to concentrate.

I think it's best to add concentrate last.

I don't know. Which do you think will mix best?

### Experiment

Salty water (colored blue)

Tap water (colored yellow)

### Predict
Draw what you think the glass will look like when filled to the top.

(Use colored markers if you like.) Try to give your reasons for your prediction.

_____

_____

### Observe

Slowly pour the salty water down the funnel. What happens?
Draw a picture of the way the glass looked full.

_____

### Explain
Try to explain what happened. _____

_____

### I Wonder ...
What would happen if we poured tap water down the funnel into salty water?

_____

Try it! What happened? Why? _____

_____

So what's the best way to mix drinks? _____

_____

## Scientific Explanation

A can of diet soda does indeed float, whereas the can of regular soda does not.

The volumes of the cans are the same. However, the can of regular soda weighs more (you can check this by weighing them) because it contains lots of sugar. Diet soda contains just a little (about 0.1 g) potent artificial sweetener. Artificial sweetener tastes sweeter than sugar, so less is needed.

The density of the can of diet soda is less than 1.0 g/ml, and the density of regular soda is greater than 1.0 g/ml.

If you squeeze the can of diet soda and put a dent in it, its volume decreases, its density increases, and it sinks. You can do this because cans contain a small amount of gas, which is compressible.

## Apparatus and Materials

- Cans of diet and regular soda (both the same size)
- Large beaker or transparent container
- Scales or balance

Lucky that's diet. It floats!

You're kidding! Does regular soda really sink?

# Does a Can of Diet Soda Float?

**On a Fishing Trip: A Can of Diet Soda Falls Overboard!**
Are they kidding?
Does a can of diet soda really float?
Does a can of regular soda sink?

## An Experiment
Can you float a can of diet soda? _____

Can you float a can of regular soda? _____

## Predict
Put a check mark [√] if you think the soda will float.
Please explain your thinking.

_____

_____

## Observe
Let's do it! Record your observations.

_____

## Explain
Try to explain what happened.

_____

_____

## Hey!
What do you think would happen if you squeezed a can of diet soda and put a dent in it?
Would it float? Please explain.

_____

_____

_____

## Scientific Explanation

As the sinker is lowered into the water, the reading on the spring balance decreases. This is because the water tries to push it up (to make it float). The more the sinker is lowered, the more water is displaced, so the more the water pushes upward. Once the sinker is completely submerged, there is nothing more for the water to push on, and from then on the scale reading remains steady.

If you use a floater instead of a sinker, the reading on the spring scale decreases to zero. When the floater is floating, the water pushes up with a force equal to its weight.

## Students' Explanations: Field Experience

This POE was used with 30 grade 9 students.

A large majority of students (90%) correctly predicted that the object would lose weight. Some of their reasons were expressed quite articulately:

> *The reading will get lighter because the water will be supporting some of the weight.*

Their language indicated that their teacher might have already taught this concept.

> *I think that the weight of the object will be lower because of the upward thrust of the water.*

When asked to consider what would happen if a floater is lowered into the water, 72% predicted that it would lose all its weight.

> *The weight would totally disappear because the water will support all its weight.*

An additional 12% said that it would lose weight but did not specify that the scale would go to zero. A few (16%) seemed confused:

> *The weight will stay the same because the object floats.*

## Students' Explanations: Research Findings

Students rarely think about forces in relation to floating and sinking and thus might have difficulty with the idea that the water provides an upward force on an object immersed in the water (Heywood and Parker 2001). This idea is addressed in FS9.

## Apparatus and Materials

- Spring scale
- Sinker
- Floater (e.g., small block of wood with a hook on it)
- String
- Beaker

# *Losing Weight?*

### In the Swimming Pool

Do you really become lighter as you walk toward the deep end?

### An Experiment

Slowly lower a sinker on a spring scale into a glass of water.

### Predict

What do you think will happen to the scale reading as you slowly lower the sinker into the water? Give your reasons.

_____

_____

### Observe

Try it! Describe what happens.

_____

_____

### Explain

In your own words, try to explain why the scale read as it did in each case.

_____

_____

_____

### *What Do You Think?*

Why do you feel lighter when your weight stays the same?

_____

What would happen to the scale if you used a floater instead of a sinker?

_____

_____

## Scientific Explanation

When you put your finger in the water, the water pushes upward on your finger: It tries to make it float! What does the water push against? The scale pan! What happens to the scale pan? It goes down!

Imagine yourself standing on a bathroom scale. What would happen to the scale if you could push upward on the ceiling?

For every action force, there is a reaction force.

Note: If students are having difficulty with this, invite them to consider what would happen if you put your hand into a Styrofoam cup and pushed this into the water. (Their familiarity with buoyancy might help them perceive that there would be a reaction force downward.)

## Students' Explanations: Research Findings

Students rarely think about forces in relation to floating or sinking and thus might have difficulty with the idea that the water provides an upward force on an object immersed in the water (Heywood and Parker 2001). This idea is addressed in FS9.

## Apparatus and Materials

- 2 beakers
- Water
- Pan balance

## *Water Force*

### Experiment
Can you tilt the scale when you put your finger in the water?

Balance two glasses of water on some scales so that they are level.

What do you think will happen if you dip your finger

(a) up to the first joint?

(b) up to the second joint?

### Predict
(a) What do you think? Try to give reasons for your first prediction. _____

_____

_____

(b) What do you think? Try to give reasons for your second prediction. _____

_____

_____

### Observe
Give it a go! What do you see?

_____

### Explain
Try to explain the reading of the balance in your own words.

_____

_____

_____

# Scientific Explanation

As the sinker is lowered, water drips out of the overflow can. The sinker displaces its own volume of liquid.

The scale reading doesn't change. Why? The weight of the liquid displaced must balance the upward push on the sinker exactly. This is Archimedes's principle.

You can check this by lowering a sinker hanging from a spring scale into a measuring cylinder partly filled with water. The rise in the water level (ml) equals the loss of weight (g) exactly.

# Students' Explanations: Field Experience

An earlier version of this POE was used with a class of 24 grade 9 students.

The majority of students (58%) correctly predicted that the scale would read the same when the sinker was lowered into the overflow can. Most of these students reasoned in terms of the sinker replacing the weight of the lost water:

> **The lost weight will be replaced by the sinker.**

A few reasoned in terms of the water exerting an upward force, e.g.,

> **... because the weight is pushing water out but it is made up for because the water is pushing up.**

Those who predicted incorrectly ignored the upward force exerted by the water:

> **... [less] because the sinker's weight is being supported by the hand.**

> **... [more] because it had a greater density than the water it displaced.**

Regarding their predictions when the sinker rested on the bottom, 67% of students correctly predicted that the scale reading would increase. They recognized that the sinker had a greater density than water:

> **... because the weight of the sinker is heavier than the weight of the water it displaced.**

Most of those who predicted incorrectly did not take this density difference into account:

> **... because the same amount of water is going out as the weight of the weight.**

One student who successfully commented on what would happen if a floater, rather than a sinker, was lowered into the can prompted the addition of an extension to this POE.

# Students' Explanations: Research Findings

Students rarely think about forces in relation to floating and sinking and thus might have difficulty with the idea that the water provides an upward force on an object immersed in the water (Heywood and Parker 2001).

# Apparatus and Materials

- Weight scale
- Overflow can
- Sinker and string
- Container to catch the displaced water
- Measuring cylinder

# Weight Gain and Weight Loss

### An Experiment
Put an overflow can on a spring scale and fill it with water. Slowly lower a sinker into the can.

It's got to weigh more …

… but it's losing water!

### Predict
(a) What do you think will happen to the scale reading as you slowly lower the sinker into the water? Give your reasons.

_____

_____

(b) What do you think will happen to the scale reading if you let the sinker settle on the bottom? Give your reasons.

_____

### Observe
Try it! Describe what happens.

(a)_____

(b)_____

### Explain
In your own words, try to explain why the scale read as it did in each case.

(a)_____

_____

(b)_____

_____

### Check It Out!
What do you think would happen if a floater was used instead of a sinker? Please explain.

_____

## Scientific Explanation

As the containers are loaded, they displace water. For the container to float, the weight of the container must be balanced by the upward push of the water. And of course, Archimedes's principle says that the upward push is equal to the weight of the water displaced. The floating container therefore displaces a weight of water (or volume) equal to its own weight (principle of flotation).

Because the containers have the same volume, they will displace the same amount of water before sinking. Hence, both containers can carry the same cargo. If you double the volume, you can double the cargo.

## Students' Explanations: Research Findings

Students rarely think about forces in relation to floating and sinking and thus might have difficulty with the idea that the water provides an upward force on an object immersed in the water. Understanding this is helped by relating the weight and volume of objects immersed in relation to the weight and volume of the displaced water (Heywood and Parker 2001). Student responses in this POE may be influenced by the commonly held student idea (see FS1T for others) that objects "in" a vessel help the vessel float (Yin, Tomita, and Shavelson 2008).

## Apparatus and Materials

- Bowl or large beaker
- Supply of glass marbles or pennies (cargo)
- 2 lightweight plastic containers (e.g., yogurt cups) cut to have same volume (50 to 100 ml)
- Third container having twice the volume of the lightweight containers

Note: Teachers may decide that their students would gain more if they carried out an investigation of how much cargo different plastic containers could hold.

## Cargo Boats

### Be a Cargo Boat Designer

There's more to being a boat designer than meets the eye.

Boats need to carry lots of cargo.

They have to be strong.

They must not capsize.

They must be cheap.

Let's look at the cargo problem! Which do you think can carry more cargo—broad boats or boats with high sides?

### An Experiment

Both plastic containers (boats) are the same volume. The tall one is fully loaded. If both are evenly loaded, do you think the broad one will be able to carry more, less, or the same?

### Predict

Check one [√].    More **[   ]**    Less **[   ]**    Same **[   ]**

Explain the reason for your prediction. _____

_____

_____

### Observe

Let's load the broad boat. What happens?

_____

### Explain

Try to explain what you saw happen.

_____

_____

### Hmm ...

How much cargo do you think a boat with twice the volume can carry? Why do you think this?

_____

_____

_____

## Scientific Explanation

Principle of flotation: The mass of a floater is equal to the mass of the liquid it displaces, or (put another way) a floater floats when it has displaced its own mass of liquid exactly.

Salty water is denser than tap water, or (put another way) salty water has a greater mass than the same volume of tap water. (This makes sense—look at all the salt you put into the water.)

Hence, when it floats in salty water, the floater displaces less volume than when it floats in tap water. Therefore, it will sink less in salty water before it floats.

Technologists use these ideas in the design of hydrometers. The weighted pencil is a simple hydrometer. It can measure density once it is calibrated by putting it in liquids of known density.

## Students' Explanations: Field Experience

This POE was used with 25 students. A large majority of students (92%) predicted correctly. However, only 28% ascribed this to the salty water being more dense.

## Apparatus and Materials

- Water
- Salt
- Beaker
- Thumbtacks
- Pencil

Follow-up question: Would it be different if the solute was sugar instead of salt? How might it be different?

## *Swimming in the Dead Sea*

### True or False?

(a) It's easier to swim in the sea than in a freshwater lake. True or false?

(b) The Dead Sea is so salty that it's almost impossible to sink. The picture (opposite) of the swimmer in the Dead Sea is not a fake. True or false?

*Man swimming in the Dead Sea*

Image provided by punchstock.com

**Tap water**      **Tap water + 1 tsp salt**      **Tap water + 3 tsp salt**

### An Experiment

Put a thumbtack (or two) in the eraser at the end of a pencil. Float the pencil in a glass of water. Mark the level on the pencil. What do you think will happen to the level mark on the pencil when it is put into saltwater?

### Predict

Try drawing the outcome (use the pictures above).

Can you explain your drawings? _____

_____

_____

### Observe

Let's check!  What happens?

(a) In tap water + 1 tsp of salt: _____

(b) In tap water + 3 tsp of salt: _____

### Explain

Try to explain what you saw happen. _____

_____

_____

### *Here's an Idea!*

I wonder if you could make a density measurer (a hydrometer) with that pencil. What do you think?

_____

_____

## Scientific Explanation

When you float the clay boat, it displaces a mass (weight) of water equal to its own mass (weight). The clay boat is denser than water, so it displaces quite a lot of water.

When you sink the clay boat, it displaces a volume of water equal to its own volume. The volume of water displaced is less than when the boat was floating. Therefore, the water level drops when you sink the boat!

## Students' Explanations: Field Experience

This POE was used with 22 grade 9 students: 19 predicted that the level would rise, 2 predicted that it would stay the same, and 1 predicted that it would go down, for a scientifically incorrect reason.

The teacher noted that after the experiment most of the students couldn't figure out what had happened, and that the "level of frustration was pretty evident during our discussion." However, "[a]fter doing this, most of the students were able to explain why the water level went down when the boat sank."

To check the students' understanding, the teacher used the POE "Don't Flood the Pool!" (FS13). She reported that "all the students were able to correctly predict and explain what would happen."

## Students' Explanations: Research Experience

Our findings are similar to those of Biddulph and Osborne (1984). They reported that in their sample of children ages 7 to 14, only 11 of 80 correctly predicted that the clay would displace more water when floating, whereas 49 predicted that the amount of water displaced would be the same. A typical reason for predicting less was,

> **If its going to be floating it wont be pushing out the same amount: there'll still be some (clay) above the surface. (14-year-old)**

They added that even after observing what happened, many were puzzled.

Note: Of 1,444 grade 9 and 11 students from 11 different high schools in Lebanon, 50.5% of the grade 9 students and 50.8% of the grade 11 students believed that ships float on water because they are made of material less dense than water (Za'rour 1975).

## Apparatus and Materials

- Modeling clay
- Glass or beaker
- Water

# Clay Boats

Get real! Steel doesn't float.

Yep! Steel boats! Don't ask me why.

Modeling clay (plasticene) doesn't float, but you can make a boat from it.

**Clay boat**

**Water**

## An Experiment
Float a clay boat in a glass of water. Mark the water level on the side of the glass.

Get ready to sink the boat. Do you think the water level will change?

## Predict
Check one [√]:

Water level goes up. **[   ]**     Water level goes down. **[   ]**     Water level stays the same. **[   ]**

Please give reasons for your prediction.

_____

_____

## Observe
Sink the boat. What happens?

_____

## Explain
Try to explain what happened. _____

_____

_____

## More Experiments
Use the same piece of clay to make boats of different shapes. How does the shape of the boat affect the water level in the glass?

_____

_____

Does this make sense to you? Explain._____

_____

_____

# Scientific Explanation

Q.1 How much will the water level rise when you put the metal weight in the boat?

A.1 When the metal is floating, it displaces its weight of water (which is a lot!). This is many times more than the volume of the metal.

Q.2 How much will the water level rise when you lower the metal into the water?

A.2 The volume of water displaced equals the volume of the metal weight. Hence, because the answer to Q.1 is much greater than Q.2, the water level in the beaker will fall when we drop the mass over the side.

If a floater is used instead of a sinker, the water level will remain the same because a floater always displaces a weight of water equal to its own weight.

# Students' Explanations: Field Experience

This POE was used with 25 grade 9 students.

Thirty-six percent (36%) thought the water level would rise. All of these students reasoned that when it was lowered into the pool, the weight would displace water:

> *... because there is more in the water.*

> *There will be too much in the pool.*

They did not seem to take into account the boat's displacing water when it was floating. Students who think this way might well be helped by observing the way the water rises (in the beaker) when the boat is loaded.

Forty percent (40%) correctly predicted that the water level would fall. Most expressed themselves very clearly and displayed excellent scientific thinking:

> *Floaters displace more than sinkers, so the level will fall.*

> *The weight will displace more water when it floats.*

Twenty-four percent (24%) thought the water level would stay the same. They reasoned in terms of the mass staying the same and did not recognize that the weight displaces more water when it is in the boat.

> *... because they are the same objects—the same mass.*

> *In order for the weight to float while it's in the boat it has to displace a certain amount. When it is out of the boat but directly in the water, it still displaces the same amount of water.*

# Students' Explanations: Research Findings

One commonly held preconception about floating and sinking that might influence students' responses in this POE is that students often believe that objects "in" a vessel help the vessel float (Yin, Tomita, and Shavelson 2008).

# Apparatus and Materials

- Large beaker
- Plastic pot or small beaker
- Weight and string
- Wooden block to fit into the plastic pot

This pool is awfully full! Don't jump in, it'll flood!

'Course it won't!

## Don't Flood the Pool!

He jumps! What do you think will happen?

### An Experiment

Put a large metal weight in a beaker or plastic pot and float it in a large bowl.

What do you think will happen if you lower the metal weight into the water with a string?

### Predict

Check one [√]:

The water level will rise. [　]    The water level will fall. [　]    The water level will stay the same. [　]

Try to explain your predictions.

_____

_____

### Observe

Gently lower the weight into the water. What happens?

_____

### Explain

Try to explain what happened.

_____

_____

_____

### *Hey!*

Metal doesn't float in water, but wood does. Try using your explanation to predict what would happen if you used a wooden block instead of a metal weight.

_____

_____

_____

## Scientific Explanation

The density of aluminum is 2.7 g/ml, and 100g occupies 37 ml.
The density of brass is 8.4 g/ml, and 100g occupies 12 ml.
The density of iron is 7.9 g/ml, and 100g occupies 13 ml.
The difference in volume between a 100 g aluminum weight and a 100 g brass weight is quite obvious. When you try to immerse the weights, you'll find that it's impossible! The aluminum is relatively buoyant and most of it remains above the water.

## Students' Explanations: Field Experience

A version of this POE (in which the teacher used brass and iron weights) was used with 25 grade 9 students.

Eighty percent (80%) predicted correctly and demonstrated sound scientific reasoning:

> **The brass will sink lower than the iron. It is more dense.**

> **The iron will displace more water so the buoyant force will be more.**

> **The iron one is less dense, so it has a greater volume and will displace more water. Therefore there is a greater buoyant force.**

Those who predicted incorrectly gave few reasons.

## Apparatus and Materials

- Simple balance arm (You can use a wooden ruler with holes drilled in it.)
- String
- 100 g aluminum weight
- 100 g brass (or iron) weight
- 2 beakers or glasses

## *Eureka!*

### The Archimedes Legend (287 BC)

The goldsmith presented King Hiero of Syracuse with his new gold crown, but strangely the king didn't appear too pleased. The king suspected the goldsmith had cheated him. He thought the goldsmith had mixed in some silver with the gold.  And he was determined to prove it!

What was he going to do? He called in Archimedes, his scientific advisor. For days, Archimedes thought about the problem. Then he had a brain wave. He placed the new crown on one pan of a balance and an equal mass of gold on the other. He then lowered the balanced pans into a tub of water.

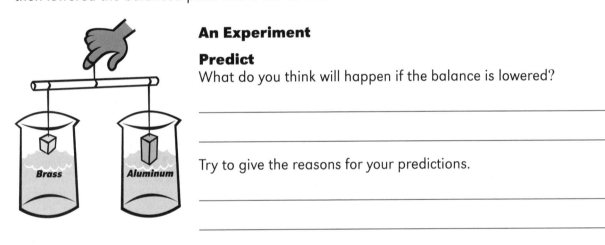

**Brass**          **Aluminum**

### An Experiment

### Predict

What do you think will happen if the balance is lowered?

_____

_____

Try to give the reasons for your predictions.

_____

_____

### Observe

Let's do it! What happens?

_____

### Explain

Try to explain what happened.

_____

_____

_____

### *Hmm ...*

After he made his discovery, Archimedes jumped out of the bath in excitement. He ran naked through the streets of Syracuse shouting "Eureka!" (I've got it!) I wonder how he explained his idea to the king?

## Scientific Explanation

Air does indeed provide a buoyant force to an object. Air and liquids are both considered fluids. All fluids provide a buoyant force.

An object displaces a volume of air equal to its own volume. The weight of the air displaced provides the buoyant force on the object. If the object weighs more than the buoyant force, it sinks.

The 100 g aluminum weight has a larger volume than the 100 g brass weight. Therefore, there is a greater buoyant force on the aluminum than the brass. When the air is removed, the buoyant forces are lost. Because there was a greater buoyant force on the aluminum than on the brass, the aluminum end of the balance will go down when the air is removed.

The scale would show a greater weight if the air was removed. There would no longer be any upward force on the weight. In reality, the loss of weight would only be a few hundredths of a gram, and this would be difficult to detect.

## Students' Explanations: Field Experience

An earlier version of this POE (in which an iron weight was used instead of an aluminum weight) was used with 25 students.

Those who predicted correctly (44%) that the brass weight would rise reasoned in terms of the buoyant force or the "support" being removed:

> *The buoyant force of the air is being removed. Since the buoyant force on the iron is greater, it will sink down.*

> *The iron is more voluminous. When the air is supporting it, it supports iron more. Without the air supporting, the iron will fall because the brass will lose more weight.*

Thirty-two percent (32%) predicted incorrectly. They recognized that the iron had a lower density or greater volume, but didn't reason successfully about the consequences:

> *The iron is less dense and the brass will go down.*

> *I think the iron will go higher up because it has greater volume.*

A lower proportion (24%) thought the scale would remain balanced. They argued either that this could be attributed to the weights having the same mass or that the lack of air wouldn't make a difference:

> *I think they will stay the same because they both have the same mass.*

> *... both losing the same thing—air.*

## Students' Explanations: Research Findings

Students rarely think about forces in relation to floating or sinking and thus might have difficulty with the idea that the water provides an upward force on an object immersed in the water (Heywood and Parker 2001).

## Apparatus and Materials

No materials needed

## *Floating in Air*

### Two Riddles
Could balloons float without air?

Would you weigh more in a vacuum?

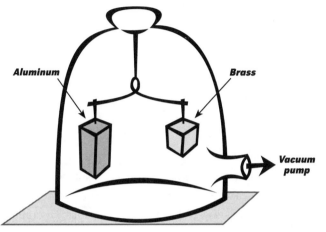

Aluminum          Brass

Vacuum
pump

### An Imaginary Experiment
It would be possible to do this if you have a bell jar and a vacuum pump. A bell jar is a glass dome that can be sealed at the bottom with a glass plate.

Here's the experiment:

Balance 100 g of aluminum with 100 g of brass.

Then the air is removed.

What do you think will happen?

### Predict
_____

Try to explain your thinking. _____

_____

_____

### Observe
Now ask your teacher what you would see. _____

_____

### Explain
Does that make sense to you? Can you explain it? _____

_____

_____

### *Hey!*

Do you mean something gains weight in a vacuum? Really?

OK! Would you see something happen if you suspended a 100 g weight from a spring scale and then took away the air?

_____

_____

# References

Biddulph, F., and R. Osborne. 1984. Pupils' ideas about floating and sinking. *Research in Science Education* 14 (1): 114–124.

Bloom, J. 2001. Discourse, cognition, and chaotic systems: An examination of students' argument about density. *Journal of the Learning Sciences* 10 (4): 447–492.

Heywood, D., and J. Parker. 2001. Describing the cognitive landscape in learning and teaching about forces. *International Journal of Science Education* 23 (11): 1177–1199.

Hitt, A. M. 2005. Attacking a dense problem: A learner-centered approach to teaching density. *Science Activities* 42 (1): 25–29.

Saunders, W. L. 1992. The constructivist perspective: Implications and teaching strategies for science. *School Science and Mathematics* 92 (3): 136–141.

Smith, C., D. Maclin, L. Grosslight, and H. Davis. 1997. Teaching for understanding: A study of students' preinstruction theories of matter and a comparison of two approaches to teaching about matter and density. *Cognition and Instruction* 15 (3): 317–393.

Stepans, W. L., R. E. Beiswenger, and S. Dyche. 1986. Misconceptions die hard. *The Science Teacher* 53 (6): 65–69.

Yin, Y., M. K. Tomita, and R. J. Shavelson. 2008. Diagnosing and dealing with student misconceptions: Floating and sinking. *Science Scope* 31 (8): 34–39.

Za'rour, G. J. 1975. Science misconceptions among certain groups of students in Lebanon. *Journal of Research in Science Teaching* 12 (4): 385–391.

# Chapter 11

## Contents

## Scientific Explanation

*Dissolve* means to mix perfectly. When a solid dissolves into a liquid, the particles of the solid intermingle perfectly with the particles of the liquid. The solution is the same all the way through.

When a reaction takes place, a chemical change occurs and new substances (new particles) are formed.

When a substance melts, it changes from a solid state to a liquid. It is still made up of the same particles. You can often get the solid back by cooling the liquid.

|  | Water | Vinegar | Alcohol |
|---|---|---|---|
| **Chalk** | nothing (insoluble) | reacts (bubbles) | nothing |
| **Ice** | melts | melts and dissolves | melts and dissolves |
| **Sugar** | dissolves | dissolves | nothing |
| **Baking soda** | dissolves | reacts (bubbles) | nothing |

## Students' Explanations: Field Experience

This POE was used with a class of 22 grade 7 students at the beginning of their study of solutions.

At the outset, the majority of students (70%) used the word *disappear* in their definitions. Some of the students (20%) included the idea that the solid was still there, even though you couldn't see it.

> **To disappear but not gone.**

Some students (20%) included the idea of particles in their definitions:

> **It means that solids like sugar or salt break up into little pieces, not big enough to be seen by the naked eye.**

With regard to their predictions, all the students knew that sugar would dissolve in water; most thought it would dissolve in vinegar and alcohol, too. A considerable proportion (more than 25%) thought chalk would dissolve in water and alcohol, ice would dissolve in alcohol, and baking soda would dissolve in water.

During the field testing, the teachers noted that the students really enjoyed doing this as a lab.

## Apparatus and Materials

- Test tubes
- Water
- Vinegar
- Ethyl alcohol and/or methyl alcohol (beware poison)
- Sugar
- Baking soda
- Chalk
- Ice

## Solution Words

### Not a Riddle

Do you know what the word *dissolve* means?

Seriously! Try to put it in your own words.

_____

_____

_____

Oh yeah! This relationship is now dissolved!

Whereupon she dissolved into tears!

All right! Yippee!

This session of the school term is dissolved indefinitely! Yay!

### Predict

Do you know what happens when different solids (on the left-hand side of the table) are mixed with the different liquids (along the top of the table). Put a *D* in the box if you think we should use the word *dissolves* to describe what happens.

|  | **Water** | **Vinegar** | **Alcohol** |
|---|---|---|---|
| **Chalk** |  |  |  |
| **Ice** |  |  |  |
| **Sugar** |  |  |  |
| **Baking soda** |  |  |  |

### Observe

Let's try some out! What do you see? Keep your eyes open for any differences in the way the solid changes.

(a) baking soda and water _____

(b) baking soda and vinegar_____

(c) baking soda and alcohol _____

(d) ice and water _____

(e) your choice_____

### Explain

People in everyday life often mix up the words *dissolve, disappear, disintegrate, react, melt,* and *destroy*. Scientists are particular. When they use the words *dissolve, react,* and *melt,* they mean different things. Which words do you think they would use to describe the following reactions:

(a) baking soda and water _____     (d) ice and water _____

(b) baking soda and vinegar _____     (e) your choice _____

(c) baking soda and alcohol _____

Can you explain the differences between dissolving, reacting, and melting?

_____

_____

### So ...

What is special about the word *dissolve*?

_____

_____

## Scientific Explanation

When the sugar dissolves, it breaks up into very, very small particles, too small to be seen. The same number of sugar particles that were in the solid cube end up being dissolved in the water. Even though some people think of the particles as being "suspended" in the water, they still have weight. Because the weight of the sugar has not changed, the two sides will remain balanced.

## Students' Explanations: Field Experience

This POE was used with 50 grade 7 students.

Thirty-two percent (32%) correctly predicted that there would be no change in weight. Fifty-four percent (54%) predicted that the sugar solution would be lighter. Not surprisingly, some thought the sugar would disappear. Others thought the cube would lose trapped air when it dissolved:

> *... because in the sugar cube there is air causing it to weigh more but once the air is crushed out it will weigh less.*

Others reasoned in terms of the sugar being spread out:

> *... because the sugar will dissolve and spread out making it lighter.*

Many students gave reasons that were difficult to interpret:

> *... the sugar molecules are smaller and so they weigh less than the larger ones.*

Fourteen percent (14%) predicted that the sugar solution would be heavier. Some associated this with the solution being more concentrated:

> *... the sugar particles will get between the water particles and make it heavier.*

The students who predicted incorrectly seemed to have little difficulty constructing the scientific explanation after they had seen the experiment.

## Students' Explanations: Research Experience

Driver (1985) has summarized the findings of a number of studies. In one study, two-thirds of English students ages 9- to 14-years-old predicted that the mass of the solution would be less. In another study, more than half of a sample of English and Swedish 15-year-olds similarly predicted that the mass would be less. Some of these students thought the sugar disappeared, others confused mass and volume, and others believed the sugar was still present, but lighter.

Holding, cited by Driver et al. (1995), found that most students at age 12 were able to appreciate that a dissolved substance was still there, but some did not consider the particles to have weight (that the weight of the sugar was now "up in the water," that it was in a "suspended state," and that it was not "pressing down" on the bottom of the container).

## Apparatus and Materials

- Sugar cubes
- 2 glasses or beakers
- 2-pan balance
- Watch glass or glass slide
- Source of heat

## *The Dissolving (Disappearing?) Sugar Cube*

### Magic or Not?

When a sugar cube dissolves in water, is it still there or has it just vanished?

If you can't see it, how do you know it's still there?

Does it still have mass?

Give me a break! Are you telling me it just disappears?

Well, you tell me what happens to it, then!

### An Experiment

Balance a scale with a beaker of water and 5 lumps of sugar on each side.

What do you think would happen to the balance if the sugar on one side is dissolved in the water?

### Predict

_____

Please explain your answer. _____

_____

_____

### Observe

Let's give it a try! Take one of the beakers off the balance. Stir in the sugar until it dissolves. Put the beaker back on the balance. What do you see?

_____

### Explain

Try to explain what you observed in the experiment.

_____

_____

### *Try This!*

Can you get the sugar back? Gently heat a drop of the solution on a watch glass or a microscope slide. Boil off the water or let it evaporate overnight. What happens?

_____

_____

_____

## Scientific Explanation

Filter paper is like a very fine sieve. It consists of wood fibers, lying across one another. The gaps between the fibers are very small indeed.

Chalk dust is far too large to pass through the filter paper and is left behind. Milk particles are smaller and are able to pass through. The particles of copper sulphate, which are blue, are so small (less than one-millionth of a millimeter across) that a solution in water appears to be clear—they pass through the filter paper easily. If the filter paper appears blue after you have filtered the copper sulphate solution, you can wash the remaining solution through the filter with water.

When you make coffee from ground beans, the brown flavored part that we drink dissolves and leaves behind the insoluble dregs or grounds. The clear brown coffee solution can pass through the paper.

## Students' Explanations: Research Findings

Biro and Zwolanski-Morovic (1992) report that some students predict that the blue color of copper sulphate will be trapped in the filter paper.

## Apparatus and Materials

- 3 beakers
- Teaspoon
- Filter funnel
- Filter paper
- Flask
- Copper sulphate
- Milk
- Powdered calcium carbonate (chalk)
- Instant coffee

Note: In addition, you might have a range of other substances available, such as soil and rust (iron oxide), with which you can experiment.

# Will It Go Through Filter Paper?

### Making Coffee
Have you ever watched filter coffee being made?

What goes through the filter?

What do you see if you hold it up to the light?

Can you see through it?

What gets left behind in the filter?

How does a filter work?

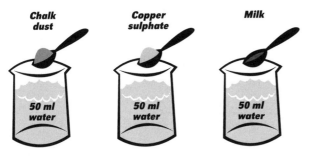

Chalk dust    Copper sulphate    Milk

50 ml water    50 ml water    50 ml water

### An Experiment
Put a teaspoon of the following substances into 50 ml water and stir them well: chalk dust, copper sulphate, and milk. Now filter them.

### Predict
What do you think will be left behind when each is filtered?

(a) Chalk dust and water mixture _____

(b) Copper sulphate and water mixture_____

(c) Milk and water mixture _____

Please give your reasons. _____

_____

### Observe
Let's do it! What gets left behind?          (a) _____

(b) _____          (c) _____

### Explain
Why do you think some parts of a mixture can pass through a filter but others can't?

_____

_____

### So?
What happens when you make filter coffee? _____

How about replacing the coffee grounds with a spoonful of instant coffee? We could try it!

_____

## Scientific Explanation

Milk does not dissolve in water even when you dilute it 1,000 times. However, it is still there—the milk particles are very tiny, too small for the eye to pick up.

You can see them at very low dilutions if you pass a beam of light through the solution. The tiny milk particles scatter some of the light. You might have seen this effect before when a beam of light is scattered by smoke, fog, or dust.

Shining a beam of light through a clear liquid can help you determine if it is truly a solution. If the particles are large enough to reflect light, then it is not a solution.

## Apparatus and Materials

- 100 ml and 10 ml graduated cylinders
- 2 beakers
- Milk
- Flashlight
- Cardboard with a hole

Note: The Tyndall effect is more readily observed in a darkened room.

## *Seeing Is Believing? The Milk Mystery*

How much can you dilute milk and still see it?

### Predict
What's your best guess? Check one[√].

(a) 10 times      [   ]

(b) 100 times      [   ]

(c) 1,000 times   [   ]

(d) More!        [   ]

Let's try it! Take 10 ml of milk and tip it into a beaker containing 90 ml of water. This dilutes 10 ml to 100 ml (10 times). Repeat using 10 ml of the already diluted milk. Repeat ... repeat ...

### Observe
What did you see?

(a) Diluting 10 times: _____

(b) Diluting 100 times: _____

(c) Diluting 1,000 times:_____

(d) Your choice: _____

### Explain
Do you think any milk is left after you have diluted it 1,000 times?_____

Do you think any milk is left when you can't see it anymore? _____

What do you think would happen to a carton of milk if you emptied it into a lake?

_____

_____

### *Interesting!*
Try shining a flashlight through the most diluted milk you made.

What do you see? _____

_____

Try to explain what you see. _____

_____

**Focused light source**

**Flashlight**

**Cardboard with hole**

Now shine the flashlight through tap water and see if there is a difference!

_____

## Scientific Explanation

Before dissolving: Notice how the solid particles are regularly spaced, with no gaps between them. Solids are like this. In contrast, there are holes between the particles of liquids. It is the presence of these holes that gives a liquid its runny quality.

After dissolving, the solute particles are now fairly evenly (randomly) scattered throughout the solution. This explains why it appears to be evenly colored all the way through.

Note: In this simplified explanation, copper sulphate is considered to consist of one type of particle.

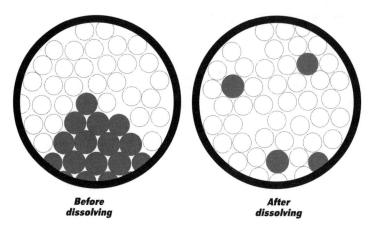

*Before dissolving*        *After dissolving*

## Students' Explanations: Field Experience

An earlier version of this POE was used with 30 grade 7 students. Seventy-five percent (75%) predicted that Dr. Y would see a homogeneous mixture under the "mega microscope":

> *The particles all moved around and mixed up.*

> *Dr. Y saw that the particles were mixed with the Jolly Rancher (candy) particles.*

> *I think Dr. Y saw tiny dots floating around in the water.*

> *The water broke up the particles and spread them around.*

## Students' Explanations: Research Findings

Prieto, Blanco, and Rodriguez (1989) asked students to portray in drawings their images of what a substance in solution would look like. More than two-thirds of grade 7 students perceived solutions as being homogeneous. However, more than half reflected a continuous vision of the dissolved substance.

Stepans and Veath (1994) asked grade 7 students what they would see if they viewed a salt solution through a "giant microscope" that showed the smallest particles. Hardly any students were able to apply particle theory in a scientifically acceptable way.

## Apparatus and Materials

- 2 beakers
- Copper sulphate (or any other colored water-soluble substance, such as candy)

# Solutions Under the Mega Microscope

Scientists think all substances consist of very tiny particles. This idea helps them explain many of the things they see happening in this world: water boiling, ice melting, crystals forming, and substances dissolving.

Scientists think these particles are very small indeed. You can't see them—not even with a very powerful microscope. Microscopes can only magnify about 1,000 times. You would need to magnify a million times to be able to see them.

### A Future Imaginary Experiment!

In the year 2030, Dr. Y invented the new mega microscope. It magnified a million times! He decided to check up on the way scientists thought substances dissolved.

He took some copper sulphate and put it in some water. He focused the microscope on the edge of the solid. Wow! Check below to see what he saw. Then he stirred the mixture. The copper sulphate dissolved. He looked down the mega microscope again. ...

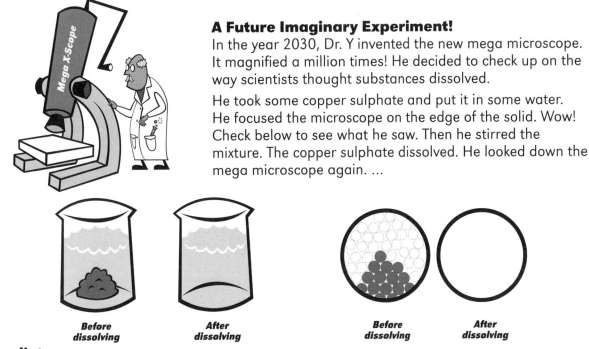

| *Before dissolving* | *After dissolving* | *Before dissolving* | *After dissolving* |

### Predict

What do you think Dr. Y sees under the mega microscope when he looks at the copper sulphate solution? Very carefully, complete his view down the mega microscope (far right).

_____

### Observe

Describe what happened when we stirred the mixture to dissolve the copper sulphate.

_____

_____

Complete the diagram after your teacher tells you what Dr. Y saw.

### Explain

Use the idea of particles to explain what happens when something dissolves.

_____

_____

**Topic:** Solutions          **Concept:** Change of volume on dissolving provides evidence for the particulate theory of matter.

## Scientific Explanation

When a solute such as salt dissolves, the particles from which it is made are able to move. The particles of solvent and solute are now able to pack together more closely than before. This results in a reduction of volume.

## Apparatus and Materials

- Flask (500 ml)
- Stopper
- Pickling salt
- Jar with a top
- Marbles of 2 different sizes (Some teachers prefer to use marbles and sand.)

NATIONAL SCIENCE TEACHERS ASSOCIATION

Stop, Mum! If you pour that sugar into the pan of water, it will overflow.

I'm sure it will be OK, Jack. Here's hoping!

## Dissolving: Is There a Volume Change?

Maybe they are discussing whether there is a change of volume when something dissolves.

Does the volume of sugar plus the volume of water equal the volume of sugar solution?

What do you think?

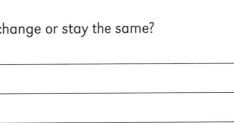

### An Experiment

Cover the bottom of a flask with crystals of pickling salt.

(These crystals are solid—they contain no air.)

Slowly fill the flask with water. Only a little salt will dissolve.

Push in a rubber stopper so the extra water overflows.

Shake it until no more salt dissolves.

Will the volume change?

Does the volume of the salt plus the volume of the water equal the volume of the salty water?

### Predict

What do you think will happen? Will the volume change or stay the same?

_____

Please give your reasons. _____

_____

### Observe

Let's do it! What do you observe? _____

_____

### Explain

Put some marbles in a jar. Fill up the jar with marbles of a different size. Put on the lid and gently shake the jar. Does this help explain what happened in our experiment?

_____

_____

_____

## Scientific Explanation

Liquids do not shrink. The particles that they are made from do not shrink. When you mix two liquids, the particles of each intermingle and pack together more closely than before. This is why there is a reduction in volume.

A similar reduction of volume can be seen if you shake a jar containing marbles of two different sizes. If ethyl alcohol or acetone is substituted for methyl alcohol, the reduction of volume is different. You would expect this because the ethyl alcohol and acetone particles are larger than the methyl alcohol particles.

A similar effect can be seen if you change the size of the marbles.

## Students' Explanations: Field Experience

During field testing of this POE with grade 7 students, students' predictions appeared to be guesswork, rather than reasoned examples. For example,

> *... there are just two liquids mixing. (Level stays the same.)*

> *... because the air goes out of the water. (Level drops.)*

> *... because there is a lot of acid in the alcohol and I think it will bubble and overflow.*

> *... because when you shake up pop it overflows. (Test tube overflows.)*

If they are to draw on pertinent understanding, then it would seem to be important for this POE to be put in the context of instruction that is related to the particulate theory of matter. For example, this POE could well follow the previous one, "Dissolving: Is There a Volume Change?"

## Apparatus and Materials

- Test tube
- Ethyl alcohol or methyl alcohol (methyl hydrate) or isopropyl alcohol (rubbing alcohol). You might dye it with food coloring.
- Jar with lid
- Marbles

Note: Some teachers prefer to use sand and marbles instead of two different sizes of marbles.

# Mixing Liquids: Is There a Volume Change?

Dr. Y is trying to make liquids shrink!

And voilà! Here's what happens.

Come on, Dr. Y! Show us how to do that!

## An Experiment

Fill a test tube halfway with water.

Pour some alcohol very carefully down the side of the test tube until it reaches the top.

Try not to mix the liquids.

What do you think will happen to the level of the liquid when it is mixed?

## Predict

Check one [√]:

Level stays the same. **[   ]**     Level drops. **[   ]**     Test tube overflows. **[   ]**

Try to explain your thinking.

_____

_____

## Observe

Let's shake it! What happens?

_____

_____

## Explain

Can you explain Dr. Y's trick? Hint: Think of the water and alcohol as being made up of different-size particles.

_____

_____

_____

## Hmm ...

What do you think would happen if you shook a jar that contained different sizes of marbles?

_____

_____

_____

# References

Biro, P., and S. Zwolanski-Morovic. 1992. *Predict, observe, explain: A children's science teaching approach*. Victoria, Australia: Monash Children's Science Group, Faculty of Education, Monash University. Booklet.

Driver, R. 1985. Beyond appearances: The conservation of matter under physical and chemical transformations. In *Children's ideas in science*, ed. R. Driver, E. Guesne, and A. Tiberghien, 85–104. Buckingham, United Kingdom: Open University Press.

Driver, R., A. Squires, P. Rushworth, and V. Wood-Robinson. 1995. Heating. In *Making sense of secondary science*, 138–142. London and New York: Routledge.

Prieto, T., A. Blanco, and A. Rodriguez. 1989. The ideas of 11 to 14-year-old students about the nature of solutions. *International Journal of Science Education* 11 (4): 451–463.

Stepans, J., and M. L. Veath. 1994. How do students really explain changes in matter? *Science Scope* 17 (8): 31–35.

**Understanding Chemical Changes**

# Chapter 12

## Contents

# Scientific Explanation

Riddles: Melting (fat) and evaporating (clothes drying) are physical changes. They can be easily reversed. On the other hand, an egg frying and paint drying are both chemical changes. Something new is made and the change cannot be reversed.

Something dissolving or something coming out of solution (the fizz) is usually thought of as a physical change. It can be reversed. On the other hand, Alka-Seltzer fizzing is a chemical change. Alka-Seltzer contains two chemicals that react together when they dissolve in water.

When a cup falls, it breaks into pieces. Nothing new is made. This is a physical change. However, if you think of a falling leaf as being in the process of dying, then this is a chemical change because the tissues start changing their molecules. We see this as changing color, the leaf becoming stiff, releasing from the tree, and so on.

The scientific answers to the changes observed in the experiments are as follows:

- Physical changes: baking soda plus water (dissolving), heating candle wax (melting)
- Chemical changes: the remainder

Nail polish drying is a physical change, whereas milk turning sour and iron rusting are both chemical changes

There are many indicators of chemical change, such as a color change, gas given off, solid formed, and heat given off. However none of these are conclusive.

# Students' Explanations: Research Findings

Driver et al. (1994) reviewed the research findings:

(a) Fizzing, exploding, changing color, and apparent changes in mass are readily used by students to recognize chemical change. However, it is doubtful whether they interpret such evidence in terms of substances changing into other substances.

(b) The idea of reversibility helps students distinguish physical change from chemical change.

(c) Students' understanding deepens when they appreciate change at the particulate level.

# Apparatus and Materials

The experiments are probably best done as a lab. Students will need

- Watch glass
- Eye dropper
- Tongs
- Tin lid
- Candle or burner
- Baking soda
- Vinegar
- Candle wax
- Salt
- Copper coin
- Bread
- Steel wool

## *Chemical Changes*

### Chemical Riddles

What's the difference between

(a) fat melting and an egg frying?

(b) clothes drying and paint drying?

(c) soda fizzing and Alka-Seltzer fizzing?

(d) a cup falling (and breaking) and a leaf falling?

Could it be that something new is being made?

Maybe it has changed forever?

In chemical changes, something new is made. New chemicals are formed. Chemical changes are usually difficult to reverse.

### Predict

Have a look at the experiments below and mark them with a *C* if you think a chemical change will take place.

### Some Experiments

Observe them carefully. Do you see any signs of a chemical change?

| Predict | Experiment | Observe Signs |
|---|---|---|
| | **Baking soda plus water** <br> Add drops of water to a teaspoon of baking soda. | |
| | **Baking soda plus vinegar** | |
| | **Cleaning a copper coin with salt and vinegar** <br> Cover the coin with a mixture of salt and vinegar. | |
| | **Heating (gently) some candle wax on a tin lid** <br> (Don't let it catch fire!) | |
| | **Heating a piece of bread on a tin lid** (Don't let it catch fire!) | |
| | **Heating a piece of steel wool** (Use tongs.) | |

### Explain

Try to explain to a friend how to tell if a chemical change takes place.

_____

_____

### *OK!*

Did you answer the riddles?

Which do you think are chemical changes? _____

_____

How about milk turning sour?  Y/N      Iron rusting?  Y/N      Nail polish drying?  Y/N

## Scientific Explanation

The chemical reaction between copper chloride solution and aluminum is an interesting one. The blue-green solution loses its color and a brown sludge—copper—forms at the bottom of the beaker. There is no change in mass.

**copper chloride (solution) + aluminum ⟶ aluminum chloride + copper**

In the follow-up example, the sodium carbonate reacts with the copper chloride to form copper carbonate (blue solid) and sodium chloride, dissolved in water.

**sodium carbonate (solution) + copper chloride (solution) ⟶**
**copper carbonate (solid) + sodium chloride (solution)**

Although there is a chemical change (or exchange), nothing is lost. The mass remains the same. The law of conservation of mass states that for chemical reactions "mass can neither be created nor destroyed."

## Students' Explanations: Research Findings

Briggs and Holding (reported in Driver et al. 1994) found that 75% of the secondary students they studied considered apparent change of mass as evidence of chemical change.

In their publication, which potentially has great significance for chemistry teachers, Horton and his colleagues (Horton 2004) identified more than 150 studies of students' alternative conceptions in chemistry. They then proceeded to categorize these by concept. Here are some of the alternative conceptions they included under the concept of conservation of matter in reactions:

(a) A large proportion of 12- to 18-year-olds do not think mass is conserved.

(b) Mass is lost in combustion.

(c) When steel wool burns inside a closed flask, its mass changes. When steel wool burns in the open, its mass decreases.

(d) A rusting nail loses weight. A rusting nail won't change weight. Some students thought that the rust was already inside the nail, and some thought that it had only reacted with oxygen in the air, which weighs nothing.

(e) A precipitation reaction results in change of mass; the mass increases because solids weigh more than liquids.

## Apparatus and Materials

- Copper chloride solution
- Aluminum foil
- Masses
- Balance
- Sodium carbonate solution

# Can Things Really Disappear?

### If an Alchemist Could Meet a Chemist

The early chemists—the alchemists—were fascinated by chemical change. It must have seemed like magic to them—things changing, things appearing and disappearing. They must have wondered, "Can things really disappear?"

Chemists today would be able to answer most of their questions. They might say, "Let's try an experiment!"

Can things really disappear?

Let's try an experiment!

*Alchemist sitting by fire*

*Chemist in a lab coat*

### An Experiment

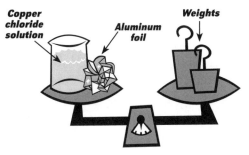

*Copper chloride solution*    *Aluminum foil*    *Weights*

Aluminum foil and copper chloride solution react chemically.

Do you think the mass will change when the aluminum foil is put into the copper chloride solution?

### Predict

Check one [√]:    Mass increases. **[   ]**    Mass decreases. **[   ]**    Mass stays the same. **[   ]**

Try to explain your thinking for your prediction.

_____

_____

### Observe

Let's do it! What are your results?_____

### Explain

Try to explain what happened. _____

_____

_____

### *Check It Out!*

Try mixing a solution of sodium carbonate (washing soda) with the copper chloride solution.

### Predict

Do you think the mass will change? _____

Try it! What happened to the scale? _____

### Explain

_____

_____

## Scientific Explanation

Many things change when you heat them. Heat is a form of energy; it often can make substances break up or decompose. All the items on the list, with the exception of salt, break up when you heat them. Chalk doesn't appear to change, but it does. Chalk, or calcium carbonate, turns into lime when it is heated. Carbon dioxide is given off. Lime is quite different chemically from chalk. It is somewhat soluble in water, and a solution will turn litmus paper blue. It doesn't fizz with acids. Lime has different chemical properties.

Wood chips, when heated, break down into charcoal (carbon) and inflammable gases.

$$wood + heat \longrightarrow carbon + inflammable\ gases$$

## Students' Explanations: Research Findings

Brendon Schollum (1981) asked 37 junior high school students to explain what happened when sugar was heated. Basically, two views were expressed.

1.  The sugar had broken up and new substances were formed; carbon, steam, and smoke were mentioned as likely products in some cases. Views compatible with the scientific position regarding this process of chemical change were spread through all age groups.

2.  The melted sugar changes to another form of sugar: The pupils made comments such as the sugar was "bubbly, boiling, burning." When students were asked for their meanings for these words, and their views of what they had observed happening when the sugar was heated, the following four types of views were evident:
    The sugar was

    (a) in another form which included a color change, or change of taste.

    (b) overcooked, but still sugar.

    (c) colored, because it was unable to "take too much heat."

    (d) changed to sugar in the gaseous state.

## Apparatus and Materials

This POE might be done in the lab.

- Salt
- Chalk
- Plastic chips (polythene)
- Sugar
- Baking soda
- Candles
- Wood clothespins
- Tin lids

Follow-up experiment: wood chips or dry twigs, can with 2 mm hole in the lid, tripod, gauze, burner or propane torch

## Beginner Chemists: Heat It!

Hundreds of years ago, the early chemists—the alchemists—were fascinated by fire. It could make all sorts of things happen. Sometimes a substance would change into something else. Magic? The dream of the alchemists was to make gold.

Today, beginner chemists often start by heating things. They want to understand how one substance changes into another.

### An Experiment

Try heating small quantities (enough to cover a fingernail) of everyday substances on a tin lid.

Don't let them catch fire.

Do you know if any of the substances below will change into new chemicals? Predictions please! Check [√] those you think will change into new chemicals.

| Predict | Substance Heated | Observe |
|---------|------------------|---------|
| | Salt | |
| | Sugar | |
| | Chalk (powder) | |
| | Polyethylene (plastic) | |
| | Sawdust or wood shavings | |
| | Baking soda | |
| | Your choice (but consult your teacher first) | |

### Explain

Do you think you observed some chemical changes? Try to explain why. _____

_____

### Awesome!

Put some wood chips in a can that has a small hole in the lid. Heat it strongly. After a minute or so, put a burning match to the hole. What happens? Can you explain it?

_____

_____

## Scientific Explanation

Most metals combine with oxygen from the air when they are heated. They form oxides:

$$\text{metal} + \text{oxygen} \xrightarrow{\text{heat}} \text{metal oxide}$$

Copper oxide (CuO) and iron oxides (FeO) are black. Aluminum, zinc, and magnesium oxides are white. Because these metals add oxygen when heated, their masses increase.

Steel wool oxidizes (burns) rapidly.

Magnesium ribbon oxidizes rapidly indeed and burns with a brilliant white flame. (You might like to demonstrate this. Careful!)

## Students' Explanations: Research Findings

Driver et al. (1994) suggest that students' ideas of chemical change deepen when they appreciate change at a particulate level.

Laverty and McGarvey (1991) asked students to describe the products of the reaction between magnesium particles and oxygen particles in both words and pictures. They categorized student responses as follows:

(a) A random mixture of magnesium and oxygen particles

(b) Magnesium particles surrounded by oxygen particles

(c) One magnesium particle joined to two oxygen particles, or two magnesiums to one oxygen

(d) An assembly of joined magnesium and oxygen particles arranged alternately and described as being "the same all the way through"

## Apparatus and Materials

- Clothespins or tongs
- Copper foil
- Test tubes
- Bunsen burner or propane torch
- Zinc foil
- Aluminum foil
- Iron foil
- Steel wool

# Heating Metals

Hey, look what happens when you heat this piece of copper foil!

Yeah! Strange, right? Where do you think the black stuff comes from? (Check one.)
___ the flame
___ the air
___ out of the copper

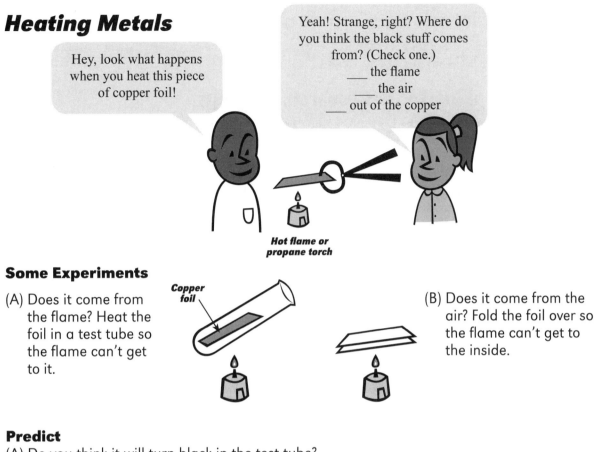

**Hot flame or propane torch**

## Some Experiments

(A) Does it come from the flame? Heat the foil in a test tube so the flame can't get to it.

*Copper foil*

(B) Does it come from the air? Fold the foil over so the flame can't get to the inside.

## Predict
(A) Do you think it will turn black in the test tube? _____
(B) Do you think the inside will turn black? _____

## Observe
Let's try it! Be careful not to burn yourself! What do you see?

(A) _____
(B) _____

## Explain
Try to explain what you saw happen. _____
_____

## More Experiments
How about doing some experiments with other metal foils? Try zinc foil **or** aluminum foil **or** iron foil (steel wool works even better).

## Hmmm?
Do you think copper foil will weigh more, less, or the same after it is heated? Try to explain why.

_____
_____
_____

## Scientific Explanation

When a substance burns, it combines with oxygen from the air. If the products are not lost as smoke or gases, the substance will always increase in weight.

## Students' Explanations: Research Findings

Of 541 British 15-year-olds who had not taken chemistry before, 16% predicted the steel wool would get heavier (Driver 1985). Andersson and Renstrom (1982; see Driver et al. 1994) and Donnelly and Welford (1988) found that a large proportion of 15-year-olds thought iron wool would lose mass when burned. Some attributed this to iron being lost in burning, others to the iron wool losing moisture, and others to the powder weighing less.

Gaining insight into students' understanding of the combustion of copper and magnesium was the focus of an action research study carried out by Valanides, Nicolaidou, and Eilks (2003). Even though all nine students were able to give correct definitions of the oxidation of copper and magnesium, three thought the mass of the copper would be less and five thought the mass of the magnesium would be less. Here is a sample of their reasoning:

> *Some of the mass of the copper has been burned ...*

> *Because the magnesium burned and ... disappeared in the air and only ashes remained.*

The student who thought there was no change of mass when magnesium was burned had this to say about the white solid magnesium oxide remaining:

> *It's just a change in its appearance and its mass is conserved.*

## Apparatus and Materials

- Balance
- Can
- Iron wool

## *Heavy Ashes*

When you burn metals, they combine with oxygen, right?

Yes, but if that's true, the ash must be heavier than the metal you started with. Hmm …

### An Experiment

Put about 1 g of iron wool in a small can and place it on a balance.

Balance it!

Take the can off the balance and light the wool inside with a long match.

Put the can back on the balance.

Do you think the can and the ashes will weigh more, less, or the same?

Try to give the reasons for your predictions.

### Predict
Check one [√].

The can and the ashes will        Weigh more **[   ]**        Weigh less **[   ]**        Weigh the same **[   ]**

Please explain your prediction.

_____

_____

_____

### Observe
Let's try it! What happens?

_____

_____

### Explain
Try to explain what happened.

_____

_____

## Scientific Explanation

The candle stays alight longer under the large bottles. Burning is a chemical change. When something burns, it combines with oxygen in the air to form new substances. After the oxygen is used, the chemical change stops. (It should be noted that this explanation is disputed; see Birk and Lawson 1999).

Heat is needed to make the change happen.

$$candle\ wax + oxygen \longrightarrow carbon\ dioxide + water$$

## Students' Explanations: Research Findings

Students hold a variety of alternative conceptions about a candle burning (Horton 2004):

(a) The wax from a burning candle (or the wood from a burning match) disappears.

(b) The wax evaporates.

(c) The wax becomes energy.

(d) The flame is caused by the wick burning.

(e) In some combustion reactions, such as burning gasoline, the role of oxygen is not recognized.

(f) The fire in a candle came out of the match and went to the candle.

(g) If water appears during burning, it was present in the candle.

## Apparatus and Materials

- 250 ml beaker
- 500 ml beaker
- 1,000 ml beaker
- Candles

Note: Glass jars of different sizes may be used instead of the beakers.

## Answers to Follow-up Questions

Some woodstoves are called airtight because the amount of air they use can be controlled.

Yes! Human beings and all living things are changing chemically all the time. The oxygen in the air we breathe combines with the food we have eaten to provide us with the energy we need.

## *Is Air Needed for Burning?*

**Airtight Woodstoves**
Don't you need air for burning?
What do you think? What would you say?

We just got a new airtight woodstove.

I thought you needed air for burning?

**Some Experiments**

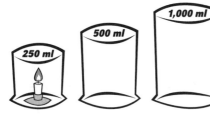

Put a 250 ml jar or beaker over a candle. Time how long it takes for the candle to go out.

Time _____ seconds

**Predict**
How long do you think the candle will stay alight?

Under the 500 ml jar _____ sec.        Under the 1,000 ml jar _____ sec.

Try to explain your thinking. _____

_____

**Observe**
Let's try it!

Time for 500 ml jar _____ sec.        Time for 1,000 ml jar _____ sec.

**Explain**
Try to explain your observations. (Bonus: Can you use the term *chemical change* in your explanation?)

_____

_____

_____

*Huh?*
Why do they call woodstoves airtight? _____

_____

I need air to live! Am I changing chemically? _____

_____

# Scientific Explanation

The water rises in the jar.

Air is, in fact, a mixture of a number of different gases: about 20% oxygen and 80% nitrogen. There are small amounts of other gases in air as well, such as carbon dioxide.

When a candle burns, oxygen from the air combines with candle wax and is used up. Carbon dioxide and water are formed from candle wax.

$$candle\ wax + oxygen \xrightarrow{\ heat\ } carbon\ dioxide\ and\ water\ (and\ some\ carbon)$$

The carbon dioxide gas, unlike oxygen, is very soluble in water. Hence, the water rises to fill the space occupied by the carbon dioxide. The water produced in the reaction condenses and therefore takes up less space than the oxygen.

# Students' Explanations: Research Findings

Schollum (1981) found that a common preconception among junior high school students was that air is not actively involved in burning. On the other hand, in their study of 400 French children ages 11 and 12, Meheut, Saltiel, and Tiberghein (1985) found that although children recognized that oxygen was necessary for combustion, some did not recognize that it was reacting with the substance being burned, and some viewed combustion as decomposition.

In his summary of the findings of seven studies that used a lit candle as an event, Johnson (2002) reported that though many pupils could state that oxygen was needed to maintain the flame, few could explain its role or, indeed, the role of the wax.

# Apparatus and Materials

- Tall jar
- Candle
- Water
- Dish

# What Is Air?

## Oxygen Riddle

How can you tell that air is used up when a candle burns? I can't tell. It looks the same to me!

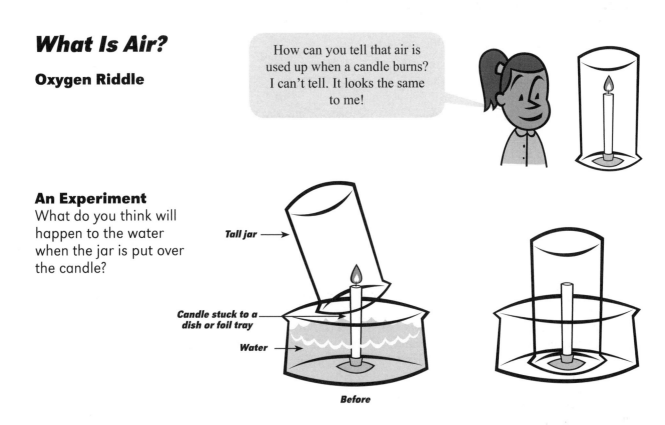

**An Experiment**
What do you think will happen to the water when the jar is put over the candle?

Tall jar →

Candle stuck to a dish or foil tray →

Water →

*Before*

## Predict
Where will the water level be after the candle has gone out? Draw your prediction above.

Please give your reasons. _____

_____

_____

## Observe
Let's try it! Draw what you observed.

## Explain
Try to explain what you observed.

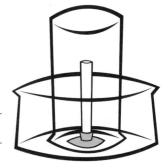

_____

_____

_____

_____

## Scientific Explanation

When a candle burns, it combines with oxygen from the air. Carbon dioxide and water vapor are formed. You can't see these products because they are colorless gases, but they do have weight.

*candle + oxygen* ⟶ *carbon dioxide + water (vapor)*

In chemical reactions, substances change into others, but there is no change in mass. This is called the law of conservation of mass: Mass cannot be created or destroyed. (This law does not apply to nuclear reactions.)

## Students' Explanations: Research Findings

Driver et al. (1994) make the simple observation that when students think gases are weightless, it is unlikely that they will understand that mass is conserved in reactions involving gases. Although this concept may seem obvious, it underlines the importance of students' understanding that gases do have mass if they are to understand the conservation of mass in chemical reactions—that is, the idea that gases have mass is an important prerequisite.

After experiencing a number of experiments on the lit candle, designed to show that wax and oxygen were changed into carbon dioxide and water, the understanding of 14-year-old students was probed through a series of questions. Of 33 students, 26 did not interpret what they saw in terms of chemical change: Some recognized that the amount of wax goes down but thought the missing wax simply evaporated or, alternatively, could not account for it. Only seven began to recognize a chemical change took place, even though the lit candle had been presented as an example of chemical change (Johnson 2002).

## Apparatus and Materials

No materials needed

## The Case of the Disappearing Candle

**Riddle**

> Where does a candle go when it's burned?

> Heaven? Heaven knows!

> Leave it to me! I'll investigate.

### Dr. Y's Awesome Experiment

Dr. Y built a huge box. He suspended it from an accurate spring scale. He put a candle inside and weighed everything. The moment of truth arrived! He lit the candle and sealed the box again. The candle burned away. It disappeared. What do you think will happen to the weight? Think carefully!

### Predict

Check one [√]. The weight of the box will    Increase [   ]    Decrease [   ]    Remain the same [   ]
Please give your reasons for your prediction.

_____

_____

### Observe

Ask your teacher to tell you what would happen.

_____

### Explain

Try to explain Dr. Y's remarkable findings._____

_____

_____

_____

### Interesting ...

I wonder what would have happened if Dr. Y had lit a fire inside the box instead of a candle.

_____

_____

## Scientific Explanation

When a solution of washing soda (sodium carbonate) is added to hard water (lime water, which is a solution of calcium hydroxide), an insoluble precipitate of calcium carbonate (chalk) is formed. It is the dissolved calcium salts that make the water hard.

*sodium carbonate + calcium hydroxide* ⟶ *calcium carbonate + sodium hydroxide*

There is no change of mass. The law of conservation of mass applies to all chemical reactions.

## Students' Explanations: Research Findings

Kind (2004) reported that 56% of 16-year-olds thought there was a change of mass in precipitation reactions, and 17% thought an increase would result from a solid weighing more than a liquid. In passing, it should be noted that many regard Kind's review of students' misconceptions in chemistry as being a "must-have and must read for anyone teaching chemistry or doing research in chemical education" (Horton 2004, p. 27).

## Apparatus

- Balance
- Washing soda
- Hard water (lime water)
- Containers

## *Hard Water*

Is your tap water hard? Hard water is more difficult to lather than soft water (rainwater).

You can soften hard water by adding washing soda. Washing soda takes out (precipitates) the dissolved calcium salts.

Let's see what happens when we mix a solution of washing soda (sodium carbonate) with hard water. (Lime water, which is a solution of lime [calcium hydroxide], is hard.)

A chemical change takes place! Do you think the mass changes?

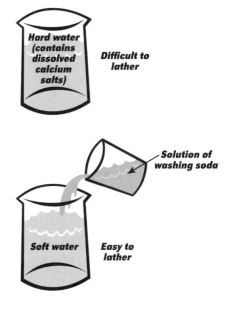

Hard water (contains dissolved calcium salts) — Difficult to lather

Solution of washing soda

Soft water — Easy to lather

### An Experiment

Hard water

Solution of washing soda

What do you think will happen to the balance if we mix the solution of washing soda with the hard water (lime water)?

### Predict
Check one [√].

Do you think the mass will      Increase **[  ]**      Decrease **[  ]**      Stay the same **[  ]**

Please give your reasons. _____

_____

### Observe
Let's do it! What did you observe? _____

_____

### Explain
Try to explain what you saw happen. _____

_____

_____

### *Hey!*
Boiling an egg is another chemical change. Do you think an egg will weigh more, less, or the same after it is boiled? Please explain.

_____

_____

# References

Andersson, B., and L. Renstrom. 1982. *Oxidation of steel wool*. EKNA Report 7, Institutionen for Praktisk Pedagogik, Univ. of Gothenburg, Sweden.

Birk, J., and A. Lawson. 1999. The persistence of the candle and cylinder misconception. *Journal of Chemical Education* 76 (7): 914–916.

Donnelly, J. F., and A. G. Welford. 1988. Children's performance in chemistry. *Education in Chemistry* 25 (1): 7–10.

Driver, R. 1985. Beyond appearances: The conservation of matter under physical and chemical transformations. In *Children's ideas in science*, ed. R. Driver, E. Guesne, and A. Tiberghien, 85–104. Buckingham, United Kingdom: Open University Press.

Driver, R., A. Squires, P. Rushworth, and V. Wood-Robinson. 1994. *Making sense of secondary science: Research into children's ideas*. London and New York: Routledge.

Horton, C. 2004. Student alternative conceptions in chemistry. Report by the Modeling Instruction in Chemistry action research team, Arizona State University. *http://modeling.asu.edu/modeling/Chem-AltConceptions3-09.doc.*

Johnson, P. 2002. Children's understanding of substances, part 2: Explaining chemical change. *International Journal of Science Education* 24 (10): 1037–1054.

Kind, V. 2004. Beyond appearances: Students' misconceptions about basic chemical ideas. Report prepared for the Royal Society of Chemistry. London: Education Division, Royal Society of Chemistry.

Laverty, D. T., and J. E. B. McGarvey. 1991. A "constructivist" approach to learning. *Education in Chemistry* 28 (4): 99–102.

Meheut, M., E. Saltiel, and A. Tiberghein. 1985. Pupils' (11–12 year-olds) conceptions of combustion. *European Journal of Science Education* 7 (1): 83–93.

Schollum, B. 1981. Chemical change. Learning in Science Project Working Paper 27, Univ. of Waikato, Hamilton, New Zealand.

Valanides, N., A. Nicolaidou, and I. Eilks. 2003. Twelfth-grade students' understanding of oxidation and combustion: Using action research to improve teachers' practical knowledge and teaching practice. *Research in Science and Technological Education* 21 (2): 159–175.

# Chapter 13

**Understanding Living Things**

## Contents

\* Notice that growth, movement, and response to stimuli are some of the characteristics of living things.

## Scientific Explanation

The seeds germinate and grow in both dark and light. Those grown in the dark are yellow, long, and straggling and eventually die. Initially, the plants get their food from the seed (the cotyledons) but cannot sustain themselves because they need light to make their food from air and water (photosynthesis). Hence, they die of starvation.

## Students' Explanations: Field Experience

This POE was used with 68 grade 9 students.

### Predictions

Nearly all of the students predicted that the seeds would grow better in the light; some mentioned that the seedlings would appear healthier, some that the plants would be greener. Forty-eight percent (48%) correctly predicted that the seedlings in the dark would die. However, 52% incorrectly predicted that those in the light would grow taller than those in the dark.

> *The first week was surprising. The ones in the dark sprouted really well ...*

### Explanations

After making their observations, 39% of students connected poor quality of growth in the dark with the plants' inability to make food (previously, only 19% had made this connection). Their responses indicated that many students were beginning to formulate scientifically acceptable explanations. Here is a sample that indicates their progress:

> *It died because of the lack of light. It first grew because light wasn't required during the germination stage.*

> *The first week was surprising. The ones in the dark sprouted really well because they don't need light to sprout but then growth slowed down when light is needed. They died. The ones in the light had all they need to grow nicely.*

> *I believe the one in the dark was desperate for light so it speeded up its growth to search for it.*

> *It grew so much in the dark because it was looking for the light. It died because it could not produce to feed.*

## Students' Explanations: Research Findings

Most 11-year-old students believe plants need light to live and grow, though a significant proportion think they need light only for good health and color (Roth, Smith, and Anderson 1983). However, after observing grass grown from seed in the dark, according to Smith and Anderson (1984), most students in grade 5 concluded that the plants in the dark were not healthy and saw no connection between the condition of the plants and lack of food. Although Barman et al. (2006) reported that a high number of K–8 students understood a plant needed sunlight to survive (93 to 99%), a much smaller proportion believed a lightbulb could be substituted (13 to 19%). However, although students may have stated that sunlight was needed, they did not necessarily understand that a light source was *required* for plant growth. Students seemed to believe that sunlight provided heat and warmth for the plant (e.g., "it warms the plant"; "gives plant heat"), but were unclear about its role in fulfilling the plant's nutritional energy requirements. This appears to persist through high school (Ozay and Oztas 2003), where some students may believe plants absorb food rather than synthesize it (Magntorn and Helldén 2007).

## Apparatus and Materials

- 2 Styrofoam cups
- Soil or sand
- Radish or mustard seeds

## *Do Plants Need Light?*
What do you think?

Put the seed tray on the windowsill. Plants need light to grow.

Seeds don't need light. They grow fine without it!

### An Experiment
Scatter some seeds in two small pots of soil or sand. Mustard or radish seeds grow fast. Keep one pot in a dark place (like a cupboard) and the other in the light. Keep the soil in the pots moist. Measure their heights and check their appearances every week for three weeks.

### Predict
Describe what you think will happen    (a) In the light      (b) In the dark

Try to explain any differences you expect. _____

_____

_____

_____

_____

### Observe

| Time | Growth in Light | Growth in Dark |
|------|-----------------|----------------|
| After 1 week | | |
| After 2 weeks | | |
| After 3 weeks | | |

### Explain
Try to explain what you observed._____

_____

_____

_____

_____

## Scientific Explanation

The seedling grows toward the light. Light acts as a stimulus to growth. This is called the *phototropic effect* (in Greek, *photos* means light and *tropos* means turning). The tip of the stem provides a growth hormone. The stem farthest from the light grows fastest because there is a greater concentration of this hormone in this area. Phototropism may also refer to plants' growth *away* from light. Vines, for instance, grow away from light so they maintain contact with the wall they grow against. If their phototropic response was to grow toward the light, they would not attach to the wall.

## Students' Explanations: Field Experience

This POE was used with 52 grade 7 students.

A large majority of students (73%) made correct predictions:

**Will grow crooked and get out.**

However, only 31% mentioned plants being drawn to the light:

**Yes, I think it will come out toward the light.**

Twenty-seven percent (27%) made incorrect predictions. Some suggested that light was required for growth:

**I don't think the plant will get any sun. After a couple of days it will die.**

Others seemed unaware of plants being drawn to the light.

**It will hit the wall and go left and just bunch up.**

**The seed will grow through the walls.**

After making their observations, 81% of the students gave explanations that referred to the plant growing toward the light.

## Apparatus and Materials

- Shoe box
- Styrofoam cup
- Soil
- Bean seed

Note: This could make an ideal home experiment.

# Effects of Light on Plant Growth

### Growing Plants on a Windowsill

People often grow plants on their windowsills. Every day or so, they turn them around. Do you know why?

### An Experiment

Will the bean seedling be able to find its way out of the box? Will it get stuck? What do you think will happen?

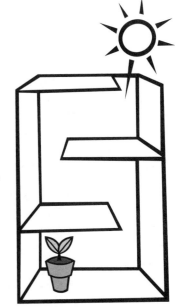

- Cut out one-third of the end of a shoe box and tape dividers to the inside (as shown in the diagram).

- Put a seedling (or plant a seed) inside and put on the lid. Stand the box on its end in the light. Water the seedling regularly.

### Predict

Using the diagram above, draw the way you think the seedling will look after about one week.

Please explain your thinking. _____

_____

### Observe

Draw the seedling every few days as it grows. Record the position of the leaves.

Date _____ _____ _____ _____

### Explain

Try to explain what you observed._____

_____

_____

_____

# Scientific Explanation

The stem of the plant grows away from gravitational pull. The plant's roots grow toward gravitational pull. Growth stimulated by gravitational pull is called the *geotropic effect*. In Greek, *geo* means Earth and *tropos* means turning. Scientists thought gravity had an effect on the hormones that control growth. However, this 1926 theory is not consistent with many later experimental observations (Firn 1990).

To show that roots actually grow in the direction of the pull of gravity, you might try the following experiment. Carefully lay a growing seedling on a bed of sand. Cover the sand with a paper towel and keep the towel and sand moist. Observe the way the roots penetrate the bed of sand.

# Students' Explanations: Field Experience

This POE was used with 54 grade 7 students.

Thirty-one percent (31%) of students correctly predicted that the stem would grow upward. However, only one student (2%) explained this in terms of the pull of gravity.

> **The stem I think will grow up because of gravity.**

Here are some examples of other predictions about the stem.

> **I think the stem will grow out straight.**

> **I think the plant will grow down because it has no support.**

> **I think the plant will die because it has no light.**

Forty-two percent (42%) correctly predicted that the root would grow downward. However, there were no indications that these students recognized the geotropic effect.

| Summary of Predictions | Stem |
|---|---|
| Grow straight | 20% |
| Grow up | 31% |
| Grow down | 24% |
| Die | 18% |
| Other | 6% |

After making their observations, 61% of the students provided explanations in terms of the pull of gravity.

# Apparatus and Materials

- Glass jar
- Bean seed
- Paper towel

Note: This would make an ideal home experiment.

## *Effects of Gravity on Plant Growth*

Plant stems grow upward! But do you know why? Check the answer you think is best.

    (a) They grow toward the **light**.

    (b) They grow away from the pull of **gravity**.

    (c) They are affected by **both light and gravity.**

What about the roots of plants?

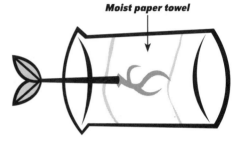

*Moist paper towel*

### An Experiment

Let's study the effects of gravity alone.

Plant a bean seed in a glass jar lined with a moist paper towel.

After the seedling has grown a few centimeters, turn the jar on its side and keep it in the dark for a few days. (Remember to keep the paper towel moist.)

### Predict

Draw the way you think the plant will look after a few days. Please explain why you drew the stem and the roots this way.

(a) Stem:_____

_____

(b) Roots: _____

_____

### Observe

Draw the plant before and after the experiment.

*Before the experiment*          *After _____ days*

### Explain

Try to explain what happened

(a) to the stem: _____

_____

(b) to the roots: _____

_____

### *Hey!*

Why do you think the roots grow downward when the jar is turned on its side—because they fall under their own weight, or because they actually grow in the direction of the pull of gravity?

Can you devise an experiment to check this out?

## Scientific Explanation

One pattern of leg movement is shown in the diagram. This pattern seems to enable the insect to keep its balance while walking. Note: A variety of insects were used in the field trials. Some were difficult to observe. Earwigs provided clear observations and exhibited this pattern of leg movement.

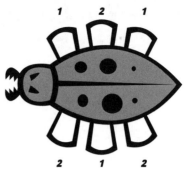

## Students' Explanations: Field Experience

This POE was used by 86 grade 7 students. These students gave a variety of predictions.

| Predictions | Percentage of Students |
|---|:---:|
| All the legs on one side move first. (1 1 1) (2 2 2) | 34 |
| Triangular movement  (1 2 1) (2 1 2) | 19 |
| Sequential movement, front to back and right to left.  (1 3 5) (2 4 6) | 13 |
| Loping movement  (1 2 3)    or    (3 2 1) (1 2 3)          (3 2 1) | 9 |
| Others or no response | 25 |

The students gave many plausible reasons for their predictions:

*So that it doesn't trip itself up.*

*I think it will move this way because it is balanced.*

*When you are on all fours you use your front right then your back left, so I'm just continuing the pattern further.*

*Like a human, one leg at a time.*

*If it moved this way it would be easier to climb and avoid small objects.*

*It would be difficult moving them one at a time and it would be a lot slower.*

*Insects move differently depending on the situation or the kind of insect.*

Only 6% mentioned balance when giving reasons for their predictions. However, after observing an earwig's "triangular" movement $\begin{pmatrix} 1 & 2 & 1 \\ 2 & 1 & 2 \end{pmatrix}$, 50% gave explanations in terms of balance.

## Apparatus and Materials

- Insect
- Glass jar or petri dish
- Some ice
- Magnifying glass (might be useful)

## If You Had Six Legs

If you had six legs, how would you walk? Which legs would you move first? Which next?

That was a tricky question. Well, how about if you had four legs? (You might try experimenting on all fours.) How do you think a cat or dog moves?

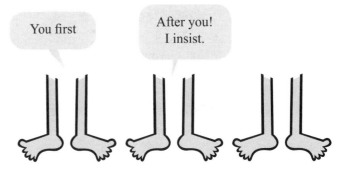

You first

After you! I insist.

### An Experiment

Insects have six legs. How does an insect move?

You can slow down fast-movers by chilling them. (Put one in a glass jar surrounded by ice.)

Which legs do you think it will move first?

### Predict

Put 1 in the appropriate boxes to indicate the legs you think will move first and 2 in the boxes you think will move second. Please give your reasons.

_____

_____

### Observe

Check out a couple of different insects. What do you see?

Insect

Insect

### Explain

Try to explain what you saw. _____

_____

_____

## Scientific Explanation

A worm doesn't have eyes or a nose as such, but it is sensitive to light, touch, and smell. Strange as it may seem, the worm does have a "brain." This is located in the third segment. The worm's brain is connected to a central nerve cord that runs the length of its body.

## Students' Explanations: Field Experience

A version of this POE was tried out with 53 grade 7 students.

| Predictions | Percentage of Students |
|---|---|
| Sensitive to touch | 96 |
| Sensitive to smell | 88 |
| Sensitive to light | 85 |

Some of the students who thought the worm would be insensitive to light associated this with the worm having no eyes:

> *I think the earthworm wouldn't react because I think it is blind.*

After making their observations, the majority of students seemed to have no difficulty accommodating the idea that a worm has a sensing system. Here is a sample of their thinking:

> *Yes, I think the worm has a nervous system because he reacts.*

> *I think the anterior end has sense but the posterior end doesn't.*

> *They have their own five senses like us. Well, maybe they have more, maybe less.*

> *Although it doesn't have a brain, it has a group of nerve endings.*

> *I don't think he has a nervous system because he doesn't know anything.*

> *I don't think worms have a nervous system. I just think it's instinctive.*

## Students' Explanations: Research Findings

There is some research suggesting that some children believe that earthworms have eyes (see Matusov 2001).

## Apparatus and Materials

- Worm
- Flashlight
- Paper towel
- Cotton swab
- Vinegar

## *Worm Sense*

### Quick Quiz
1a. Can a worm see? _____     1b. Does it have eyes? _____

2a. Can a worm feel? _____     2b. Does it have nerves? _____

3a. Can a worm smell? _____     3b. Does it have a nose? _____

### Experiment 1: Effects of Light
Lay the worm on a damp paper towel. Let it rest a while. Shine a narrow beam of light on its head. It's best to carry out this experiment in a darkened room or box.

### Predict 1
What do you think will happen? _____

_____

### Observe 1
Let's try it! Try other parts of the body too! _____

_____

### Experiment 2: Effects of Touch
Gently touch different parts of the worm with a pencil (not a pen).

### Predict 2
What do you think will happen? _____

_____

### Observe 2
Let's try it! What does the worm do?_____

_____

### Experiment 3: Effects of Vinegar
Dip a cotton swab in some vinegar. Hold the cotton swab a centimeter away from different parts of the worm's body. (Don't touch it, though. That would be mean.)

### Predict 3
What do you think will happen? _____

_____

### Observe 3
Let's try it!_____

_____

### Explain 1, 2, 3
Can you explain your observations? How do you think a worm manages when it doesn't have eyes or a nose? _____

_____

## Scientific Explanation

The smaller bottle cools down faster. The amount of heat lost depends on the surface area. For its volume (size), the smaller bottle has a larger surface area.

## Students' Explanations: Research Findings

Any concept involving ratio and proportion, such as the relationship of surface area to size and volume, can be difficult for students to understand (Smith et al. 1997).

## Apparatus and Materials

- 2 glass bottles, one of which contains twice as much hot water as the other
- Woolen cloth to wrap each bottle (or some other kind of insulator)
- 2 thermometers

# Chilling Out

Do you think small children feel the cold more than adults?

In winter, animals grow thick coats to keep them warm. Is it an advantage to be a big animal or a small animal? Which cools down faster?

### An Experiment

Make two artificial animals by wrapping two bottles with a layer of cloth. (Choose bottles such that one contains twice as much as the other.)

Fill the bottles with hot water and take their temperatures every five minutes (put the tops on between readings).

### Predict

Which do you think will cool faster? Check one [√]:

The small bottle **[   ]**          The large bottle **[   ]**          Both will be the same. **[   ]**

Please give your reasons. _____

_____

_____

### Observe
Let's try it!

| Time (min.) | | | | | | |
|---|---|---|---|---|---|---|
| **Temperature of Small Bottle (°C)** | | | | | | |
| **Temperature of Large Bottle (°C)** | | | | | | |

### Explain
Try to explain what happened. _____

_____

_____

_____

# References

Barman, C. R., M. Stein, S. McNair, and N. S. Barman. 2006. Students' ideas about plants and plant growth. *The American Biology Teacher* 68 (2): 73–79.

Firn, H. 1990. Phototropism. *Journal of Biological Education* 24: 153–157.

Magntorn, O., and G. Helldén. 2007. Reading new environments: Students' ability to generalize their findings between different ecosystems. *International Journal of Science Education* 29 (1): 67–100.

Matusov, E. 2001. Intersubjectivity as a way of informing teaching design for a community of learners classroom. *Teaching and Teacher Education* 17 (4): 383–402.

Ozay, E., and H. Oztas. 2003. Secondary students' interpretation of photosynthesis and plant nutrition. *Journal of Biological Education* 37 (2): 68–71.

Roth, K. J., E. L. Smith, and C. W. Anderson. 1983. Students' conceptions of photosynthesis and food for plants. Paper presented at the American Educational Research Association, Montreal, Canada.

Smith, C., D. Maclin, L. Grosslight, and H. Davis. 1997. Teaching for understanding: A study of students' preinstruction theories of matter and a comparison of two approaches to teaching about matter and density. *Cognition and Instruction* 15 (3): 317–393.

Smith, E. L., and C. W. Anderson. 1984. Plants as producers: A case study of elementary science teaching. *Journal of Research in Science Teaching* 21 (7): 685–698.

# Chapter 14

**Understanding Life Processes in Plants**

## Contents

*Refer to Living Things 1 (LT1) for LP4. They are identical. LP4 was duplicated here on account of it being a natural part of this sequence.

## Scientific Explanation

The seeds in the sealed jar do not germinate well. Seeds need water and oxygen from the air to germinate. Seeds contain food. Oxygen is needed to change this food into energy. Energy is necessary for the seed's living processes to work.

$$food + oxygen\ (from\ the\ air) \longrightarrow energy$$

This process is called *respiration*.

## Students' Explanations: Research Findings

Driver et al. (1984) found that less than half of 15-year-olds thought oxygen was required for respiration.

This is in accord with the findings of Simpson and Arnold (1982b), who found that among 12- to 16-year-olds there was little understanding that respiration was a continuous process and that plants use energy released from food to support their living processes.

Students may believe that respiration only occurs during some periods of the day and not throughout the entire day (Ozay and Oztas 2003).

In a broad study in which participants were solicited through an article in *Science and Children*, Barman et al. (2006) reported that almost two-thirds of students in grades 6 through 8 indicated that plants needed oxygen and carbon dioxide to grow (although it may not have been the same two-thirds for each gas). Student understanding of the roles of oxygen and carbon dioxide in respiration and photosynthesis was not clear.

## Apparatus and Materials

- Corn seeds
- 2 test tubes
- Rubber stopper
- Paper towel

# Do Seeds Need Air to Germinate?

Which of the following substances do you think seeds need to germinate?
Check [√] all that apply.

(a) Water **[   ]**        (b) Light **[   ]**        (c) Air **[   ]**        (d) Minerals from the soil **[   ]**

### An Experiment

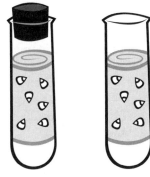

What do you think will happen if you deprive seeds of air?
Lay about six corn seeds along a crumpled piece of paper towel.
Carefully load the arrangement into a large test tube.
Moisten the paper towel thoroughly with water.
Prepare a second tube in the same way and seal it with a rubber stopper.

### Predict

Do you expect to see any difference in the germination of the seeds?

_____

_____

Please explain. _____

_____

### Observe

Record the number of seeds that germinate as the days go by. Continue your observations for about two weeks. Draw a table on the back of this page to record your data.

_____

_____

### Explain

Try to explain what happened. _____

_____

_____

_____

### *Interesting ...*

How about designing some other experiments to find out more about seed germination?

## Scientific Explanation

When they are deprived of air, plants appear healthy for a few days but then begin to die. Plants need water, light, air, and minerals from the soil to grow. They make their food by photosynthesis from water and carbon dioxide (from the air) in the presence of light. Without food, they cannot keep their life processes going.

## Students' Explanations: Research Findings

In a broad study in which participants were solicited through an article in *Science and Children*, Barman et al. (2006) reported that almost two-thirds of students in grades 6 through 8 indicated that plants needed oxygen and carbon dioxide to grow (although it may not have been the same two-thirds for each gas). Student understanding of the roles of oxygen and carbon dioxide in respiration and photosynthesis was not clear.

When interviewed about their understanding of photosynthesis, a high proportion of non-science-major college students did not mention that carbon dioxide was a necessary starting material, that sugar or starch was a product of photosynthesis, or that oxygen was released in the process (Käpylä, Heikkinen, and Asunta 2009). However, biology majors did not demonstrate this misunderstanding.

## Apparatus and Materials

- 2 large test tubes
- Rubber stopper
- Perlite or sand

## Do Plants Need Air to Grow?

Which of the following substances do you think plants need to grow?
Check any [√] you think apply.

(a) Water **[   ]**          (b) Light **[   ]**          (c) Air **[   ]**          (d) Minerals from the soil **[   ]**

### An Experiment

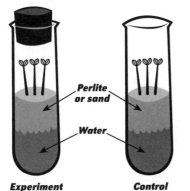

**Perlite or sand**

**Water**

**Experiment**          **Control**

What do you think will happen if you deprive plants of air?

Scatter a few radish seeds in two large test tubes, each filled halfway with perlite or sand. Keep the sand moist. Keep about 1 cm of water in the bottom of each test tube. Leave them to grow for about one week. Then seal one test tube with a rubber stopper.

### Predict

Do you expect there will be any differences after another week? _____

_____

Please explain. _____

_____

### Observe

What differences do you observe as the days go by?_____

_____

### Explain

Try to explain what happened. _____

_____

_____

### Hey!

Can you devise experiments to find out

(a) if plants need light?

(b) if plant growth is improved by adding minerals to the soil?

(c) which part of the air (oxygen, carbon dioxide, or nitrogen) plants need for growth?

## Scientific Explanation

The weight of the soil decreased very slightly (about 5 g). Van Helmont concluded that the tree got its mass from the water. However, he failed to recognize that air was involved. As students will find out later, plants need water, carbon dioxide from the air, and sunlight to make the food they need to grow.

## Students' Explanations: Field Experience

This POE was used with 67 grade 9 students.

Sixty-two percent (62%) expected the mass of the soil to decrease, and 31% thought it would stay the same. Although there was some ambiguity in what they wrote, about one-third of those predicting a decrease (20% of all students) thought the plant obtained its nutrients from the soil:

> *I think the soil got lighter because the plants ate the minerals in the soil.*

> *I think the weight of the soil decreased by 74 kg because it takes nutrients from the soil.*

> *Because the soil has dead things in it and he didn't let anything in it.*

After being told of Van Helmont's observations, nearly all the students gave expanded answers about where they think plants get the food they need to grow.

Some students (10%) concluded that the food materials were contained in the rainwater:

> *The plant gets food from the soil and after the plant takes all the nutrients out of it, the water restores the nutrients.*

The majority (70%) mentioned water and light (sun) as important sources, but only 15% mentioned air:

> *They get their food from water and dead animals and light.*

Twenty-one percent (21%) displayed a shallow prior knowledge of photosynthesis:

> *I think that they make their own food using photosynthesis, chlorophyll, water and nutrients.*

> *I think plants must get their food from the rain, sun, also they must have some food in their leaves and stem (starch).*

## Students' Explanations: Research Findings

Some 15-year-old students think of plants eating, drinking, and digesting their food (Driver et al. 1984). In a study of 11-year-olds, 80% thought soil was the source of food (fertilizers being considered as plant food), 25% thought water was the source, and 5% air (Roth, Smith, and Anderson 1983). By the age of 14 to 16 years old, as many as one-third of the students might still think plants get their food from the soil (Simpson and Arnold 1982b). Refer to Bell (1985), Barman et al. (2006), or Wang (2004) for good summaries of students' ideas about plant nutrition.

## Apparatus and Materials

No materials needed

## Plant Food

Where do plants get the food (called *nutrients*) they need to grow?

*Do they get it from the soil or what?*

This was the question that puzzled Van Helmont 400 years ago. He carried out the first experiment on living plants.

Hamburger and fries, please.

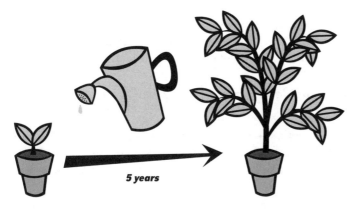

*5 years*

### Van Helmont's Experiment

Van Helmont wondered if plants got their food from the soil, so he planted a small willow tree in a tub of dry soil. Before planting it, he weighed both the tree and the soil. He gave the tree nothing but rainwater to keep it alive. After five years, he dug it up and weighed it again. He found that it had gained about 74 kg. He then dried the soil and weighed it.

### Predict

What do you think happened to the weight of the soil? _____

_____

Can you give an explanation?_____

_____

### Observe

You might be able to find out about Van Helmont's experiment in a book in the library. Otherwise you could ask your teacher.

_____

_____

### Explain

So where do you think plants get the "food" they need to grow?

_____

_____

### Guess What!

Van Helmont thought plants made their wood, stem, bark, and leaves from water! What would you have said to him?

_____

_____

## Scientific Explanation

The seeds germinate and grow in both dark and light. Those grown in the dark are yellow, long, and straggling and eventually die. Initially, the plants get their food from the seed (the cotyledons) but cannot sustain themselves because they need light to make their food from air and water (photosynthesis). Hence, they die of starvation.

## Students' Explanations: Field Experience

This POE was used with 68 grade 9 students.

### Predictions

Nearly all of the students predicted that the seeds would grow better in the light; some mentioned that the seedlings would appear healthier, some that the plants would be greener. Forty-eight percent (48%) correctly predicted that the seedlings in the dark would die. However, 52% incorrectly predicted that those in the light would grow taller than those in the dark.

> *The first week was surprising. The ones in the dark sprouted really well ...*

### Explanations

After making their observations, 39% of students connected poor quality of growth in the dark with the plants' inability to make food (previously, only 19% had made this connection). Their responses indicated that many students were beginning to formulate scientifically acceptable explanations. Here is a sample that indicates their progress:

> *It died because of the lack of light. It first grew because light wasn't required during the germination stage.*

> *The first week was surprising. The ones in the dark sprouted really well because they don't need light to sprout but then growth slowed down when light is needed. They died. The ones in the light had all they need to grow nicely.*

> *I believe the one in the dark was desperate for light so it speeded up its growth to search for it.*

> *It grew so much in the dark because it was looking for the light. It died because it could not produce to feed.*

## Students' Explanations: Research Findings

Most 11-year-old students believe plants need light to live and grow, though a significant proportion think they need light only for good health and color (Roth, Smith, and Anderson 1983). However, after observing grass grown from seed in the dark, according to Smith and Anderson (1984), most students in grade 5 concluded that the plants in the dark were not healthy and saw no connection between the condition of the plants and lack of food. Although Barman et al. (2006) reported that a high number of K–8 students understood a plant needed sunlight to survive (93 to 99%), a much smaller proportion believed a lightbulb could be substituted (13 to 19%). However, although students may have stated that sunlight was needed, they did not necessarily understand that a light source was *required* for plant growth. Students seemed to believe that sunlight provided heat and warmth for the plant (e.g., "it warms the plant"; "gives plant heat"), but were unclear about its role in fulfilling the plant's nutritional energy requirements. This appears to persist through high school (Ozay and Oztas 2003), where some students may believe plants absorb food rather than synthesize it (Magntorn and Helldén 2007).

## Apparatus and Materials

- 2 Styrofoam cups
- Soil or sand
- Radish or mustard seeds

## Do Plants Need Light?
What do you think?

Put the seed tray on the windowsill. Plants need light to grow.

Seeds don't need light. They grow fine without it!

### An Experiment
Scatter some seeds in two small pots of soil or sand. Mustard or radish seeds grow fast. Keep one pot in a dark place (like a cupboard) and the other in the light. Keep the soil in the pots moist. Measure their heights and check their appearances every week for three weeks.

### Predict
Describe what you think will happen   (a) In the light      (b) In the dark

Try to explain any differences you expect. _____

_____

_____

_____

_____

### Observe

| Time | Growth in Light | Growth in Dark |
|------|-----------------|----------------|
| After 1 week | | |
| After 2 weeks | | |
| After 3 weeks | | |

### Explain
Try to explain what you observed._____

_____

_____

_____

## Scientific Explanation

Plants make their food (starch) from carbon dioxide (in the air) and water. They use this food to grow and to give them the energy they need to keep them working.

(a) After some time, all the carbon dioxide is used up and the plants die—"starve to death."

(b) There is no change in weight. Nothing can get in or out of the greenhouse. Water and carbon dioxide are changed into "plant."

## Students' Explanations: Field Experience

This POE was used with 17 grade 9 students toward the end of their study of photosynthesis.

The majority of the students (61%) predicted that the mass of the greenhouse would increase, 24% predicted no change, and 10% predicted a decrease. The teacher remarked that the POE prompted some good discussion. The students provided a variety of interesting reasons for their different predictions:

*I think it will get heavier because the plants are growing and there will be more matter.*

*It will stay the same. The plants take in water and let it out as vapor.*

*I think the mass will get lower because it will use up the $H_2O$ and $CO_2$.*

*I think it will decrease in mass. The water will dry up slowly and wet soil is heavier than dry soil.*

Many of the student responses seemed to reveal difficulties in understanding the conservation of matter during physical or chemical change rather than difficulties in understanding photosynthesis. Predictions about whether the plants would grow or die were fairly evenly divided. Even when they differed, the students' reasoning was frequently acceptable:

*All ingredients are necessary for plants to grow.*

*They would use up all the $CO_2$.*

After observing the experiment performed in a "Mason" jar, many students apparently enhanced their understanding of the conservation of matter. Many accounted for the plants dying in terms of the carbon dioxide being used up.

## Students' Explanations: Research Findings

Simpson and Arnold (1982a) found that even those students who have had two years of secondary science education may have difficulty understanding the basic concepts of food, living, gases, and energy. These concepts are, of course, a prerequisite to understanding photosynthesis.

## Apparatus and Materials

- A Mason jar or clear 2 L soda bottle
- Soil
- Seeds (e.g., radish, corn, or mustard)
- Laboratory scales

Note: Field experience suggests that it is important to seal the jar well.

## Dr. Y's Greenhouse

Dr. Y decided to carry out an enormous experiment on plant growth. He built a greenhouse on top of a huge weighing machine. He dropped in a load of soil, scattered all sorts of seeds, and soaked the seeds with plenty of water. He sealed the greenhouse to make it airtight. The plants began to grow! Then he went on a long holiday.

What do you think he saw when he returned?

### Predict

Check one [√]:

(a) The plants had grown. **[   ]**   The plants appeared unhealthy. **[   ]**   The plants had died. **[   ]**

Please give your reasons. _____

_____

_____

Check one [√]:

(b) The mass increased. **[   ]**   The mass decreased. **[   ]**   The mass stayed the same. **[   ]**

Please give your reasons. _____

_____

_____

### Observe

If you have time, you could carry out a similar experiment in a Mason jar or a 2 L soda bottle. If not, ask your teacher what would happen to the plants and the mass.

(a) The plants: _____

_____

(b) The mass:_____

_____

### Explain

What would you say to Dr. Y? _____

_____

_____

_____

## Scientific Explanation

The potted plant loses weight and the soil begins to dry out. Because no water can escape through the plastic bag surrounding the pot, it must escape through the plant.

The roots of the plant take up water. The water moves up the stem and escapes through the leaves. This process is called *transpiration*.

If you put a clear plastic bag over the plant, you can see condensation forming on the inside of the bag. This is further evidence of transpiration.

## Students' Explanations: Field Experience

This POE was used with 65 grade 9 students.

Twenty-six percent (26%) correctly predicted a **decrease in weight**, but only 14% gave acceptable reasons in terms of transpiration.

> *The pot would weigh less. This would happen because the water would go up the stem and leave through the leaves.*

Thirty-one percent (31%) predicted an **increase in weight**. Half of these students argued that the plant would continue to grow.

> *I think it will [get heavier] because the leaves have light, $CO_2$, $H_2O$ and there is no reason why it should not grow.*

Other reasons for an increase in weight indicated that the students were encountering significant difficulties with the problem:

> *The bag might get heavier from the heat.*

> *It will get heavier because the moisture will get in the bag.*

Many (41.5%) predicted that the weight would stay **the same.** Some suggested that the system behaved as if it were closed.

> *No way for anything to get through the bag.*

Others thought there could be an exchange of gases but that an equilibrium would exist.

> *It will stay the same because of the carbon dioxide going out and the oxygen coming in.*

In sum, transpiration seemed to be a conceptually new experience to most of these students. However, after observing the loss in weight (about 15 g per day), the majority (60%) were apparently successful in accommodating the idea.

> *It lost weight because no water is getting in, therefore it's gaining no weight. The water's getting out through the leaves.*

## Students' Explanations: Research Findings

In a study of student understandings of transpiration, Barker (1998) reported that three-quarters of students believe that water enters a plant only through the roots but not through the leaves or stomata. Nearly 50% of the students believed that plants retain all of the water they absorb.

## Apparatus and Materials

- Potted plant (e.g., geranium) with single stem
- 2 large transparent plastic bags
- Tape

## Do Plants Drink?

If we put a potted plant into a clear plastic bag, seal the bag, and leave it in the light to grow, we know that there will be no change in weight. Nothing can get in or out.

But what do you think might happen if you just put the pot into the bag and leave the remainder of the plant out? Will the plant absorb the water in the soil?

### An Experiment

Water a potted plant. Put the pot in a plastic bag. Tie the bag around the stem of the plant.

What do you think will happen to the weight?

### Predict

Check one [√]:

Weight increases. **[ ]**   Weight decreases. **[ ]**   Weight stays the same. **[ ]**
Please provide your reasons. _____

_____

### Observe

Let's do it! What happens? Weigh the potted plant daily for a number of days.

| Day 1 | Day __ | Day __ | Day __ |
|-------|--------|--------|--------|
|       |        |        |        |

### Explain

Can you explain what happened? _____

_____

_____

### Try This!

Put a clear plastic bag over the plant and put the plant in sunlight. What happens to the inside of the bag? Can you explain what you observe?

_____

_____

_____

_____

## Scientific Explanation

Plants lose water rapidly on hot days. The rate of loss increases when the wind is blowing. Water escapes and evaporates through tiny openings (called *stomata*) on the underside of the plants' leaves. You can see these under a microscope.

## Students' Explanations: Field Experience

An earlier version of this POE was used with grade 9 students. The majority appeared to understand how the apparatus worked:

> ***The water level rose inside the tube. The water is pulled up the tube against gravity because the plant is drinking the water.***

## Students' Explanations: Research Findings

In a summary of a number of studies of students' understanding of plant nutrition, Bell (1985) suggested that students have poor understanding of the relationships between photosynthesis, water uptake, and respiration. In a study of student understandings of transpiration, Barker (1998) reported that three-quarters of students believe that water enters a plant only through the roots and not through the leaves or stomata and that almost 50% of the students believed that plants retain all of the water they absorb.

## Apparatus and Materials

- Leafy stems
- 30 cm length of capillary tubing of different internal diameters
- Large bowl
- Fan
- Petroleum jelly

### Notes

(a) The size of the leafy stem and the internal diameter of the glass tube need to be carefully balanced for the apparatus to work well. Try it beforehand.

(b) Cut off 1 cm of the stem underwater and assemble the apparatus under the water.

# Watching Plants "Drink"

Plants wilt on hot days. They seem to lose water fast. What about windy days? Anyone know? What would you expect?

### An Experiment

Here's a neat experiment to try. You can measure how fast plants lose water.

Pick a leafy stem so that it fits snugly into a short rubber tube.

Join a piece of glass capillary tubing to the stem with the rubber tube. Do this in a bowl of water so that no air bubbles get in.

Measure how fast the water level moves: _____ mm/min.

Now what do you expect to happen if we turn on a fan?

### Predict

Check one [√]. When the fan is turned on, the water level will move

(a) Faster **[   ]**      (b) Slower **[   ]**      (c) At the same rate **[   ]**

Please give your reasons. _____

_____

### Observe

Let's measure how fast the water level moves with the fan on. _____ mm/min.

### Explain

Do you have any comments on your observations? _____

_____

_____

### Wow!

A great idea for another experiment! Take a guess about which part of the leafy stem is letting the water escape.

_____

Check it out by smearing your predicted "escape route" with petroleum jelly (this stops water from passing through). What happened?

_____

_____

# Scientific Explanation

Water travels up plant stems through long cells contained in the "vascular bundles." The "strings" in celery stalks and the veins in leaves and flowers are vascular bundles. Hence, it's possible for colored water to travel through these bundles to the leaves and flowers. Dr. Y succeeded in making a red-and-blue carnation because the veins are not connected—they branch out.

# Students' Explanations: Field Experience

This POE was used with 62 grade 9 students.

Sixty-nine percent (69%) correctly predicted that a red-and-blue carnation would result. Twenty-seven percent (27%) predicted that a purple carnation would be produced.

Most of the students predicting correctly provided limited explanations for their prediction:

> *... because we know that water can travel through a plant.*

Indeed, only 12% of these students provided extended explanations in terms of vein structure.

After making their observations, 90% of all the students enhanced their initial explanations and frequently mentioned vein structure.

The following examples provide some indication of the ways in which the students elaborated on and enhanced their explanations.

(a) Student predicting correctly (red and blue)

> *Initial explanation: Yes, because the coloring will travel up the stem.*

> *Final explanation: Because the veins don't meet. They branch out at the top but don't come together.*

(b) Student predicting incorrectly (purple)

> *Initial explanation: ... the carnation will turn purple because of the red and blue colors will blend together.*

> *Final explanation: The veins go up the stem and then branch out. They do not connect at the top or anywhere else.*

# Students' Explanations: Research Findings

In a summary of a number of studies of students' understanding of plant nutrition, Bell (1985) suggested that students have poor understanding of the relationships between photosynthesis, water uptake, and respiration. Some students are reported to believe that plants have animal-like circulatory systems with active pumping occurring (Barker 1998).

# Apparatus and Materials

- Celery (stand overnight in colored water)
- White carnation
- Red and blue food coloring
- Sharp knife or razor blade

# A Red and Blue Carnation

Dr. Y was experimenting to find out how water traveled up plants. He took some celery sticks and dipped them in colored water. He was surprised when he sliced up the celery. The water seemed to be traveling up long, thin tubes.

## An Experiment

Dr. Y had a fiendish idea. He wondered if he could make red and blue carnations. He split the stem of a white carnation: He put half in water containing red food coloring and the other half in water containing blue food coloring. Do you think his experiment will succeed?

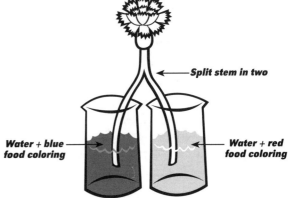

Split stem in two

Water + blue food coloring

Water + red food coloring

## Predict

Will Dr. Y succeed? Please explain. _____

_____

## Observe

Let's do it! _____

## Explain

_____

_____

_____

## *Hey!*

Could you make a tricolored carnation? How about red, white, and blue?

_____

_____

_____

# References

Barker, M. 1998. Understanding transpiration—More than meets the eye. *Journal of Biological Education* 33 (1): 17–20.

Barman, C. R., M. Stein, S. McNair, and N. S. Barman. 2006. Students' ideas about plants and plant growth. *The American Biology Teacher* 68 (2): 73–79.

Bell, B. 1985. Students' ideas about plant nutrition: What are they? *Journal of Biological Education* 19 (3): 213–218.

Driver, R., D. Child, R. Gott, J. Head, S. Johnson, C. Worsley, and F. Wylie. 1984. Science in schools at age 15: Report No. 2. Report to the DES, DENI, and the Welsh Office on the 1981 survey of 15 year olds. London: Assessment of Performance Unit.

Käpylä, M., J.-P. Heikkinen, and T. Asunta. 2009. Influence of content knowledge on pedagogical content knowledge: The case of teaching photosynthesis and plant growth. *International Journal of Science Education* 31 (10): 1395–1415.

Magntorn, O., and G. Helldén. 2007. Reading new environments: Students' ability to generalize their findings between different ecosystems. *International Journal of Science Education* 29 (1): 67–100.

Ozay, E., and H. Oztas. 2003. Secondary students' interpretation of photosynthesis and plant nutrition. *Journal of Biological Education* 37 (2): 68–71.

Roth, K. J., E. L. Smith, and C. W. Anderson. 1983. Students' conceptions of photosynthesis and food for plants. Paper presented at the American Educational Research Association, Montreal, Canada.

Simpson, M., and B. Arnold. 1982a. Availability of prerequisite concepts for learning biology at certificate level. *Journal of Biological Education* 16 (1): 65–72.

Simpson, M., and B. Arnold. 1982b. The inappropriate use of subsumers in biology learning. *European Journal of Science Education* 4 (2): 173–183.

Smith, E. L. and C. W. Anderson. 1984. Plants as producers: A case study of elementary science teaching. *Journal of Research in Science Teaching* 21 (7): 685–698.

Wang, J.-R. 2004. Development and validation of a two-tier instrument to examine understanding of internal transport in plants and the human circulatory system. *International Journal of Science and Mathematics Education* 2 (2): 131–157.

## Contents

## Scientific Explanation

In a similar experiment, the following results were obtained.

| | In the Woods | In a Field | In a Lawn |
|---|---|---|---|
| **Number of Worms** | 5 | 15 | 50 |

A number of biotic and abiotic conditions affect some populations:

(a) Worms do not thrive in very acid soils (often found in woods).

(b) Worms are sensitive to soil consistency. They choose soil that can be traveled through easily.

(c) Worms need moist conditions.

(d) Worms feed on dead vegetable matter (e.g., grass clippings).

## Students' Explanations: Research Findings

Hogan and Fisherkeller (1996) report that students do not have a strong understanding of the important role of decomposers (including earthworms) in food webs and ecosystem energy flow. In their summary of student beliefs about ecology, Driver et al. (1994) report that many students do believe that dead material rots away without the need for decomposing agents, or believe that abiotic (nonbiological processes) alone are responsible for this decay. More than half of students do not believe that earthworms are necessary for plant growth (Barman et al. 2006).

## Apparatus and Materials

If you have six groups of students, you will need

- 6 2 L soda bottles with holes in their caps
- 6 metersticks or tape measures
- Mustard powder
- Teaspoons of washing-up liquid
- Bucket of water (for washing worms)

Note: To take into account local soil conditions, it is recommended that you first try the experiment yourself, varying the quantity (and possibly the strength) of the solutions as necessary.

## Worm Count

Going fishing? Need some worms? Where would you most likely find them—in the woods, in a field, or in a lawn? What do you think?

### An Experiment: Doing a Worm Count

With your classmates, choose about three different locations to search. Divide into groups (about two groups per location). You can bring worms to the surface by spraying with soapy water (about 2 squirts of washing-up liquid in 2 L of water) or mustard powder in water (about 2 tsp in 2 L). Mark out a square meter and spray it evenly. Wait 10 to 15 minutes and count the number of worms that appear. Afterward, wash the worms and return them to the soil. Then flood the treated area with water.

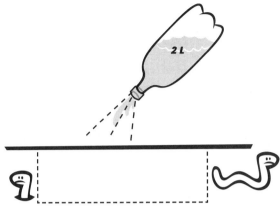

### Predict

Where do you think you will find the most worms? The least? Please give your reasons.

_____

_____

_____

### Observe

| Describe Each Location as Best You Can. | Number of Worms |
|---|---|
| (i) | |
| (ii) | |
| (iii) | |

### Explain

Try to explain why worms choose to live where they do (their habitat).

_____

_____

_____

_____

## Scientific Explanation

Sow bugs choose damp, dark places. They are better adapted to these places. They respire (i.e., breathe) more easily in damp places because the "gills" they have for breathing require a moist environment for a gas exchange to occur. They are normally safer in dark places because predators cannot see them. They eat rotting vegetable matter. This, of course, is also found in damp dark places.

## Students' Explanations: Research Findings

Munson (1994) reported that students tend to have poor understandings of the concept of "niche" and may believe that the needs of any species are related to their perceived role in the ecosystem. For instance, when one finds coyotes and wolves living in the same area, students might assume that they have identical diets because both are predators.

## Apparatus and Materials

- 2 shoe boxes
- At least 12 sow bugs (or a number divisible by two)
- Damp paper towel
- Plastic wrap
- Sandpaper

# Sow Bug Habitats

If you could choose any place in the world to live, what would it be like? Would it always be sunny? How hot would it be? Would it rain at all? What food would you want to eat? Anything else? What is your ideal habitat?

What do you think a sow bug chooses?

Make a choice chamber by dividing a shoe box in two. Cut a small opening in the divider. Put an equal number of sow bugs into each side (maybe six).

### Experiment 1: Dark or Light?
Cover one side of the box to make it dark.

### Experiment 2: Wet or dry?
Put a piece of damp paper towel in one side (lay it on plastic to stop the box from getting wet). Cover the box with clear plastic wrap or the lid.

### Predict
Which places do you think the sow bug will choose? Do you have any ideas why?

_____

_____

_____

### Observe
What happens? You might need to wait awhile.

_____

_____

_____

### Explain
Try to explain what happened. _____

_____

_____

_____

### *More Experiments!*
You might like to explore other preferences of habitat that sow bugs might have. How about rough versus smooth surfaces, or flat surfaces versus surfaces with elevations. Or … ?

## Scientific Explanation

If all the woodland was logged, the squirrel, deer, mouse, and rabbit populations would decrease. It's likely that the wolf, owl, and snake populations would decrease as well. The populations of all animals would be affected in the same way.

Trees are at the bottom of the food pyramid. They are producers of food. Cutting down all the trees would have a dramatic effect. Because they provide the main source of food for mice and deer, these populations could disappear. In addition, the populations of other animals that depend on them (e.g., the wolf) might be seriously reduced.

If all the wolves were shot, the populations of deer, mice, and rabbits would increase rapidly at first but would then drop off. The owl population would also increase.

Wolves are at the top of the food pyramid and have no natural predators. At first, you would expect their prey to flourish (mice, deer, and rabbits). However, these populations cannot go on expanding forever, as they will be limited by the available food supply (grass and trees).

## Students' Explanations: Field Experience

This POE was tested with 40 grade 8 students. Sixty percent (60%) made acceptable predictions. Students seemed to find it easier (by a factor of 2) to conceptualize the effects of eliminating a predator (the wolf) versus losing a food supply (the trees).

Students who had difficulty making correct predictions appeared to be depending on their everyday knowledge rather than attempting to interpret the food web:

> *If all the wolves were shot, all the little animals, such as rats and others would not be eaten so they would be pests and eat your plants and vegetables, etc.*

> *[If the woodland was logged], then some animals would die and birds would lose their homes.*

Only 18% of students mentioned secondary or indirect effects:

> *The population of all living things the wolf eats (rabbit, mouse, deer) would go up which would affect the rest of the animals in the food web directly or indirectly.*

Only 10% (of the predictions about wolves) predicted that the growth of the populations of their prey would be influenced by food supply:

> *... the deer, mouse, and rabbit population would go up then down when their food supply goes down and so on.*

## Students' Explanations: Research Findings

Researchers have identified a variety of difficulties encountered by students with this concept:

- Some students do not understand that changing the population of one component of a food web will affect several different web pathways (Barman, Griffiths, and Okebukola 1995).

- Some students often view the effect of relationships in the web as unidirectional (Palmer 1997; Green 1997; Hogan 2000).

- Some students are confused by how abiotic components are integrated (Eyster and Tashiro 1997).

- Some students have a poor understanding of the role of a decomposer (Hogan and Fisherkeller 1996).

## Apparatus and Materials

No materials needed

## Food Web

The diagram below shows a variety of typical plants and animals that live in a woodland. Let's turn it into a food web by drawing arrows from a plant or animal to those who use it as food—from prey to predator. Ecosystems like this one are very sensitive to climatic change and interference by humans.

Maple tree    Deer    Hawk    Mouse

Grass    Rabbit    Frog    Wolf

Grasshopper    Snake

### Predict

Choose one. What do you think would happen if the woodland was logged, or what do you think would happen if all the wolves were shot? Please explain.

_____

_____

### Observe

It's unlikely that you would be able to observe such an event. However, your teacher would be able to tell you what to expect.

_____

_____

### Explain

_____

_____

_____

## Scientific Explanation

At first, the mice began to multiply. The population increased. Then, as food became scarce, the birth rate dropped, and the population stopped growing.

## Students' Explanations: Field Experience

This POE was used with 40 grade 8 students. It appeared to be well within their capacity.

Forty-three percent (43%) predicted that the population would increase. Some anticipated a higher population would be established, and some anticipated the operation of natural selection:

> *I predict that the mouse population will increase until there are so many mice, each one gets less and less food until the population is down again—only the strong will survive.*

What limits the population increase? Seventy-five percent (75%) of the students made reasonable hypotheses: starvation, fighting, lower birth rate, increased disease, higher death rate among newborns and the young, cannibalism. Thirty-three percent (33%) anticipated starvation would limit the population, and 10% thought the birth rate would drop.

Why was a lower reproduction rate observed? Again, there was a wide range of thoughtful explanations (65%): lower fertility of females on account of weakness or disease, reduced sex drive, stress, slower sexual maturation, reduced quality of gene pool, instinct. A few students (8%) suggested that the mice might be capable of a rational response:

> *The birth rate went down because they know they can't produce as many animals.*

## Students' Explanations: Research Findings

Students may believe that populations might increase until limits are reached and then crash and become extinct. If they believe that ecosystems are a limitless resource, they may not have ever considered scenarios like this one (see the review by McComas [2002] for further details).

## Apparatus and Materials

No materials needed

## Mice Population I: When Food Becomes Scarce

This is the story of a famous research study. Dr. John Emlen became interested in a colony of mice that lived in some old buildings. He began feeding them 250 g of food every day and watched what happened.

The mice reproduced rapidly and the population increased. But as food became scarce, some mice left. Dr. Emlen found that the number leaving was about the same as the birth rate.

### Experiment 1: Food Scarcity

Dr. Emlen wondered what would have happened if he had stopped the mice from leaving.

He did an experiment in a "closed system" and supplied a fixed amount of food every day.

*Closed system*

### Predict

What do you think happened? Please give your reasons.

_____

_____

_____

### Observe

Your teacher will be able to tell you what Dr. Emlen observed.

_____

_____

_____

_____

### Explain

How would you explain Dr. Emlen's findings?

_____

_____

_____

_____

## Scientific Explanation

The mouse population increased rapidly and then stabilized. Their living conditions became overcrowded, the mice began fighting, and the females stopped taking care of their nests and their offspring. Although the birth rate remained high, the young mice did not survive.

## Students' Explanations: Field Experience

This POE was used with 40 grade 8 students. A large majority of students (80%) anticipated that an abundance of food in a closed system would result in population growth and overcrowding.

There was a wide range of speculations as to how the mice would respond or be affected. The most frequently mentioned were fighting, overeating (sometimes resulting in death), and increased disease. One student suggested that they might stop breeding, another that there might be mass suicides (like for lemmings). (Note that this is incorrect. Lemmings do not commit mass suicide; their population dramatically changes because of cycling of food availability.)

After being informed of the results of the experimental study, the majority of students concluded that mice need space. Many suggested that a lack of space creates stress.

## Apparatus and Materials

No materials needed

# Mice Population II: When Space Is Limited

### Experiment 2: Limited Space

Dr. Emlen wondered what would have happened if food supply was not a problem. He carried out a similar experiment in a closed system but provided lots of food.

*Closed system*

### Predict

What do you think happened? Please give your reasons. _____

_____

_____

_____

### Observe

Your teacher will be able to tell you what Dr. Emlen observed.

_____

_____

_____

_____

### Explain

How would you explain Dr. Emlen's findings? _____

_____

_____

_____

_____

## Scientific Explanation

| Date | 1905 | 1910 | 1915 | 1920 | 1925 | 1930 | 1935 | 1940 |
|------|------|------|------|------|------|------|------|------|
| Number of deer | 4,000 | 10,000 | 25,000 | 60,000 | 90,000 | 30,000 | 15,000 | 10,000 |

In the early years, the plan seemed to work well. The deer population exploded. The predator control program continued. However, by 1925, it became clear that there was a food shortage. That winter was especially long and cold. Moreover, overgrazing had seriously damaged the ecosystem. It considerably reduced the amount of food available and the number of deer the forest could support.

## Students' Explanations: Field Experience

This POE was used with 40 grade 8 students.

Seventy-five percent (75%) correctly predicted that the deer population would increase and then decrease.

Some students (15%) attempted to link this POE with the understanding they had gained from previous POEs:

> **The population increased at first but I think that it would decrease because they would eat all the food, etc., quickly. The rabbits, mice and squirrels wouldn't have as much food.**

> **... this would cause a decrease in food and space and they would get stressed and start fighting.**

## Students' Explanations: Research Findings

In their summary of the literature, Driver et al. (1994) reported that many studies have found that most students interpret food web problems (a multicomponent predator-prey relationship) in a limited way. This was evident when students were asked to predict what would happen when the population of an organism was changed in a hypothetical web.

(a) Some thought the effects of removing a top predator would have fewer links with the rest of the web than the removal other predators.

(b) Some did not recognize that the effects of removing a species extended beyond the species' immediate predator or prey.

(c) Some did not recognize that the size of the prey population affected the size of the predator population.

Insufficient understanding of the variety of prey items of a predator may influence how students perceive the effect of removing the predator from the ecosystem. For instance, Prokop and Kubiatko (2008) report that students may believe that wolves only eat deer and not also rabbits (whose population might then also increase and affect this ecosystem and, subsequently, the deer population).

## Apparatus and Materials

No materials needed

## Save the Deer?

This is a true story! In 1906, the Kaibab Plateau in northern Arizona was declared a national park. About 4,000 deer lived in the park. The park managers decided that it would be good to try to increase the deer population. So, in 1907, they put a bounty on all the deer's natural enemies (predators). In a very short time, hunters killed nearly all the wolves, coyotes, mountain lions, and bobcats. What do you think of this plan?

### Predict
What do you think happened to the deer population? Please give your reasons.

_____

_____

_____

_____

### Observe
Every year, the park managers carried out a deer census. The data they obtained can be found in many books (e.g., Keating 1988). Your teacher will help you fill in the table below, which shows how the deer population changed.

| Date | 1905 | 1910 | 1915 | 1920 | 1925 | 1930 | 1935 | 1940 |
|---|---|---|---|---|---|---|---|---|
| **Number of deer** | 4,000 | | | | | | | |

### Explain
Why do you think the deer population changed the way it did?

_____

_____

_____

_____

# References

Barman, C. R., A. K. Griffiths, and P. A. O. Okebukola. 1995. High school students' concepts regarding food chains and food webs: A multinational study. *International Journal of Science Education* 17 (6): 775–782.

Barman, C. R., M. Stein, S. McNair, and N. S. Barman. 2006. Students' ideas about plants and plant growth. *The American Biology Teacher* 68 (2): 73–79.

Driver, R., A. Squires, P. Rushworth, and V. Wood-Robinson. 1994. *Making sense of secondary science*. London and New York: Routledge.

Eyster, L. S., and J. S. Tashiro. 1997. Using manipulatives to teach quantitative concepts in ecology. *The American Biology Teacher* 59 (6): 360–364.

Green, D. W. 1997. Explaining and envisaging an ecological phenomena. *British Journal of Psychology* 88: 199–217.

Hogan, K. 2000. Assessing students' system reasoning in ecology. *Journal of Biological Education* 35 (1): 22–28.

Hogan, K., and J. Fisherkeller. 1996. Representing students' thinking about nutrient cycling in ecosystems: Bidimensional coding of a complex topic. *Journal of Research in Science Teaching* 33 (9): 941–970.

Keating, J. 1988. *Population growth and balance*. New York: Trillium Press.

McComas, W. F. 2002. The ideal environmental science curriculum: History, rationales, misconceptions and standards (Part I of II). *The American Biology Teacher* 64 (9): 665–672.

Munson, B. H. 1994. Ecological misconceptions. *Journal of Environmental Education* 25 (4): 30–34.

Palmer, D. H. 1997. Students' application of the concept of interdependence to the issue of preservation of species: Observations on the ability to generalize. *Journal of Research in Science Teaching* 34 (8): 837–850.

Prokop, P., and M. Kubiatko. 2008. Bad wolf kills lovable rabbits: Children's attitudes toward predator and prey. *Electronic Journal of Science Education* 12 (1): 55–70.

# Index

# Index

NATIONAL SCIENCE TEACHERS ASSOCIATION

# Index

NATIONAL SCIENCE TEACHERS ASSOCIATION

# Index

NATIONAL SCIENCE TEACHERS ASSOCIATION

# Index

## M

Magnetism

NATIONAL SCIENCE TEACHERS ASSOCIATION

# Index

# Index

NATIONAL SCIENCE TEACHERS ASSOCIATION

# Index

**W**